BYRON AND THE FORMS OF THOUGHT

LIVERPOOL ENGLISH TEXTS AND STUDIES 61

BYRON AND THE FORMS OF THOUGHT

ANTHONY HOWE

LIVERPOOL UNIVERSITY PRESS

First published 2013 by
Liverpool University Press
4 Cambridge Street
Liverpool
L69 7ZU

Copyright © 2013 Anthony Howe

The right of Anthony Howe to be identified as the author of this book has been asserted by him in accordance with the Copyright, Designs and Patents Act 1988.

British Library Cataloguing-in-Publication data

A British Library CIP record is available

ISBN 978-1-84631-971-6 cased

Typeset by Carnegie Book Production, Lancaster
Printed and bound by CPI Group (UK) Ltd, Croydon CR0 4YY

Contents

Abbreviations

CPW   *Lord Byron: The Complete Poetical Works*, ed. Jerome J. McGann and Barry Weller, 7 vols (Oxford: Clarendon Press, 1980–93). Byron's poetry is quoted from this edition unless otherwise stated.

BLJ   *Byron's Letters and Journals*, ed. Leslie A. Marchand, 13 vols (London: John Murray, 1973–94)

BMW   *Lord Byron: The Major Works*, ed. Jerome J. McGann (Oxford: Oxford University Press, 2008)

CMP   *Lord Byron: The Complete Miscellaneous Prose*, ed. Andrew Nicholson (Oxford: Clarendon Press, 1991)

HVSV *His Very Self and Voice: Collected Conversations of Lord Byron*, ed. Ernest J. Lovell, Jr. (New York: Macmillan, 1954)

Preface

This book has not come easily, nor would it have come at all were it not for quite a lot of other people. Listing them makes me realize that it might just have been worth it. A special mention goes to Bernard Beatty who is still teaching me about Byron and thought and poetry. For help of various hues I thank the following (none of you deserve alphabetical order): Michael O'Neill, Howard Erskine-Hill, Fred Parker, Simon Jarvis, Robert Douglas-Fairhurst, Corinna Russell, Duncan O'Connor, Alexander Regier, Gabriel Heaton, Peter Cochran, Patrick McGuinness, Geraldine Hazbun, Katherine Sutherland, Madeleine Callaghan, Philip Smallwood, Antoinette Renouf, Fiona Robertson, Gregory Leadbetter, Anthony Mellors, Stacey McDowell, Moira Redmond, Emma Weatherill and my family. You have all helped me write a book about Byron. I promise never to do it again.

The doctoral thesis behind this book was supported financially by the Arts and Humanities Research Council. Finishing the book was made possible by a period of research leave and the support of my colleagues at Birmingham City University. Liverpool University Press and Anthony Cond have been more than patient and more than very good. It's an honour to keep up old connections.

In memory of Margaret Mary Howe MBE

Introduction

In Julian Farino's two-part BBC dramatization *Byron* (2003), the only writing of Byron's to feature significantly is the manuscript of the poet's memoirs, a work that only a handful of people ever read. The scene, we assume, is John Murray's drawing room in Albemarle Street; present are Murray himself, John Cam Hobhouse, and other associates of the recently deceased poet. The book, amidst a series of uncertain and frightened looks, is thrown onto the fire, in the process burning into the biographical record one of its more famous holes. It is an effective opening scene, one that suggests a fruitful unshackling from history and an opportunity creatively to overwrite some intriguing blank spaces. But there is also in it something sadly symptomatic of how we have come to think of one of our greatest poets.

Byron persists in the popular imagination. He made himself – and has been made into – one of the defining qualities of his own tumultuous age: Romantic, passionate, radical and mysterious. 'Byronic' has a cultural immediacy that is not there with 'Wordsworthian' or 'Shelleyan'. Biographies of the poet are produced with unfailing energy. He regularly features on television and film where his life needs few fictional additives to stimulate twenty-first century appetites. He is a seminal figure respecting the modern obsession with celebrity.[1] This afterlife, however, has been a very different affair to that of other eminent nineteenth-century literary figures such as Dickens or Jane Austen, writers identified primarily with their books and characters. Byron, we might easily conclude from his broader cultural status, was not really important as a writer at all. As a thinker he barely registers.

Byron's reconstruction as the definitive non-intellectual Romantic, as a poet of passion but not of thought, begins with weighty opinions such as Goethe's: 'Lord Byron is only great when he is writing poetry; as soon as he reflects, he is a child.'[2] Matthew Arnold came to similar conclusions:

> Byron, it may be said, was eminent only by his genius, only by his inborn force and fire; he had not the intellectual equipment of a supreme modern

poet; except for his genius he was an ordinary nineteenth-century English gentleman, with little culture and no ideas.³

For Arnold, Byron represented something from which the national life of the mind needed to shift away; he stood for a redundant emotivism summarized by words such as 'force', 'genius' and 'fire' when what was needed was 'intellectual equipment' and 'ideas', neither of which Byron had to offer. T. S. Eliot agreed, identifying Byron's apparent linguistic poverty as the sign of his secondariness:

> Of Byron one can say, as of no other English poet of his eminence, that he added nothing to the language, that he discovered nothing in the sounds, and developed nothing in the meaning, of individual words. I cannot think of any other poet of his distinction who might so easily have been an accomplished foreigner writing in English. The ordinary person talks English, but only a few people in every generation can write it; and upon this undeliberate collaboration between a great many people talking a living language and a very few people writing it, the continuance and maintenance of a language depends. Just as an artisan who can talk English beautifully while about his work or in a public bar, may compose a letter painfully written in a dead language bearing some resemblance to a newspaper leader, and decorated with words like 'maelstrom' and 'pandemonium': so does Byron write a dead or dying language.⁴

Byron may be a good storyteller, but he writes an ersatz poetry of surfaces in the 'dead' language of Romantic poetic diction; he works in decorative words lacking the modes of awareness essential to the poet's grasp of things. What is perhaps puzzling about Eliot's resonant criticism is his determination to read Byron in the singular, as if the Oriental Tales, all four cantos of *Childe Harold's Pilgrimage* and *Don Juan* were all made of the same stuff. The distinctness of the latter, which is decidedly proto-Modernist in so far as it picks up the baton from *Tristram Shandy*, is not allowed.⁵ After all, it was Byron among the major Romantics who came to insist that one should be able to make a poem about a fried egg as well as a sunset. It was Byron, also, who subjected the linguistic deadness Eliot identifies in Romanticism to its most extensive interrogation in its own day. Where Auden, in his brilliant 'Letter to Lord Byron', threw out the 'trash' of *Childe Harold's Pilgrimage* but held to the 'fine' *Don Juan*,⁶ Eliot wants to purge us wholesale of a monotone Byron who is ridiculously stuck to his time.

Byron criticism is a history of more or less comprehensible swerves from Byron. The poet's self-mythologizing has been taken on and extended by others to the extent that he has become one of the most *written* poets in the language. Bertrand Russell, who devoted an entire chapter of his *History of Western Philosophy* to Byron, picked up on this twinning of Byron and 'Byron'. For Russell, however, the latter was the significant one: 'Like many other prominent men, he was more important as a myth than as he really was. As a myth, his importance, especially on the Continent, was enormous'.[7] Whether Byron 'as he really was' can be distinguished from Byron the myth is another question, but Russell is certainly right that Byron had been overtaken by his cultural and political attributions.

The rewriting of Byron as his own pre-eminent text continued with the rise of the English literature professional: 'He lives that eternity which is art. He is more than a writer [...]. He is poetry incarnate. The others are dreamers: he is the thing itself'.[8] The academic study of Byron, however, while maintaining this sense of the cultic, also allowed more space in which to acknowledge the poet's fractures and contradictions as well as to ponder his place in the canon. Leavis, for instance, saw Byron not as a defining Romantic genius, but as a poet with a strong 'eighteenth-century element', something which is identified as 'essential to his success'. The main effect of this 'success', however, was, according to Leavis, to bring out 'how completely the Augustan order had disintegrated'.[9]

The 1950s and 60s were, on the whole, less backhanded in their appreciation and, while concerns remained about the poet being 'an essentially uneducated spirit',[10] Byron studies had, by the late 60s at least, flourished as a serious academic concern, especially, although not exclusively, in the United States.[11] As Jerome McGann pointed out from its midst, however, some of this work, and especially where influenced by the New Critics, was made uncomfortable by the sceptical, fragmentary and contradictory modes of thought characteristic of Byron's *oeuvre*. These critics sought forms of intellectual and aesthetic coherence that Byron rarely provides, and their judgements of individual poems often hinged on whether or not they found what they wanted.[12] With Byron's poetry we often stumble into quiet clearings of lucidity, but we are rarely allowed to stray too far from the truths of disorder.

Byron again found himself at a disadvantage when critics turned to the idea of a Romantic canon. Although the problems and continuities of visionary experience are central to Byron's thought, it remains difficult to place the poet in relation to the seriousness of High Romantic literary culture. He may be a definitive Romantic, but Byron also lampooned Wordsworth, championed Pope, and wrote much of his best poetry in satirical and serio-comic modes. Thus we pick up M. H. Abrams's magisterial 550-page *Natural Supernaturalism*, a defining work of Romantic period literary criticism, and find only one index reference to the literary colossus of Regency England: 'Byron I omit altogether; not because I think him a lesser poet than the others but because in his greatest work he speaks with an ironic counter-voice and deliberately opens a satirical perspective on the vatic stance of his Romantic contemporaries'.[13] This wasn't necessarily a value judgement, just an acknowledgement that Byron did not fit with the Anglo-German, secularized-theological literary history that Abrams wanted to describe. As a massive reinforcement of the 'vatic' as a pre-eminent poetic quality, however, Abrams's work did nothing for Byron's reputation as a serious poet and thinker. His sidestepping of Byron, moreover, was followed by some of the most intellectually ambitious Romanticists of the 1970s, who found Shelley's evanescent symbolism more germane to their theoretical ambitions.[14]

If Byron's critical stance on the incipient aesthetic ideologies of his historical moment made him a misfit for Abrams, then for the Marxist-influenced 'new' historicists of the 1980s it made him a prescient ally (of sorts). Byron's exclusion was for these critics not a necessary preparative to the understanding of literary history, but an unhistorical act of misdescription. The canon makers of the 60s and 70s were culpable ideologists, their work, as McGann put it, being 'dominated by a Romantic Ideology, by an uncritical absorption in Romanticism's own self-representations'.[15] To exclude Byron from our readings of the period is to extend rather than analyse the assumptions of literary Romanticism. It was to fail Byron, but it was also to fail to learn from his clear-sighted critique of acculturation as a form of blindness. What was needed, in McGann's view, was a more accurate understanding of the socio-historical realities of Romantic period literature and culture, one free from the tacit value judgements of the vatic critical tradition. This shift of emphasis from canon to history meant that Byron, a figure of enormous historical and cultural importance, could easily be reinte-grated into the scholarship of the period.

This re-inclusion of Byron, however, has in turn been doubted due to its reliance upon interpretative frameworks that homogenize critical reading in the interests of non-literary analysis.[16] Its price, as Jane Stabler puts it, has been 'the realization of [Byron's] poetry at the level of the reading experience'.[17] The recovery of this experience, as Stabler and others have stressed, must now be seen as a priority. The reasons for this, as well as having specific things to do with Byron's thought, relate to fundamental questions about what literary criticism is for and what it tells us about. When we engage the scriptings of literary form the event in which we participate, as Derek Attridge puts it, 'exceeds the limits of rational accounting'.[18] Such a claim leads to another about the meliorative force of literature in compensating the shortfall of modernity in its reading of the human. Christopher Ricks writes of the

> endemic and valuable resistance, not hostility, that literary studies (no less than literature) have always needed, of their nature, to put up to the fellow-humanities philosophy and history: history, with its claim that the establishing of facts is its province, and (more pressingly of late) philosophy, with its claim that the pursuit of truth is its province.[19]

In acknowledging the resistance of human experience to the discourses of fact, attentive reading liberates us from, in arresting, the rush to settle things in words. Literary form, as Angela Leighton has put it, 'stops us in our tracks of thinking, and inserts itself in that moment of stillness. To attend to form is thus to admit some other kind of mental attention, which is not the quick route to a name or the knowledge of an object'.[20] Form has claims to make in those places where to name is always to misname.

Ricks's missable aside – '(no less than literature)' – seems crucial here. It reminds us that the study of literature, if it is to follow its object for any distance, cannot depart entirely from that object's ways of being. A poem's projection beyond the remit of category cannot be tracked by critical discourse that insists upon an assimilation to scientific or quasi-scientific method. Literary criticism, as has been recognized since at least Horace, thus needs to be an act of participation as well as an act of contextual investigation. We need not go as far as Schlegel in dismissing reflexive analysis entirely,[21] but neither should we miss the point of his mischief. The following study of Byron, while in part a work of historical and intertextual scholarship, tries to keep this in mind in its address of the poet's forms. It also wants to argue that this approach is of especial importance in Byron's case because of the part played by such thinking in the poet's achievement. Byron, that is, can be placed – and, at times, consciously places himself – in a version of the critical tradition I have been describing with reference to Ricks, Leighton and others. He understood that any serious apprehension of poetry is unavailable to writing with no sense of form. To read Byron's thinking is to be drawn into a poetics that is both enriched and withheld by the problems of literary singularity. Byron's poetry, rather than being reproducible as a discrete branch of philosophy, engages philosophical thought as a prelude to self-understanding. It becomes its own investigation into the thoughtfulness and knowledge of form.

* * *

This is to touch upon some of the central claims of this book and where they come from. Some further words about the book's manner, structure and aims may be useful. The book is self-consciously essayistic. It does propose an argument or set of linked arguments, but it also allows itself to think against their grain and against the grain of argumentation in general. There is a degree of accident in this in so far as the pursuit of poetic meanings is not a science and (perhaps especially so in the case of Byron) likely to generate a degree of mess and misfitting. The deliberate side to the book's essayistic approach has to do with an attempt to shape its thinking to Byron's own. Byron, as is well known, places *Don Juan* in an essayistic tradition by bringing to our attention his debt to writers such as Montaigne and Sterne. Such formal choices, which also relate to Byron as a writer of prose, make their own claims about knowledge. This book is minded of and in agreement with Byron's thinking on this matter.

I agree with recent studies by Hoagwood and Bernhard Jackson in their claim that the sophistication of Byron's thought has been consistently underestimated. Where I differ with both of these critics is in my approach to rectifying the apparent oversight. I try to avoid, that is, subjugating the reading of poetry to the purposes of claiming Byron as a particular species of philosopher. Hoagwood's specific argument about Byron's thought as a type of vivified Pyrrhonism will be considered in due course; his methodology is of more immediate concern. Hoagwood makes a determined point of privileging Byron's prose because he views it as a clearer and more reliable source of his subject's philosophical ideas.[22] Such an approach, as well as making questionable assumptions about the relative reliability of Byron's prose voice(s), can only ever give us a limited account of Byron's thought for precisely the reasons I have been discussing. The poet's mistrust of direct argumentation and his corresponding faith in poetic form renders problematic any notion that his 'philosophical' importance can be understood with primary or exclusive reference to his attempts to articulate philosophical positions.

For Byron, such ways of knowing often seem secondary to the animation discovered in the processes of writing and reading poetry.

Bernhard Jackson, while rightly leaving behind Hoagwood's disavowal of intention as well as his suspicion of poetry, does maintain and build upon the latter's assumption that Byron's recovery as an intellectual depends upon our capacity to (re)discover him as a philosopher, as a thinker with a 'well thought-out and fully articulated philosophy of knowledge, one with significant practical implications'. This coherent philosophy, moreover, is seen as resulting from a process of intellectual development; it 'arrives', that is, by a 'process of gradual intellectual consideration that begins early in [Byron's] career and [which] solidifies by means of progressive speculation and testing'.[23] The instincts forged in reading Byron leave me sceptical about such definitive assertions about the poet's intellectual development.[24] I also disagree with the claim that Byron's 'philosophical stance' fixes *Don Juan* as a consistent, practical means of demonstrating to the reader that he is 'faced with a world in which there is no objective or universal ground' and thus that the individual is 'free to determine what is understood, what is accepted, even what will be true'.[25] I don't think we can tie Byron to an individualistic, rationally determined 'freedom' of this kind. I also question the idea that the 'philosophical' function of a poem such as *Don Juan* is consistently to break down generalized knowledge claims. First, this turns poetry into a predictable, readily paraphrased system. As well as missing the poem's undetermined uniqueness, such an approach cancels its surprizingness and reassigns it to the critic's argument. Second, as I read it at least, *Don Juan* is deeply interested in trans-individual sublime states and their relation to human cognition. Granted, the poem does not put forward a coherent theory of universalized knowing, but it does think about (and through) poetry in terms of its collective, emancipatory and imaginative possibilities (I discuss this in my fourth essay). It would be fair to say that Byron is the major British Romantic who puts most pressure on objective knowledge claims at the level of poetic form, but he also knew that scepticism does not rule things out. Part of Byron is a seriously moral Romantic poet concerned with the role of poetry in tracing the forgotten paths between human culture and states of origin. What is interesting and unique in Byron's thought is closer to Shelley's poetics than Hume's philosophy.

* * *

The book is divided into three main parts, each subdivided into two extended, linked essays. Part I considers Byron's relation to philosophical scepticism, the area of philosophy most commonly associated with the poet. Rather than describing Byron as a particular species of philosophical sceptic I trace the ways in which scepticism, particularly through the ideas of Montaigne, leads to an understanding of poetry as something with a 'philosophical' agency of its own (although not one we can understand by returning to the set terms of intellectual history). Form, for Byron, becomes a way of reading the world against the grain of its objectification. It offers the possibility of reinvigorating thought as a mode of existential and political challenge. I proceed to test these incipient ideas about a Byronic poetics with reference to Byron's religious thought and also his famous critique of intellectual rigidity or 'system'.

My second essay considers as a case study Byron's most obvious work of 'philosophical poetry', *Cain*. In reading against those who have interpreted the play as a manifesto, I explore *Cain* (as Byron urges us to do) more as an encounter between 'argument' and 'drama' than as a political work interested in literary form only for purposes of disguise and misdirection. I read the play through its interest in the meeting point of rational speculation and literary cognition. While developing the argument of Essay I in retracing Byron's shift from scepticism to poetics I also make specific claims about *Cain* as a unique intervention in vatic tradition.

Building upon the ideas of Part I, the book's central essays confront Byron's thinking about literary writing more directly and from two different points of view. The first asks what Byron thought it meant to write about poetry through a detailed study of the poet's attempts at prose literary criticism during his career, in the early 1820s, as a pamphleteer and controversialist. I argue that to understand Byron's critical prose we need to place it in a tradition of reflexive critical writing that was most present to Byron in the figure of Samuel Johnson. Johnson's literary scepticism is read as an important source for Byron's ideas about the resistance of poetry to theoretical apprehension. I also, following the lead of Andrew Nicholson and others, wonder what a Byronic prose poetics might look like. Essay IV asks the same question, but with primary reference to poetry rather than prose. It (re) assesses, that is, Byron's position within the territory of post-Lockean and Romantic poetics. Beginning with Byron's shifting apprehension of the sublime I ask how Byron aligns his poetry with states of origin acknowledged as beyond description. Poetry for Byron, I argue, stands in a similar relation to 'Eternity' as true criticism does to its object. Vatic agency, in this sense, is for Byron inherently critical, an idea I explore with reference to Romantic literary culture more broadly but also in relation to Byron's self-critical shift from *Childe Harold's Pilgrimage* to *Don Juan*.

Part 3 takes some of the principal ideas identified in Part 2 and explores them with reference to *Don Juan* both as a narrative and a political poem. The first essay suggests that thinking about poetry in *Don Juan* is something that happens not just in the narrator's philosophical digressions but in the very forms of the poem's narrative. Narrative's self-knowledge, its acknowledgement of its own selectiveness, becomes a mode of reflecting upon what the poem cannot contain. The final essay construes this act of visionary reflection as inherently political through a consideration of Byron as a narrative war poet. Byron's engagement of the sublime, I suggest, is echoed in the poem's critical apprehension of political truth. His re-visioning of war poetry specifies a poetics of lyric immediacy as a necessary context for social melioration. To argue thus is also to challenge the dominant assumption that Byron's politics is primarily or even exclusively available to the methods of historical scholarship.

Notes

1 See Tom Mole, *Byron's Romantic Celebrity: Industrial Culture and the Hermeneutic of Intimacy* (Basingstoke: Palgrave Macmillan, 2007).

2 Quoted in E. M. Butler, *Byron and Goethe: Analysis of a Passion* (London: Bowes and Bowes, 1956), 115.

3 'Lectures and Essays in Criticism', ed. R. H. Super (Ann Arbor: University of Michigan Press, 1962), 132.

4 T. S. Eliot, *On Poetry and Poets* (London: Faber and Faber, 1957), 200–1.

5 Eliot's first appearance in print, 'A Fable for Feasters' (1905), was an *ottava rima* poem in the style of *Don Juan*. See *Poems Written in Early Youth*, ed. Valerie Eliot (London: Faber and Faber, 1967), 13–16. Eliot recalls his verses with embarrassment in *On Poetry and Poets*, 193.

6 *The English Auden: Poems, Essays and Dramatic Writings 1927–1939*, ed. Edward Mendelson (London: Faber and Faber, 1977), 169 (ll. 2, 5).

7 Bertrand Russell, *A History of Western Philosophy and its Connections with Political and Social Circumstances from the Earliest Times to the Present Day* (London: Unwin, 1946), 780.

8 G. Wilson Knight, *The Burning Oracle* (Oxford: Oxford University Press, 1939), 198.

9 F. R. Leavis, *Revaluation* (New York: Norton, 1936), 153.

10 W. W. Robson, 'Byron as Poet' (Chatterton Lecture), in *Proceedings of the British*

Academy, 1957; reprinted in *Byron: A Collection of Critical Essays*, ed. Paul West (Englewood Cliffs, NJ: Prentice Hall, 1963), 94.

11 Andrew Rutherford, *Byron: A Critical Study* (Edinburgh: Oliver and Boyd, 1962); F. Gleckner, *Byron and the Ruins of Paradise* (Baltimore: Johns Hopkins University Press, 1968); W. Paul Elledge, *Byron and the Dynamics of Metaphor* (Nashville: Vanderbilt University Press, 1968); M. G. Cooke, *The Blind Man Traces the Circle: On the Patterns and Philosophy of Byron's Poetry* (Princeton: Princeton University Press, 1969).

12 Jerome J. McGann, *Fiery Dust: Byron's Poetic Development* (Chicago: University of Chicago Press, 1968), 65–6.

13 M. H. Abrams, *Natural Supernaturalism: Tradition and Revolution in Romantic Literature* (Oxford: Oxford University Press, 1971), 13. Harold Bloom found space for a smallish chapter on Byron (less than half the size of the chapter on Blake) in *The Visionary Company: A Reading of English Romantic Poetry* (London: Faber and Faber and Faber, 1962), where he notes that Byron's is the 'most social of Romantic imaginations and so the least Romantic' (p. xv).

14 Notably in *Deconstruction and Criticism* (London: Routledge & Kegan Paul, 1979), a seminal collection of essays by Bloom, Paul de Man, Jacques Derrida, Geoffrey Hartman and J. Hillis Miller, in which an interest in Shelley's *The Triumph of Life* dominates.

15 Jerome J. McGann, *The Romantic Ideology: A Critical Investigation* (Chicago: University Of Chicago Press, 1983), 1.

16 See Susan J. Wolfson, *Formal Charges: The Shaping of Poetry in British Romanticism* (Stanford, CA: Stanford University Press, 1997), 2–3 and *passim*. Also see Alan Rawes's Introduction to *Romanticism and Form*, ed. Alan Rawes (Basingstoke: Palgrave Macmillan, 2007).

17 Jane Stabler, *Byron, Poetics and History* (Cambridge: Cambridge University Press, 2002), 5.

18 Derek Attridge, *The Singularity of Literature* (London: Routledge, 2004), 3.

19 Christopher Ricks, 'The Pursuit of Metaphor', in *Allusion to the Poets* (Oxford: Oxford University Press, 2002), 241–60 (242).

20 Angela Leighton, *On Form: Poetry, Aestheticism, and the Legacy of a Word* (Oxford: Oxford University Press, 2007), 21.

21 'It is not necessary for anyone to sustain and propagate poetry through clever speeches and precepts [...]; one cannot really speak of poetry except in the language of poetry'. Friedrich Schlegel, *Dialogue on Poetry and Literary Aphorisms*, trans. Ernst Behler and Roman Struc (University Park, PA: Pennsylvania State University Press, 1968), 54.

22 Terence Allan Hoagwood, *Byron's Dialectic: Skepticism and the Critique of Culture* (Lewisburg, PA: Bucknell University Press, 1993), 23.

23 Emily A. Bernhard Jackson, *The Development of Byron's Philosophy of Knowledge* (Basingstoke: Palgrave Macmillan, 2010), 2.

24 I am thinking in particular of Byron's instinctive refusal of linearity and his tendency to write of his own work within dialectical narratives of nostalgia and loss. His most important and self-conscious intellectual 'development', I would suggest, is the one that takes us from the style of *Childe Harold's Pilgrimage* to that of *Don Juan*, a move informed by Byron's recognition that 'we are upon a wrong revolutionary poetical system' (*BLJ*, v, 265). I would not want to suggest, however,

that we should construe this change in simple progressive terms. Byron certainly did not. We could only understand this as the symptom of a developing 'philosophy of knowledge', moreover, with reference to a Byronic poetics that is evolving away from the claims of philosophy.

25 Bernhard Jackson, *The Development of Byron's Philosophy of Knowledge*, 180.

PART 1

PHILOSOPHY

'I doubt if doubt itself be doubting'
Scepticism, System and Poetry

What kind – or kinds – of thinker was Byron? What were his philosophical sources and how did these shape the peculiar structures of thought exhibited in his poems, letters and more formal prose? Those who have discussed such questions have usually identified philosophical scepticism, something about which the poet was demonstrably informed, as an important point of reference. M. G. Cooke somewhat reluctantly concluded that Byron 'is so strongly disposed to mistrust strictly clean categories that the primary bent of his philosophy must be termed skeptical'. For Cooke, scepticism is something to be admitted rather than celebrated: it 'becomes a question', Cooke worries, 'and indeed a vexed question, whether we can find in Byron's verse some affirmative philosophic position, befitting a poet of his rank and of his years'.[1] Donald H. Reiman was less concerned about the fittingness of Byron's scepticism, finding in it a philosophical correlate for the situation of Byronic exile: 'as a universal outsider, Byron self-consciously employed Academic or Pyrrhonist skepticism to distance himself from the creeds that competed for his allegiance'.[2] Hoagwood goes further to claim this universal distancing as an intellectually coherent and sophisticated response to the world:

> Byron's rehearsal of the traditional skeptical principles and tendencies is more than a reproduction of a source or of sources. It is rather the articulation (often a disorderly articulation) of a critical method of greater intellectual sophistication than has been normally allowed to the poet.[3]

Byron does more than toy with the ideas of philosophical scepticism; he articulates, rather, a distinct critical practice or 'method', one that allows us to place him in intellectual history with more confidence than has traditionally been the case. Contrary to Cooke's sense of Byron's scepticism as problematic, moreover, Hoagwood associates it, via the

Pyrrhonist's *ataraxia*, with 'delight' and the 'enrichment of human experience'.[4]

While there can be no doubt about Byron's interest in philosophical scepticism or its importance for his writing, no clear consensus has emerged about how best to describe this aspect of the poet's thought. Not helpful here is the fact that 'scepticism' is a rather nebulous term, both in its popular (ranging through various senses of wariness, cynicism and pessimism) and technical uses;[5] it is not always clear, in this respect, that critics have used it to mean the same thing. There are historical considerations also. In the eighteenth century, the word, mainly due to its anti-religious ramifications, was often associated not with a successful mode of life (as for Hoagwood) or even reasoned caution (although it can be for Hume), but with optimistic intellectual programmes, 'enthusiasm', or even fanaticism. The outlandish schemes of Walter Shandy, for instance, are described as 'sceptical, and [...] far out of the high-way of thinking'.[6] For Pope, the 'sceptic', mired in his doubt, lacks vigour and presence; he is no more than a footnote to the life of the mind:

> Know then thyself, presume not God to scan;
> The proper study of Mankind is Man.
> Placed on this isthmus of a middle state,
> A being darkly wise, and rudely great:
> With too much knowledge for the Sceptic's side,
> With too much weakness for the Stoic's pride,
> He hangs between; in doubt to act, or rest,
> In doubt to deem himself a God, or Beast;
> In doubt his mind and body to prefer,
> Born but to die, and reas'ning but to err;[7]

This kind of 'sceptic' is an intellectually atrophied extremist, one who programmatically doubts everything. He is too certain, too closed down in his thinking, to grasp the non-categorical truths of Man's 'middle state', the energized but wearing inbetweeness that Pope captures in the rhythms of his punctuation.

Byron, who at no point identifies himself as a sceptic, takes a similar if less theologically certain line: 'I have formed no decided opinion – but I should regret any *sceptical bigotry* as equally pernicious with the most credulous intolerance' (*BLJ*, iv, 60). 'Sceptics' for Byron tend to be either militant bigots or risible reactionaries, such as the 'sceptics who would not believe Columbus' (*Don Juan*, xvi, 4).[8] When Byron does become interested in scepticism it tends to be at those moments where it collapses into its own definitions. This is famously and deliberately the case with the Socratic 'I know nothing except the fact of my ignorance'. At the same moment Socrates claims to 'know nothing' and also to know a 'fact' (that Socrates is 'ignorant'). By loading his words beyond their capacity the philosopher turns a static epistemological claim into a shifting experiment in thought.

Byron knew this famous crux from Diogenes Laertius's *Lives of the Eminent Philosophers* and quoted a version of it in *Don Juan* (vii, 5). He was fascinated by its implications and placed them at the intellectual centre of his poem, notably in this stanza which he spins out of Montaigne:

> 'Que sçais-je?' was the motto of Montaigne,
>   As also of the first Academicians:
> That all is dubious which Man may attain,
>   Was one of their most favourite positions.
> There's no such thing as certainty, that's plain
>   As any of Mortality's Conditions:
> So little do we know what we're about in
> This world, I doubt if doubt itself be doubting.

(Don Juan, ix, 17)

Rather than reproducing conventional sceptical arguments ('all is dubious which Man may attain'), Byron writes them only in order to cross them out again.[9] His interest lies in those moments where argument breaks down – or flourishes – into paradox and form. Thus it is 'plain' (or certain) that 'There's no such thing as certainty', a reflection intensified and escalated in the gleeful alliteration of 'I doubt if doubt itself be doubting'. This wriggling out of normative argument into absolute possibility is also a nod to tradition in so far as it participates in the ironic, dialogic status of Montaigne's physically inscribed but uncertain motto. Byron's printed and vocally dense utterance becomes a perfectly timed claim on behalf of literary presence. At precisely the moment in which philosophy – as Locke understood it at least – seems to lose its grip, the evasions of poetic form assume a quasi-tactile immediacy that offers to mitigate what might seem a dismal epistemological predicament.

This connection between scepticism and poetics, a major concern of what follows, will be easier to understand if we first assemble some context.[10]

* * *

Philosophical scepticism can be dated back at least as far as Arcesilaus of Pitane (c.315–242 BC), founder of the Middle Academy, and later Carneades (c.213–129 BC). Pyrrhonism, a development of this 'Academic' scepticism that takes its name from the peripatetic philosopher Pyrrho of Elis (born c.365–270 BC) – who travelled to India with Alexander the Great, and whose teachings were based upon a sceptical sense of cultural difference – is concerned more with ethics than epistemological procedure. It was later codified (c.AD 200) by Sextus Empiricus. Byron knew about classical scepticism from a range of sources, including Montaigne, Bayle and Hume; he also (as has been noted) read Diogenes Laertius's *Lives of the Philosophers*,[11] which includes an account of Pyrrho's life and thought, and which refers to the apocryphal stories about the philosopher's refusal to avoid, on extreme sceptical grounds, onrushing chariots and steep precipices, and his constantly having to be saved by a contingent of dedicated followers.

Classical scepticism can be subdivided into a number of stages or procedures. The first is *isostheneia*, a sceptical balancing that involves juxtaposing conflicting views with the aim of undermining belief in any single opinion or system. Traditionally, this was carried out through a series of standard arguments or 'tropes', which balance, as Diogenes Laertius has it, 'the equal value of contradictory sayings'.[12] The sceptic may argue, for instance, that the fact that there are many different forms of religious belief itself undermines the likelihood of any particular form being true. This process justifies for the sceptic a situation of suspended judgement or *epoche*, a complete indecision with respect to any definitive claims about the nature of reality. He does not argue that a particular system is necessarily false, only that it appears to be impossibly difficult, given our unreliable and limited resources, to say with certainty that it is true. Academic scepticism, which sought to undermine (primarily Stoic) dogma, found in *epoche* an end in itself: since certainty can be challenged on any question, the sceptic refuses to assent to his opponent's claims and also withholds any dogmatic alternative. Gibbon read Bayle as a determined sceptic of this kind, as a universal critic of religious and philosophical systems:

> His critical Dictionary is a vast repository of facts and opinions; and he balances the *false* religions in his sceptical scales, till the opposite quantities, (if I may use the language of Algebra) annihilate each other [...]. 'I am most truly (said Bayle) a protestant; for I protest indifferently against all Systems, and all Sects'.[13]

The very constitution of Bayle's *magnum opus*, its being a 'vast repository of facts and opinions', entails a huge act of *isosthenia*; sceptical activity, as with Montaigne, seems an inevitable consequence of amassed learning. The sceptic's wisdom, moreover, is expressed not through a direct argument but through an act of form: it is the dictionary's textual fabric, its manner of compilation, that determines the direction of its meaning.

Another version of the argument from variety – again an important one for Byron – is Hume's case against miracles.[14] Hume's probabalistic relativism appealed to Byron as a strongly reasoned response to the world, but also as a rich store of comically pliant imagery. This is Hume:

> in matters of religion, whatever is different is contrary; and that it is impossible the religions of ancient ROME, of TURKEY, of SIAM, and of CHINA should, all of them, be established on any solid foundation. Every miracle, therefore, pretended to have been wrought in any of these religions (and all of them abound in miracles), as its direct scope is to establish the particular system to which it is attributed; so has it the same force, though more indirectly, to overthrow every other system.[15]

With Byron, here in *Beppo*, the stamped presence of argument – which is so clear in Hume's prose – is modulated and energized by the mind of the poet and ironist:

> And there are dresses splendid, but fantastical,
>   Masks of all times and nations, Turks and Jews,
> And harlequins and clowns, with feats gymnastical,
>   Greeks, Romans, Yankee-doodles, and Hindoos;
> All kinds of dress, except the ecclesiastical,
>   All people, as their fancies hit, may choose,
> But no one in these parts may quiz the clergy,
> Therefore take heed, ye Freethinkers! I charge ye.
>
> *(Beppo, 3)*

Byron borrows Hume's Romans and Turks and swells their ranks to create a vibrant pluralism that stands in contrast to an authoritarian establishment determined to assert its exemption from the threatening energies of variety. The question of what Byron is arguing, however, seems a difficult one to answer. We could take the stanza as a critique of organized religion from the perspective of the 'Freethinker', as an assertion of the individual's right to 'choose' without the coercion of a morally unreliable and philosophically unjustified Church. This, however, as well as being too straightforward for Byron's complex take on religion, would be to crowbar deft and tonally evasive poetry into a position of over-easy liberalism. The first problem is that Byron is not thinking straightforwardly in philosophical terms in the way Hume is. What for Hume is the space of argument is for Byron crammed full of life and the questionable, participated truths of carnival as an ethically particular form of human activity. The idea of choice, moreover, is not given a clear philosophical outcome: if we wish to construe our ability to 'choose' as our 'fancies hit' as a straightforwardly good thing then we do so because of what we have already decided rather than because of anything that has happened in the process of reading Byron's poetry. The question of how desirable such freedom might be is left unanswered behind the poet's irony. Second, Byron is interested in his language as its own form of comic life; the rhymes that carry through 'fantastical' and 'gymnastical' and that link up 'doodles' and 'Hindoos' don't argue anything, but they contribute to a reading experience that projects beyond the assumptive framework of the argued.

One of the most provocative questions thrown up by classical scepticism is where we go (if anywhere) from the suspended state of *epoche*. Hume argued that in the absence of certainty we should weigh the merits of each case and decide which is most likely. The classical Pyrrhonist takes a rather different line. Pyrrhonism is conceived of by its followers as a way of life outside the Academy; it is more concerned with the broken surfaces of life than the procedures of theory. Academic scepticism, it has been said, 'leads nowhere', whereas 'Pyrrhonism is a universal attitude'.[16] The Pyrrhonist withholds belief about the nature of reality as it is presented to him through the senses, but he does (*contra* the amusing but misleading stories about Pyrrho and onrushing chariots) 'assent to appearances, over which he has no control',[17] as well as accepting the social and cultural configurations within which he finds himself (in this sense it is a conservative philosophy). He is not, as the stories suggest, a lunatic who refuses instinct, will and nature at the behest of philosophical principles, but one who seeks a life untroubled by what are seen as fruitless conflicts over questions that cannot in any case be settled in a philosophically satisfactory manner. Pyrrhonists 'follow', as Sextus Empiricus writes, 'a line of reasoning which, in accordance with appearances, points us to a life comfortable to the customs of our country and its laws and institutions, and to our instinctive feelings'.[18] The end of Pyrrhonism is not to win an argument but to achieve a state of *ataraxia*;[19] it encourages, that is, a way of life grounded in a 'suspension of judgment [that] brings with it tranquillity like its shadow'.[20]

For Byron, Pyrrhonism was just another crazy pre-Christian sect he had read about in Bayle (and others), as we see in this pointedly double suspension:

I am no Platonist, I am nothing at all; but I would sooner be a Paulician, Manichean, Spinozist, Gentile, Pyrrhonian, Zoroastrian, than one of the seventy-two villainous sects who are tearing each other to pieces for the love of the Lord and hatred of each other. (*BLJ*, ii, 89)[21]

Influenced by Hume's sense of Pyrrhonism as irrelevant, as something that will 'vanish like smoke' when exposed to the realities of life,[22] Byron would have thought of the Pyrrhonist as a version of the philosopher in Johnson's *Rasselas*.

On the other hand Hume (arguably) misrepresents Pyrrhonism by conflating it with Academic scepticism, the latter, seemingly, being more susceptible to his accusations of excessive abstractness and irrelevance to real life.[23] The Pyrrhonist has in fact thought about his inability to deny the 'principles of our nature' and his *ataraxia*, especially where developed (as Hoagwood does in Byron's case) away from simple conformism, is perhaps not quite as hopeless as Hume suggests. If Hume does misunderstand Pyrrhonism then he also bequeaths his misunderstanding to Byron who, as Hoagwood and others note, makes a number of claims that seem (at least partly) consistent with the tripartite Pyrrhonian structure described above. His insistence upon being 'nothing at all', for instance, sounds just like the kind of non-dogmatic disengagement typical of classical scepticism. Byron frequently self-diagnoses such states of mental disengagement, thus falling more or less into line with the procedures recommended in Diogenes Laertius and by Sextus Empiricus: 'I will neither read *pro* nor *con*. God would have made His will known without books, considering how very few could read them when Jesus of Nazareth lived, had it been His pleasure to ratify any peculiar mode of worship' (*BLJ*, ii, 98). Such refusals to 'read' either way (especially if we ignore the complications entered by Byron's devout tones) might certainly be extrapolated into a state of *epoche*. Whether we want to go as far as to commit Byron, with Hoagwood, to a neo-Pyrrhonist 'conceptual and preconceptual frame' is another question.[24]

Hoagwood, it seems to me, overcommits his subject through a selective use of evidence. He cites this extract from a pre-wedding letter to Annabella Milbanke:

The only part [of mathematics] I remember which gave me much delight were those theorems (is that the word?) in which after ringing the changes upon – A–B & C–D. &c. I at last came to "which is absurd – which is impossible" and at this point I have always arrived (*BLJ*, iii, 159)

Of this it is claimed that 'Byron intensifies the pleasure of mental suspension, putting "delight" where the ancients put "tranquillity", but the total suspension of mind is welcomed by Byron no less than the early philosophical sceptics'.[25] In another letter to Annabella, Byron writes: 'in the midst of myriads of the living & the dead worlds – stars – systems – infinity – why should I be anxious about an atom?' (*BLJ*, iv, 78). Of this Hoagwood claims that the 'deficit of a conclusion, comforting or otherwise, can generate a sceptical *ataraxia* and a freedom from angst. [Byron] expresses in his own voice – not in the fictionality of a poetic projection – this skeptical quietude and its basis'.[26] The first problem here is the assumption that in these letters we encounter a more authentic, stable or reliable voicing of Byron's philosophical views than we do in the poetry. Byron's pre-wedding letters to Annabella emerge from a very specific and complex set of social and psychological factors, and project a different personality to the one encountered, for instance, in the letters to Hodgson. They are certainly a performance, and not necessarily less of one than the often movingly honest narrator of *Don Juan*, who also represents a more intellectually developed Byron. It is true that a form of rational suspension is welcomed in the case of mathematics (part of a larger joke about Byron's future wife) and in the second example Byron plays the world-weary philosopher who has apparently given up in the face of his own insignificance; but, taken as a whole, his articulations are too richly contradictory and evasive to justify any conceptual privileging of 'skeptical quietude' or 'freedom from angst' (intended or otherwise). Byron often suggests the opposite, as when he (allegedly) remarked to the composer Isaac Nathan, in 1814, that 'they accuse me of atheism – an atheist I could never be – no man of reflection, can feel otherwise than doubtful and anxious, when reflecting on futurity' (*HVSV*, 83).

Hoagwood is right to draw attention Byron's 'vitality' and 'life-enhancing power',[27] but while these energies certainly draw from the imagery and structures of the sceptical tradition they also exceed that tradition's frames. Byron's philosophical significance will not be found by invoking (or adapting) established philosophical descriptors, but in following the ways his poetry transforms linear thought amidst the energizing possibilities of language:

> For ever and anon comes Indigestion,
>   (Not that most 'dainty Ariel') and perplexes
> Our soarings with another sort of question:
>   And that which after all my spirit vexes,
> Is, that I find no spot where man can rest his eye on,
>   Without confusion of the sorts and sexes,

Of being, stars, and this unriddled wonder,
The World, which at the worst's a glorious blunder –

(Don Juan, xi, 3)

For Byron, the world's 'wonder' and 'blunder' are firmly linked, and while the former may be glimpsed in passing there remains nowhere 'man can rest his eye'. Vexation, which is the opposite of the Pyrrhonist's aim, is for Byron a necessary precondition of speculative and spiritual action and defines the environment in which true attentiveness and engagement become possible. The narrator of Don Juan may find moments of tenuous stability – 'I perch upon an humbler promontory, / Amidst life's infinite variety' (Don Juan, xv, 19) – but to be perched is not to suggest the kind of committed intellectual residency assumed by the notion of having a philosophical position or 'stance' such as the Pyrrhonist's. Byron is not writing philosophy here but transforming its terms as part of a critical investigation into thought and its relation to metaphor. To write 'For ever and anon comes Indigestion' is not to commit to scepticism but to wonder (with Montaigne) about the staging of such commitments in language.

Pyrrhonism is important in Don Juan, not because it provides an intellectual frame for the poem, but because it suggests images to the poet. Where the narrator, imperilled but not quite overwhelmed, sails 'In the Wind's Eye' upon the 'Ocean of Eternity' (Don Juan, x, 4), the Pyrrhonist (in a stanza not discussed by Hoagwood), is hopelessly becalmed:

> It is a pleasant voyage perhaps to float,
>   Like Pyrrho, on a sea of speculation;
> But what if carrying sail capsize the boat?
>   Your wise men don't know much of navigation;
> And swimming long in the abyss of thought
>   Is apt to tire: a calm and shallow station
> Well nigh the shore, where one stoops down and gathers
> Some pretty shell, is best for moderate bathers.

(Don Juan, ix, 18)

Pyrrho's 'sea of speculation' may offer the prospect of a 'pleasant float' (ataraxia), but, in what looks a version of Hume's critique, it is questioned as an ethical conclusion. Byron places limits on speculative philosophy ('swimming long in the abyss of thought') in the direction of life. Where Hume turns away from philosophy to the benefits of sociability, however, the Byronic poet and exile drives on towards the eternal. He also allows his metaphors to complicate things, to invite paraphrase but to resist its wish for conclusion. Alongside the hard-pressed poet and the hapless philosopher he introduces another figure, the 'moderate bather' (Byron was of course anything but); this seemingly ordinary fellow is counselled to stay 'well nigh the shore' and content himself with a 'pretty shell'. Rather than ditching philosophy entirely, however, this returns us to it by suggesting another version of Pyrrhonism. Rather than the tranquillity-directed procedures recommended by Sextus Empiricus, Byron seems to be thinking more of the artefact-mediated ('pretty shell') fideism he encountered in Montaigne. To complicate things further, the object of Byron's apparent condescension is associated with one of the poem's great symbols of genius and intellectual humility, Isaac Newton.[28]

Where classical Pyrrhonism, as we find it in Sextus Empiricus, can only take us so close to Byron because it isn't interested in writing, Montaigne's version offers a more plausible line of enquiry. Byron found in Montaigne a philosopher whose meanings are conditioned by the ironies of ego and (essayistic) form. He also found a thinker fascinated by the sublunary, but never content with its boundaries.

Montaigne's influential playing of theology was dictated by the intellectual turmoil of his times. When the writings of Sextus Empiricus, which had largely disappeared from the European intellectual scene, were published by Henri Étienne (in a Latin translation) in 1562, they caused a 'sensation' amidst the intellectual ferment of the Reformation.[29] From the perspective of the Catholic Church, assailed as it was by energetic reformers, philosophical scepticism threatened to create a 'crise pyrrhonienne' in religion.[30] In response, Catholic intellectuals, including Pierre Charron, Pierre-Daniel Huet and, less straightforwardly, Montaigne, turned Pyrrhonism to their own advantage; they accepted the sceptical impasse identified by their classical forbears but, instead of using it to attack religion, used it to argue that there can be no rational basis for departing from the established Church. Adapting the classical Pyrrhonist's conformism, these Christian Pyrrhonists proposed that the only alternative to the chaos of absolute relativism is obedience to what is established.

Montaigne admired classical Pyrrhonism, claiming that there is 'nothing in human Invention, that carries so great a shew of Likelyhood and Utility'.[31] In his 'Apologie de Raimond Sebond', an important text within the Christian Pyrrhonist tradition, he follows classical procedure by compiling an extensive list of religious forms that he uses to undermine confidence in any one particular system. Faced with this diversity, he challenges the would-be dogmatist to 'brag, that you have *found the Bean in the Cake*' (*Essays*, ii, 277). At this crucial point (*epoche*), however, he departs from classical precedent to assert the necessity of placing our faith in a metaphorically vibrant Church:

> She [reason] *does nothing but err throughout, but especially when she meddles with Divine things.* [W]e daily see [...] that if she swerve never so little from the ordinary Path; and that she strays from, or wander out of the way, set out and beaten by the *Church*, how soon she loses, confounds and fetters herself, tumbling and floating in this vast, turbulent and waving Sea of Human Opinions, without restraint, and without any determinate end. (*Essays*, ii, 283–4)

Montaigne's 'turbulent and waving Sea of Human Opinions' flows into Byron's 'sea of speculation'. The latter's 'pretty shell', moreover, by offering something reassuringly comprehensible (and aesthetically pleasing) to hold to in the face of boundlessness, touches the metaphorical space occupied by Montaigne's rock-like Church. This also recalls Byron's comments on the Italian Catholicism in which he was immersed for much of his adult life.[32] Sharply contrasting the cold, austere doctrines of the 'Calvinistic Scotch School' with which he was 'early disgusted' and for which he was 'cudgelled to Church for the first ten years of [his] life' (*BLJ*, iii, 64),[33] the vibrant presences of Catholicism sparked and held Byron's imagination: 'I am really a great admirer of tangible religion', he wrote to Thomas Moore from Pisa, 'and am breeding one of my daughters a Catholic, that she may have her hands full [...]. What with incense, pictures, statues, altars, shrines, relics, and the real presence, confession, absolution, – there is something sensible to grasp at'. Byron continues this well-known letter by withholding earnestness while at the same time foregrounding the kind of metaphorical language already noted in *Don Juan*: 'Besides it leaves no possibility of doubt; for those who swallow their Deity, really and truly, in transubstantiation, can hardly find anything else otherwise than easy of digestion' (*BLJ*, ix, 123). The simple yet profound idea that the aesthetics of faith might hold off the claims of scepticism is typically complicated by the (comic) possibilities of metaphor. This leaves us on shaky ground if we want to claim Byron for Catholicism in any straightforward way, but we should also notice that in the very process of scrambling his voice Byron is participating in precisely the kind of dynamic he describes. By activating his own poetic imagination he projects an aesthetic construct (of sorts) between the site of thought and its ultimate, unknowable object. If 'pictures, statues, altars, shrines, relics' have a common capacity to mitigate the void, then might not the shapings of the poet do something similar?

Another way of approaching this begins with the observation that Byron makes a poor show, in his pre-Italian years, of being a non-Catholic fideist. Without 'something sensible to grasp at' he runs into tensions between official morality and poetic presence, as here in the Gibbon and Voltaire stanza of *Childe Harold's Pilgrimage*:

> Lausanne! and Ferney! ye have been the abodes
> Of names which unto you bequeath'd a name;
> Mortals, who sought and found, by dangerous roads,
> A path to perpetuity of fame:
> They were gigantic minds, and their steep aim,
> Was, Titan-like, on daring doubts to pile
> Thoughts which should call down thunder, and the flame
> Of Heaven, again assail'd, if Heaven the while
> On man and man's research could deign do more than smile.
>
> (*Childe Harold's Pilgrimage*, iii, 105)

The bottom line certainly looks fideist in bestowing a kindly smile upon the greatest efforts of human reason. What comes across, however, is not God's infinite wisdom, mercy or compassion, but His blandness. All of the interest is with Gibbon and Voltaire who are recast as Promethean heroes, their Babel-like pile of doubts and intrepid pursuit of 'dangerous roads' (rather than Montaigne's beaten path) dominating the stanza. Byron was not a scoffer at religion, but his attempt at orthodoxy here is failed by the distribution of poetic force. With no tangible presence available from his theological context he is left to create his own on terms that seem unflattering to doctrine.

What is missing here is not any openness to religion on Byron's part but the opportunity to align it with the mediating efforts of the imagination. By way of comparison we might take the description in the later, Italian-written cantos of *Don Juan*, of Norman Abbey, a version of Byron's own Newstead. The place is described through a fine historical, aesthetic and reflexive awareness, its riven statues attesting to a now-stilled, diachronic violence:

> Within a niche, nigh to its pinnacle,
>   Twelve saints had once stood sanctified in stone;
> But these had fallen, not when the friars fell,
>   But in the war which struck Charles from his throne,
> When each house was a fortalice – as tell
>   The annals of full many a line undone –
> The gallant Cavaliers, who fought in vain
> For those who knew not to resign or reign.
>
> (*Don Juan*, xiii, 60)

Unlike the massive and massively political fragments of Shelley's 'Ozymandias' which crumble beneath the absolute of time, Byron's statues register a graded sense of history; they survived the machinations of Thomas Cromwell only to fare less well amidst the ravages of Oliver. In relation to this we may detect a few Cavalier sympathies and even a touch of the house-proud aristocrat ('fortalice' is a little technical and not a little Shandean), but nothing in the way of clear theological positioning. As the narrator rattles on, however, the statues, which have witnessed history's passing and absorbed it shocks, persist in their inscrutable but tangible profundity. They make their own silent claim (upon us). Their partial erasure, moreover, is compensated by the sheer verbal presence of Byron's poetry. That concentration of stress – 'stood sanctified in stone' – participates in eroded meanings that hover between presence and absence.

This recalls us, also, to the densities of (Byron's) Montaigne's motto, the background to which is worth looking at. When Leigh Hunt arrived in Pisa to live with Byron in June 1822 he brought with him Charles Cotton's translation of Montaigne. Byron had read the philosopher before he left England (and owned 1802 and 1811 editions), but now returned to the essays, extensively rereading them over a summer in which he was also occupied with cantos viii and ix of *Don Juan*.[34] It was Hunt's copy that the poet apparently read and in which he marked several pages that appear to have particularly interested him with 'a double dog's ear'.[35] On one of these dog-eared pages Montaigne discusses, in the essay 'Use Makes Perfectness' (usually translated 'On Practice'), his Byronic choice of subject: "Tis now many Years since, that my Thoughts have had no other aim and level than myself, and that I have only pry'd into and study'd myself' (*Essays*, ii, 71). In developing this discussion, Montaigne reveals the difficulties that have attended his endeavour: 'I chiefly paint my Thoughts, an Inform Subject, and incapable of Operative Production. 'Tis all that I can do to couch it in this airy body of the Voice' (*Essays*, ii, 72). Thought is an 'Inform Subject' and as such is not easily captured by the writer's words. A similar problem crops up in the 'Apologie de Raimond Sebond' when Montaigne is discussing how the ancient sceptics tried to describe the attitudes or mental states that characterize their philosophy:

> The *Pyrrhonian* Philosophers, I discern, cannot express their general Conception in any kind of speaking: For the World requires a new language on purpose. Ours is all form'd of affirmative Propositions, which are totally antartick to them. Insomuch that when they say, I doubt, they are presently

taken by the Throat, to make them confess, that at least they know, and are assured that they *do doubt*. By which means they have been compell'd to shelter themselves under this medicinal Comparison, without which, their Humour would be inexplicable. When they pronounce, *I know not*: Or, *I doubt*; they say, *that this Proposition carries off it self with the rest, no more, no less, than* Rhubarb, *that drives out the ill Humours, and carries it self off with them.* This Fancy will be more certainly understood by Interrogation: *What do I know?* (as I bear it in the Emblem of a Balance). (*Essays*, ii, 295–6)

Language is an accumulation of 'affirmative Propositions' and as such fundamentally unsuited to expressing the Pyrrhonist's philosophical attitude, something that would require a 'new language'. Lacking any such thing, these philosophers enlist the suggestiveness of metaphor to hint at what cannot be described directly. Similarly, Montaigne suggests that we might approach his own thought not in terms of arguments and answers, but by forming in our minds the question that Byron carries forward into his poem. The motto, which Montaigne (in or around 1576) had stamped on a medal with the image of a balance or weighing scales, is posited between subject and indefinable object as an acknowledgement of scepticism that is also a prompt to mental attentiveness.

Unlike later philosophers, such as Locke, who downplay literary language as mere entertainment, Montaigne invests such language with a distinct philosophical agency:

Why will not *Nature* please once and for all to lay open her Bosom to us, and plainly discover to us the Means and Conduct of her Movements, and prepare our Eyes to see them? Good God, what Abuse, what Mistakes should we discover in our poor Science! I am mistaken, if that weak Knowledge of ours hold any one thing, as it really is, and I shall depart hence more Ignorant of all other things than my own Ignorance. Have I not read in *Plato* this Divine Saying, That, Nature is nothing but an Aenigmatick Poesie! As if a Man might peradventure say, a veil'd and shady Picture, breaking out here and there with an infinite Variety of false Lights to puzzle our Conjectures [...] And certainly *Philosophy* is no other than a falsified *Poesie*. (*Essays*, ii, 310–11)

Echoing Socrates, as Byron would in *Don Juan*, Montaigne admits the certainty of his 'Ignorance'. The truths of nature are not laid open to us and are thus like an 'Aenigmatick Poesie' that will always 'puzzle our Conjectures'.[36] Literary cognition thus occupies and describes the moment in which conventional philosophy breaks down. The latter, in its selectiveness, is correspondingly relegated to the status of 'falsified *Poesie*'.

In *Don Juan*, Byron comes very close to such a view of things through his own questions – 'But what's reality? Who has its clue?' – and rejected answer: 'Philosophy? No; she too much rejects' (*Don Juan*, xv, 89).[37] He also, as we have seen, follows Montaigne in recognizing the potential for certain linguistic formulations to mitigate epistemological breakdown. Where Montaigne's motto is a question, however, Byron's 'I doubt if doubt itself be doubting' raises the stakes by pressurizing affirmation into paradox. Montaigne's question seeks to render his meaning sufficiently 'Inform' to express his (adapted) Pyrrhonism. Byron's paradox doesn't stay with anything so philosophically determined and is thus both more radically sceptical and more open to undetermined possibility. It would not be correct, therefore, to understand *Don Juan*'s uptake of Montaigne, with Lilian Furst, as articulating 'resignation in the face of an impenetrable enigma'.[38] Poetry may resign on behalf of an autonomous 'Philosophy' on the grounds that it is a 'falsified *Poesie*', but in so doing it rescripts its own role as 'philosophical' agent, as tenuous intervention upon the 'Ocean of Eternity'.

* * *

Scepticism, as presented in *Don Juan*, enters the problematic moment of encounter between philosophy and poetry. To limit this self-disowning 'scepticism' to non-literary frames of analysis is thus to miss its imaginative trajectory. I now want to think more about what scepticism might mean for Byron and specifically about how his doubts about the written practice of others shape his own writing.

If we ask what Byron is being sceptical *about* in places such as *Don Juan* then one word that immediately springs to mind is 'system', that most flexible and persistent of Byronic pejoratives. During his courtship of 1814 Byron complained, in a letter to Lady Melbourne, that with Annabella, his future wife, 'the least word – or alteration of tone – has some inference drawn from it – sometimes we are too much alike – & then again too unlike – this comes of *system* – & squaring her notions to the Devil knows what' (*BLJ*, iv, 231). Annabella's systematic mind, rather than taking things as they come, pre-decides a world it is not used to encountering on its own terms. Her squaring of the unshaped writes small something Byron would come to understand as a profound cultural and moral malaise.

Although Byron's critique of 'system' is often conflated with his 'scepticism', the two emerge from distinct traditions. David Simpson has described the anti-systematic attitude as one which continues to be available even today for the articulation of a British (and, with some differences, an Anglo-American) way of doing and seeing things, one based on common-sense, on a resistance to generalized thought, and on a declared immersion in the minute complexities of a 'human' nature whose essence is usually identified in an accumulation of mutually incomprehensible details rather than in a single, systematized personality.[39]

A classic example of this attitude is that of Shaftesbury, who took issue with progressive, but, as he saw them, humanly unrealistic philosophical theories concerned with abstruse, generalized concepts rather than specific ethical realities:

> But for the philosopher who pretends to be wholly taken up in considering his higher faculties, and examining the powers and principles of his understanding, if in reality his philosophy be foreign to the matter professed, if it goes beside the mark and reaches nothing we can truly call our interest or concern, it must be somewhat worse than mere ignorance or idiotism. The most ingenious way of becoming foolish is by a system. And the surest method to prevent good sense is to set up something in the room of it.[40]

Voltaire, in similar terms, laid the blame for 'system' at the door of Descartes, who, he claimed, was 'born not to discover the errors of Antiquity, but to substitute his own in the Room of them; and [was] hurried away by that systematic Spirit which throws a Cloud over the Minds of the greatest Men'.[41] 'System' can be the mark of the weak mind, but it can also be an expression of the powerful mind's hubris and involution. It involves an act of replacement or insertion that, unlike Byron's use of motto and paradox, lacks the self-knowledge bequeathed by scepticism. Byron traced the problem back further than Voltaire did:

> Oh Plato! Plato! you have paved the way,
>   With your confounded fantasies, to more
> Immoral conduct by the fancied sway
>   Your system feigns o'er the controlless core
> Of human hearts, than all the long array
>   Of poets and romancers: – You're a bore,
> A charlatan, a coxcomb – and have been,
> At best, no better than a go-between.
>
> (*Don Juan*, i, 116)

For Byron, as for Pope, to be human is to be a 'Chaos of Thought and Passion, all confus'd' (*Essay on Man*, ii, 13); we are not built around a coherent and explicable centre, but a 'controlless core' that defies reason. 'Systems' such as Plato's are in these terms fundamentally dishonest in their feigning ('to fashion fictitiously or deceptively' (*OED*)) over or will to control an unforthcoming human nature. Where Plato's original swerve into 'system' involves a brilliant untruth, however, its legacy has been at best ambivalent. Using the same allusion to Milton's Satan through which Shelley weaves subtle menace into the apocalyptic ending of his *Ode to Liberty*,[42] Byron concludes that the great philosopher has 'paved the way' for lesser minds to enervate where he has energized.

As Simpson makes clear, the critique of 'system' is politically freighted. In Byron's day it was central to the British establishment's response to revolutionary politics, 'repeatedly defined as French obsession' and seen as 'explicitly un-English'.[43] Somewhere behind this attitude was Burke's argument against the theorization of complex and particularized human situations:

> I cannot stand forward, and give praise and blame to any thing which relates to human actions, and human concerns, on a simple view of the object, as it stands stripped of every relation, in all the nakedness and solitude of metaphysical abstraction. Circumstances (which with some gentlemen pass for nothing) give in reality to every political principle its distinguishing colour, and discriminating effect. The circumstances are what render every civil and political scheme beneficial or noxious to mankind.[44]

Byron's politics have generated much debate,[45] and it would be a brave commentator who seeks to pin them down.[46] It seems fair to speculate, however, that the poet would have approved Burke's suspicion of any attempt to manage human 'concerns' through thinking that is better suited to the 'solitude of metaphysical abstraction'. He despised what he saw as Malthus's attempts to bring human specifics under the rule of scientific generalization, scorning his 'turning marriage into arithmetic' (*Don Juan*, xv, 38).[47] He also objected, on similar grounds, to the attempts of the Benthamite Philhellene Leicester Stanhope, 'a mere schemer and talker', to manage revolutionary Greece; the latter's ideas, Byron apparently complained, were conceived 'without reference to any body, or any thing'.[48] But where Burke, who blamed 'system' for the bloody implosion of the French Revolution, fixes such problems to anti-establishment politics, Byron could see them at both ends of the politcal spectrum. He could construe reformist and revolutionary ideas as thoughtlessly bent on destruction, but he also recognized the post-Waterloo European political structure as 'A prop not quite so certain as before' (*Don Juan*, ix, 3).

As Byron was acutely aware, sceptical thought is always vulnerable to its own energies. If the anti-systematic impulse becomes as predictable as the systematic activity to which it is opposed, then it has undone itself. 'System' thus cannot be dismissed without thought and must, in some cases, be embraced, as Byron does through system-driven figures such as Plato and Napoleon. Systems offer energy, drive and verve; they are, moreover, the basis of life and provide the psychological and formal contexts within which life's vitality is expressed. This may result in foolishness – or worse – but such aberrations need to be understood with reference to the formidable and enervating alternatives. Sterne recognizes this in the comic and sympathetic psychology of Walter Shandy, an amateur philosopher described as 'all uniformity; – he was systematical, and, like all systematick reasoners, he would move both heaven and earth, and twist and torture every thing in nature to support his hypothesis'.[49] These mental oddities, however, are not merely held up to ridicule (as we might get with Swift), but are analysed within a comic frame that acknowledges 'systematical' tendencies to be necessary psychological adaptations in the face of a life that is hurtling inescapably towards the unspeakable fact of death. Walter and Toby may ride their hobby horses roughshod over the gardens of common sense, but in the process they generate energy, empathy and optimism; they stumble into a life of comedy that offsets the immediacy of an otherwise, for Sterne, containing and undeniable tragedy.

Similar patterns can be traced in *Don Juan*, a poem strongly indebted to Sterne:[50]

> The evaporation of a joyous day
>   Is like the last glass of champagne, without
> The foam which made its virgin bumper gay;
>   Or like a system coupled with a doubt;
> Or like a soda bottle when its spray
>   Has sparkled and let half its spirit out;
> Or like a billow left by storms behind,
> Without the animation of the wind;
>
> (*Don Juan*, xvi, 9)

As Shaftesbury tells us, the narrative of experience leads to wisdom; it is also, Byron recognized, a story of loss. The sceptic's puncturing of 'system' with his doubts can be no simple victory; it may be justified philosophically, but for the nostalgic poet it maps onto the ways in which life is leached from the world. If, in the final analysis, 'system' is a mode of delusion, then it is only so in the sense that pleasure is a frivolity when measured against the cold span of experience. Poetry, in these terms, both describes the problem and musters a defence. Scepticism is built into the form of the stanza in its listing acknowledgement that each individual simile must fail. Their very proliferation, however, discovers new energies where bland theoretical prose would find none. Scepticism remains intact, but it is not allowed to inscribe defeat.

Byron's critique of 'system' is more complex and sympathetic than is sometimes thought. Where it often seems most aggressively direct is in the poet's attacks on some of his prominent literary contemporaries. If 'system' lays claim to the unique grounds of poetic meaning, he concluded, then we risk losing one of our most profound challenges to the narrowing of apprehension in which modernity is busily involved. Although unlikely allies, Byron would in these terms have had some sympathy with Hazlitt's attack on the literary 'system-maker' as one who lacks a 'tremulous sensibility to every slight and wandering impression' and who thus cannot 'follow all the infinite fluctuations of thought through their nicest distinctions'.[51] Among those Byron saw as missing these fluctuations in his writing was Leigh Hunt, to whom he wrote: 'I have not time nor paper to *attack* your *system* – which ought to be done – were it only because it is a *system*' (*BLJ*, iv, 332).[52] There was also Wordsworth, 'the great Metaquizzical poet' (*BLJ*, viii, 66) with his 'new system to perplex the sages' (*Don Juan*, 'Dedication', 4) as well as Coleridge:

And Coleridge, too, has lately taken wing,
    But, like a hawk encumber'd with his hood,
Explaining metaphysics to the nation –
I wish he would explain his Explanation.
                    (*Don Juan*, 'Dedication', 2)[53]

The problem here, as Byron saw it, was the extent to which philosophy and theory, in works such as Wordsworth's Preface and Coleridge's *Biographia Literaria*, were assuming responsibility for poetry (and poetics). This had to be a bad thing for poetry, Byron thought, because it is precisely in breaking free from the assumptions of philosophy that poetic writing finds its epistemological value.

The intelligent critique of system is a double-edged sword. As one of the defining poets of his day, Byron could not insulate himself entirely from his own critique of Romantic overdetermination. We sense this when he claims of his (relatively Wordsworthian) third canto of *Childe Harold's Pilgrimage* that he had been 'half mad during the time of its composition, between metaphysics, mountains, lakes, love unextinguishable, thoughts unutterable, and the nightmare of my own delinquencies' (*BLJ*, v, 165). Writing of the same poem's final canto, Thomas Love Peacock complained to Shelley, in May 1818, that it is 'really too bad. I cannot consent to be an *auditor tantum* of this systematical "poisoning" of the mind of the reading public'.[54] When Peacock made a point of satirizing Byron on these grounds in his *Nightmare Abbey* (1818), Byron took the criticism with good grace, even sending Peacock a rosebud with a message that he bore him no ill will for his satire.[55] Indeed, Byron had, by this stage, been questioning the 'systematical' tendencies of his own work for some time, notably in this well-known letter to Murray:

> With regard to poetry in general I am convinced the more I think of it – that he [Moore] and *all* of us – Scott – Southey – Wordsworth – Moore – Campbell – I – are all in the wrong – one as much as another – that we are upon a wrong revolutionary poetical system – or systems – not worth a damn in itself – & from which none but Rogers and Crabbe are free – and that the present & next generations will finally be of this opinion. (*BLJ*, v, 265)

Written in September 1817, around the time Byron was moving away from *Childe Harold's Pilgrimage* and towards *Don Juan*, Byron's letter is intriguingly poised between reaction and innovation. Byron praises the old-fashioned couplets of Rogers and Crabbe for being free from the contemporary malaise of 'system',[56] yet the last thing he has in mind is any suggestion that either writer should be taken as a model for the present or the future. *Don Juan* is a strikingly original poem, one that is 'wholly new & relative to the age',[57] as Shelley, the period's most exhilarating invocator of poetic possibility, describes it.

Byron's attack on literary 'system' is not a curmudgeonly or reactionary reflex; it is informed, rather, by the poet's acute sensitivity to the generic priorities of his day.[58] His critique was thus not simply a question of indulging a genius for *ad hominem* satire; it was about, and needed to come through, the claims of literary form. This is most obviously indicated by Byron's self-conscious placement of *Don Juan* in the essayistic tradition: 'Read, or read not, what I am now essaying / To show ye what ye are in every way' (*Don Juan*, vii, 7). Byron witnessed and admired the critical force of essay in Montaigne, Sterne and (among others) Johnson.[59] Take, for instance, Johnson's definition of 'systematic', which quotes Bayle on one side of the question: 'I treat of the usefulness of writing books of essay, in comparison of that of writing systematically'. Bayle, as a profuse sceptic, was naturally drawn to essayistic modes, and would have associated their philosophical 'usefulness', as Montaigne did, with their provisional and incomplete formal suggestiveness. As well as quoting Bayle, however, Johnson also quotes Isaac

Watts (a favourite author of his) complaining about the eighteenth-century vogue for hammering 'system': 'now we deal much in essays, and unreasonably despise *systematical* learning; whereas, our fathers had a just value for regularity and systems'.[60] Johnson's definition becomes genuinely essayistic – or unpredetermined – by keeping in mind the fact that even a preference for the essay can become systematic (and thus disempowered), depending upon cultural norms. By setting aside the claims of category Johnson ironically, but powerfully, enlists for his cause forces that threaten the very possibility of meaningful definition.[61]

Don Juan, with a similar if more chaotic kind of irony, articulates the challenge of essay in the very process of philosophical speculation:

> IF from great Nature's or our own abyss
>   Of thought, we could but snatch a certainty,
> Perhaps mankind might find the path they miss –
>   But then 'twould spoil much good philosophy.
> One system eats another up, and this
>   Much as old Saturn ate his progeny;
> For when his pious consort gave him stones
> In lieu of sons, of these he made no bones.
>
> But System doth reverse the Titan's breakfast,
>   And eats her parents, albeit the digestion
> Is difficult. Pray tell me, can you make fast,
>   After due search, your faith to any question?
> Look back o'er ages, ere unto the stake fast
>   You bind yourself, and call some mode the best one.
> Nothing more true than *not* to trust your senses;
> And yet what are your other evidences?
>
>   (*Don Juan*, xiv, 1–2)

The intellectual skeleton of this comes from philosophical scepticism in its identification of systematic philosophy as a long trail of delusion and hubris, one 'system' consuming and usurping the next, thus reversing 'the Titan's breakfast'. If this is all that results from our reading, however, then we are not reading what has been written. What is arresting here is the reach of the language and imagery beyond philosophical positioning into the surrounding richness of human history and imagination. Byron's metaphors do not think of themselves as cloudy inconveniences but as assertions against the static; his 'bind' and 'stake', for instance, remind us of the terrors that attend the history of intellectual dispute. Where Locke would consider himself forced to accept the physical basis of intellectual language,[62] Byron revels in the comic and expansive possibilities thrown up by linguistic dependence. He constructs his stanzas in order to call into question the autonomy of mind and its pretensions to abstract objectivity: to write 'our own abyss / Of thought' is not the same as writing 'our own abyss of thought'. Neither Byron nor Saturn can digest what they eat, but between them they oversee the breakdown of metaphoric function. There is no skilful, elegant, mutually elucidating compression of physical and mental of the kind we might get from Shakespeare,[63] only an increasingly messy, energetic language found in the process of throwing off the duties of description imposed by intellectual history. It is the words themselves ('stones' cannot make 'bones' but the word can be broken down into 'sons') rather than their apparent objects that come to dominate.[64]

Byron is less interested in making philosophical arguments than he is in acknowledging the world through the process of recognizing what such arguments leave out:

> WHEN Bishop Berkeley said 'there was no matter,'
>   And proved it – 'twas no matter what he said:
> They say his system 'tis in vain to batter,
>   Too subtle for the airiest human head;
> And yet who can believe it! I would shatter
>   Gladly all matters, down to stone or lead,
> Or adamant, to find the World a spirit,
> And wear my head, denying that I wear it.
>
> What a sublime discovery 'twas to make the
>   Universe universal Egotism!
> That all's ideal – *all ourselves*: I'll stake the
>   World (be it what you will) that *that's* no Schism.
> Oh, Doubt! – if thou be'st Doubt, for which some take thee,
>   But which I doubt extremely – thou sole prism
> Of the Truth's rays, spoil not my draught of spirit!
> Heaven's brandy, – though our brain can hardly bear it.
>
> For ever and anon comes Indigestion,
>   (Not that most 'dainty Ariel') and perplexes
> Our soarings with another sort of question:
>   And that which after all my spirit vexes,
> Is, that I find no spot where man can rest his eye on,
>   Without confusion of the sorts and sexes,
> Of being, stars, and this unriddled wonder,
> The World, which at the worst's a glorious blunder –
>
> (Don Juan, xi, 1–3)

Again the bare bones come from identifiable philosophical sources but to call this a 'materialist critique of [...] philosophical idealism' (*BMW*, 1060) is to push it into precisely the kind of misapprehension it would resist. It is true that Byron has Johnson's famous rebuff to Berkeley in mind, but rather than kicking a stone (and knowing exactly what will happen), he crashes into language without any comprehensive overview of the likely results. Any success the stanzas might claim as a riposte to Berkeley derives not from argument but from the creative and dislocating energies of language and form that Byron sets in motion. The object of criticism here is not Berkeley's brilliant theory, but the more general assumptions of 'system' about how mind and language apprehend the world.[65] Thus Byron scatters, in enriching, the word 'matter' by associating it with at least three concepts (substance, relevance, individual cases). By unfitting the word for the purposes of systematic philosophy he suggests that the problem lies not with language but with our assumptions about how we know things. Nothing has been proven and no epistemological stance established. A challenge, however, has been entered, one we feel in our receptiveness to the possibilities of literary language. Poetry suggests to us that we don't need to despair just because we can't get past the arguments of the sceptic on the sceptic's own grounds. This means hope, and thus where we might expect to end on 'at the best is' we get a more promising 'at the worst's'.

Notes

1 Cooke, *The Blind Man Traces the Circle*, 144, 175. Before Cooke, the only sustained study of Byron's scepticism of which I am aware is Edward Wayne Marjarum, *Byron as Skeptic and Believer*, Princeton Studies in English, 16 (Princeton: Princeton University Press, 1938).

2 Donald H. Reiman, *Intervals of Inspiration: The Skeptical Tradition and the Psychology of Romanticism* (Florida: Penkevill, 1988), 309.

3 Hoagwood, *Byron's Dialectic*, 23.

4 Hoagwood, *Byron's Dialectic*, 36. Broadly in agreement, Bernhard Jackson suggests that *Don Juan* is an 'ample demonstration that for Byron skepticism, and the relativism it engenders, are liberating and empowering' (*The Development of Byron's Philosophy of Knowledge*, 6).

5 *The Cambridge Dictionary of Philosophy* notes that scepticism 'can be either partial or total, either practical or theoretical, and, if theoretical, either moderate or radical, and either of knowledge or justification' (846).

6 Laurence Sterne, *The Life and Opinions of Tristram Shandy, Gentleman*, Florida Edition, ed. Melvyn New and Joan New, 3 vols (Florida: Florida University Press, 1978), I, 170. All quotations from *Tristram Shandy* taken from this edition.

7 *An Essay on Man*, ii, 1–10. Pope's poetry is taken from *The Poems of Alexander Pope*, one-volume Twickenham edition, ed. John Butt (London: Methuen, 1963; repr. 1996).

8 Compare *Don Juan*, viii, 108.

9 Compare Beatty's observation that *Don Juan* 'exhibits scepticism in operation' but also keeps it 'at bay'. Bernard Beatty, *Byron's Don Juan* (London: Croom Helm, 1985), 79.

10 Some of what follows overlaps with helpful work in this area (among others) by Hoagwood and Reiman (especially on Byron and classical scepticism) and Bernhard Jackson (notably on Byron and British Empiricism).

11 *CPW* notes allusions to the work at *Don Juan*, ii, 84 and xiv, 1–9.

12 Diogenes Laertius, *Lives of the Eminent Philosophers*, Loeb Classical Library, trans. R. D. Hicks, 2 vols (London: Heineman, 1965), II, 487. Also see Gisela Striker, 'The Ten Tropes of Aenesidemus', in *The Skeptical Tradition*, ed. Myles Burnyeat (Berkeley: University of California Press, 1983), 95–115.

13 Edward Gibbon, *Memoirs of My Life*, ed. Georges A. Bonnard (London: Nelson, 1966), 64–5.

14 As 'to miracles', Byron wrote, 'I agree with Hume that it is more probable men should *lie* or be *deceived*, than that things out of the course of nature should so happen (*BLJ*, ii, 97). The lawyer Thomas Smith, who met Byron in Cephalonia in 1823, reported that Byron 'had just been reading, with renewed pleasure, David Hume's Essays. He considered Hume to be by far the most profound thinker and clearest reasoner of the many philosophers, and metaphysicians of the last century. "There is," said he, "no refuting him, and for simplicity and clearness of style, he is unmatched, and is utterly unanswerable." He referred particularly to the Essay on Miracles' (*HVSV*, 418).

15 David Hume, *An Enquiry Concerning Human Understanding*, ed. Tom L. Beauchamp (Oxford: Oxford University Press, 1999), 178.

16 Pierre Couissin, 'The Stoicism of the New Academy', trans. Jennifer Barnes and Myles Burnyeat, in *The Skeptical Tradition*, 31–63 (57).

17 David Sedley, 'The Motivation of Greek Scepticism', in *The Skeptical Tradition*, 9–29 (19–20).

18 Sextus Empiricus, *Outlines of Pyrrhonism*, Loeb Classical Library, trans. R. G. Bury, 4 vols (London: Heinemann, 1933–49), I, 13.

19 See Sedley, 'The Motivation of Greek Scepticism', 21–2.

20 Diogenes Laertius, *Lives of the Eminent Philosophers* II, 517–19.

21 Compare *Don Juan*, xiii, 84.

22 Hume, *An Enquiry concerning Human Understanding*, 206.

23 See Richard H. Popkin, *The High Road to Pyrrhonism*, ed. Richard A. Watson and James E. Force (San Diego: Austin Hill Press, 1980), 126. On the wider issue of eighteenth-century responses to ancient scepticism see Constance Blackwell, 'Diogenes Laertius's *Life of Pyrrho* and the interpretation of ancient scepticism in the history of philosophy: Stanley through Bruckner to Tennemann', in *Scepticism and Irreligion in the Seventeenth and Eighteenth Centuries*, ed. Richard H. Popkin and Arjo Vanderjagt (Leiden: Brill, 1993), 324–57.

24 Hoagwood, *Byron's Dialectic*, 15.

25 Hoagwood, *Byron's Dialectic*, 39.

26 Hoagwood, *Byron's Dialectic*, 41.

27 Hoagwood, *Byron's Dialectic*, 36.

28 'I don't know what I may seem to the world, but as to myself, I seem to have been only like a boy playing on the sea shore, and diverting myself in now and then finding a smoother pebble or a prettier shell than ordinary, whilst the great ocean of truth lay all undisclosed before me'. Joseph Spence, *Anecdotes, Observations, and Characters, of Books and Men. Collected from the Conversations of Mr. Pope, and other Eminent Persons of his Time* (London: John Murray, 1820), 54. Byron also alludes to Newton's (alleged) famous words at *Don Juan*, vii, 5 and x, 1–4.

29 Sextus Empiricus, *Outlines of Scepticism*, ed. Julia Annas and Jonathan Barnes (Cambridge: Cambridge University Press, 2000), xi.

30 Richard H. Popkin, *The History of Scepticism from Erasmus to Spinoza* (Berkeley: California University Press, 1979), 4.

31 *Essays of Michael Seigneur de Montaigne*, trans. Charles Cotton, 4th edn, 3 vols (London, 1711), II, 261. Hereafter referred to in the text as *Essays*.

32 On Byron's 'fundamental seriousness about religion' see M. K. Joseph, *Byron the Poet* (London: Gollancz, 1964), 305 and G. Wilson Knight, *Lord Byron: Christian Virtues* (London: Routledge and Kegan Paul, 1952). On Byron's Catholicism see Beatty, *Byron's Don Juan* (especially Chapter 4).

33 According to William Harness, who stayed with the poet at Newstead Abbey from December 1811 to January 1812, 'Byron, from his early education in Scotland, had been taught to identify the principles of Christianity with the extreme dogmas of Calvinism. His mind had thus imbibed a miserable prejudice, which appeared to be the only obstacle to his hearty acceptance of the Gospel' (*HVSV*, 44). Also see Bernard Beatty, 'Calvin in Islam: A Reading of *Lara* and *The Giaour*', *Romanticism*, vol. 5, no. 1 (1999), 70–86 and Truman Guy Steffan, *Lord Byron's Cain: Twelve Essays and a Text with Variants and Annotations* (Austin: University of Texas Press, 1968), 26–8.

34 James Hamilton Browne, who travelled with Byron by sea from Leghorn to Cephalonia towards the end of Byron's life, and later published his conversations with the poet, recalled that Byron 'made it a constant rule to peruse every day one or more of the Essays of Montaigne. This practice he said, he had pursued for a long time; adding his decided conviction, that more useful general knowledge and varied information were to be derived by an intimate acquaintance with the writings of that diverting author, than by a long and continuous course of study' (*HVSV*, 387).

35 Hunt reproduced, with some modernization and commentary, the pages thus marked for *The New Monthly Magazine and Literary Journal*, 19 (Jan and March 1827), 26–32; 240–5. Also see Richard I. Kirkland Jr., 'Byron's Reading of Montaigne: A Leigh Hunt Letter', *Keats-Shelley Journal*, 30 (1981), 47–51.

36 Again Montaigne has Socrates in mind, specifically *Alcibiades*, II in which Socrates remarks that 'poetry as a whole is by nature inclined to riddling, and it is not every man who can apprehend it'. *Plato* (vol viii), *Loeb Classical Library*, trans. W. R. Lamb (London: Heinemann, 1955), 261.

37 Compare Keats: 'I have never yet been able to perceive how any thing can be known for truth by consequitive reasoning – and yet it must be – Can it be that even the greatest Philosopher ever (when) arrived at his goal without putting aside numerous objections'. *The Letters of John Keats*, ed. Hyder Edward Rollins, 2 vols (Cambridge, MA: Harvard University Press, 1958), I, 185.

38 Lilian R. Furst, *Fictions of Romantic Irony in European Narrative, 1760–1857* (London: Macmillan, 1984), 118.

39 David Simpson, *Romanticism, Nationalism, and the Revolt against Theory* (Chicago: University of Chicago Press, 1993), 4.

40 Anthony, Earl of Shaftesbury, *Characteristics of Men, Manners, Opinions, Times, etc.*, ed. John M. Robertson, 2 vols (London: Richards, 1900), I, 189.

41 Voltaire, *Letters concerning the English Nation*, 55.

42 'As waves which lately paved his watery way / Hiss round a drowner's head in their tempestuous play' (*Ode to Liberty*, 284–5). Unless otherwise stated Shelley is quoted from *Shelley's Poetry and Prose*, ed. Donald H. Reiman and Neil Fraistat (New York: Norton, 2002). The original is *Paradise Lost*, ii, 1026–7: 'Paved after him a broad and beaten way / Over the dark abyss'. *Paradise Lost* is quoted from John Milton, *Paradise Lost*, ed. Alistair Fowler, 2nd edition (London: Longman, 1998).

43 Simpson, *Romanticism, Nationalism, and the Revolt against Theory*, 43.

44 *The Writings and Speeches of Edmund Burke*, general editor Paul Langford; vol. 8 'The French Revolution 1790–1794', ed. L. G. Mitchell (Oxford: Clarendon Press, 1989), 58.

45 Contrast Malcolm Kelsall, *Byron's Politics* (Brighton: Harvester, 1987) with Michael Foot, *The Politics of Paradise: A vindication of Byron* (London: Collins, 1988).

46 'Our sentiments agreed a good deal, except upon the subjects of religion and politics, upon neither of which I was inclined to believe that Lord Byron entertained very fixed opinions' (Sir Walter Scott, after meeting the poet in 1815; *HVSV*, 114).

47 Compare *BLJ*, ii, 98, *BLJ*, ix, 19 and *Don Juan*, vi, 19.

48 William Parry, *The Last Days of Lord Byron* (1825); quoted in *HVSV*, 563. Also see F. Rosen, *Bentham, Byron, and Greece* (Oxford: Clarendon Press, 1992), 301 and *passim*.

49 *Tristram Shandy*, I, 61.

50 'I mean it for a poetical T[ristram] Shandy – or Montaigne's Essays with a story for a hinge' (*BLJ*, x, 150).

51 Quoted in Roy Park, *Hazlitt and the Spirit of the Age: Abstraction and Critical Theory* (Oxford: Clarendon Press, 1971), 37.

52 Byron also complained to Thomas Moore, after questioning Hunt about Hunt's own poetry, that his 'answer was, that his style was a system, or *upon system*, or some such cant; and, when a man talks of system, his case is hopeless: so I said no more to him, and very little to any one else' (*BLJ*, vi, 46).

53 Coleridge, perhaps unwisely, wrote to Byron, of the *Biographia*, that 'my object [is] to reduce criticism to a system, by the deduction of the Causes from the Principles involved in our faculties'. *Collected Letters of Samuel Taylor Coleridge*, ed. Earl Leslie Griggs, 6 vols (Oxford: Clarendon Press, 1956–71), IV, 598.

54 Quoted in Carl van Doren, *The Life of Thomas Love Peacock* (New York: Russell, 1966), 112–13.

55 He also remembered *Nightmare Abbey* when writing the English cantos of *Don Juan*. See, for instance, xv, 97.

56 For some of Byron's other (mixed) comments on both authors see *BLJ*, iii, 107 and v, 266.

57 *The Letters of Percy Bysshe Shelley*, ed. Frederick L. Jones, 2 vols (Oxford: Clarendon Press, 1964), II, 323 (To Mary Shelley, 10 August, 1821).

58 As Clifford Siskin has pointed out, the 'system', as a literary genre (one traditionally contrasted with the essay), was on the rise in the period. 'Through most of the [eighteenth] century', Siskin notes, 'the number of works that explicitly called themselves "systems", or invoked "system" in their titles, trailed – in a ratio of 1 to 3 (or higher) – the total of those efforts self-identified as, or with, essays. After 1798, however, production of self-described systems regularly outpaces essay output'. Clifford Siskin, 'The Year of the System', in *1798: The Year of the Lyrical Ballads,* ed. Richard Cronin (London: Macmillan, 1998), 9–31 (12).

59 The 'antisystematic impulse', writes Adorno, in its 'relationship to scientific procedure and its philosophical grounding as method [...] draws [its] fullest conclusions from the critique of system'. It 'allows', Adorno continues, 'for the consciousness of nonidentity, without expressing it directly; it is radical in its non-radicalism, in refraining from any reduction to a principle, in its accentuation of the partial against the total, in its fragmentary character'. 'The Essay as Form', in *Notes to Literature*, ed. Rolf Tiedemann, trans. Shierry Weber Nicholsen, 2 vols (New York: Columbia University Press, 1991), I, 3–23 (12, 9).

60 Samuel Johnson, *A Dictionary of the English Language*, 2 vols (London: J. Johnson, 1806).

61 Fred Parker describes such thinking-through-form as something that 'cannot be expressed as an intellectual position, a completed thought; it cannot be registered as a simple item within the history of ideas, or translated into a moral exhortation'. Fred Parker, *Scepticism and Literature: An Essay on Pope, Hume, Sterne, and Johnson* (Oxford: Oxford University Press, 2003), 29–30.

62 '[W]e can find no word or description for any of the intellectual operations which, if its history is known, is not seen to have been taken, by metaphor, from a description of some physical happening'. I. A. Richards, *The Philosophy of Rhetoric* (London: Oxford University Press, 1936), 91.

63 As with Richard Gloucester's invitation to Buckingham: 'Come, let us sup betimes, that afterwards / We may digest our complots in some form'. *Richard III*, III.i.196–7. Shakespeare is taken from *The Norton Shakespeare*, ed. Stephen Greenblatt et al. (New York: Norton, 1997).

64 Byron directs his language towards what John Gibson describes as 'a territory of understanding that is left unmentioned by our standard talk of knowledge'. 'Between Truth and Triviality', *British Journal of Aesthetics*, vol. 43, no. 3 (July 2003), 224–37 (231). Gibson has in mind Cavell's distinction between knowing and acknowledgement: 'we think skepticism must mean that we cannot know that the world exists', Cavell writes, 'and hence that perhaps there isn't one [...]. Whereas what scepticism suggests is that since we cannot know that the world exists, its presentness to us cannot be a function of knowing. The world is to be *accepted*; as the presentness of other minds is not to be known, but acknowledged'. Stanley Cavell, *Must we Mean what we Say? A Book of Essays* (Cambridge: Cambridge University Press, 1976), 324.

65 I am fairly close here to Bernhard Jackson's reading of the stanza (*The Development of Byron's Philosophy of Knowledge*, 175–6), but differ from her sense (as I understand it) that Byron both agrees and disagrees with Berkeley in the interests of breaking down objective knowledge claims in order to promote 'individual determination'. This is to place the work of form in the service of a coherent, clearly articulated

(positive, individualistic) sceptical position, thus limiting Byron's language by precisely the kind of macro-assumption it wants to challenge. If we want to theorize what is happening here then our frames need to be those of (visionary) poetics rather than philosophical scepticism.

A 'Voice from out the Wilderness'
Cain and Philosophical Poetry

To read Byron's poetry as philosophy without reference to form is to miss the poetry's philosophical significance. This seems most pressingly true in the case of *Don Juan*, a poem in which language is untethered within the precincts of intellectual history with effects that are at once critical and creative. In what follows I want to think about this complicated meeting of philosophy and poetry, something, I suggest, in which Byron was deeply interested, with primary reference to what seems in many ways the poet's most obviously 'philosophical' literary work, *Cain*.

Byron began writing *Cain* in Ravenna on 16 July 1821. Six months later he would resume *Don Juan* after having written nothing of his sprawling epic for over a year.[1] The new cantos of *Don Juan*, beginning with canto vi, would display several significant changes from previous instalments, notably an increase in digressive material and a closer integration of this into the narrative of the story.[2] These newly extensive digressions, which punctuate (and frequently open) the later cantos of the poem, have a strong philosophical flavour, a fact it seems reasonable to connect with the composition of *Cain* and its strong speculative themes. Despite their chronological and thematic proximity, however, *Cain* and *Don Juan* appear to have little in common in terms of scope, tone and form. *Don Juan* is on the whole a much fuller, more diverse and more comically evasive poem, one wonderfully uncontained by its philosophical interests and brimming with energies that seem the antithesis of argumentative rigour. *Cain*, by comparison, looks far more obviously and directly like something we can call a 'philosophical poem'; it is easier to read, that is, as a vehicle for its grounding polemical commitments than as a poetic shaping to the unargued contours of life. These differences have tended to mean that critics have approached the two works not only in isolation from one another, but with very different assumptions and aims: where serious critics of *Don Juan* have been minded of the poem's fragmentariness and resistance to systematic thought, *Cain's* commentators have often looked at the play as something closer to a manifesto, as containing a definite philosophical or religious message. For this reason the play, or 'Mystery' as Byron termed it, has assumed an especial significance among those interested in Byron's philosophical position(s). Largely this is right: much of the play is driven by argument and polemical force and we feel these energies as dominant within a literary frame that feels, by contrast, unsure of itself. In particular the play has a strong political voice, one that dominates within standard interpretations of the play. On the other hand, argument is not left untouched by dramatic staging; it is altered and unsettled at the edges in ways that raise questions about the sufficiency of rational explication. Other kinds of intelligence – dramatic form, irrational action, tradition and allusion, love and vatic apprehension – enter and complicate the play. We need to understand the play's dominant argument (one forged in linguistic scepticism and political dissent); but we also need to understand the literary awareness through which argument is made alive to its own limitations in the face of existence.

One of the earliest responses to *Cain*, by the clergyman Reginald Heber, came in an unsigned review of Byron's dramas in the *Quarterly Review* of July 1822. Heber looks at the play from an intelligent, orthodox perspective,[3] reading it as a work of radical scepticism and thus as an attempt to undermine all forms of organized religion: the 'sarcasms of Lucifer and the murmurs of Cain', he suggests, 'are directed against Providence in general; and proceed to the subversion of every system of theology'.[4] A more intriguing response came from William Blake, who, after reading *Cain*, wrote *The Ghost of Abel*, his first known attempt at drama for over forty years. Byron, who is addressed in strikingly direct terms, has, according to Blake, missed his way as a poet and prophet. He has been seduced by the scepticism that drives the world of reason and science and has lost touch with the permanent forms of spirit and imagination:

TO LORD BYRON IN THE WILDERNESS:
                              What doest thou
  here, Elijah? Can a poet doubt the visions of Jehovah?
  Nature has no outline; but Imagination has. Nature
  has no time; but Imagination has! Nature has no
  supernatural and dissolves: Imagination is Eternity.[5]

Byron has strayed into a wilderness of 'doubt' and apprehends only the physical world of 'Nature', which 'dissolves' and which has 'no outline';

he has lost sight of the eternal, permanent realm of 'Imagination' that should be the true object of the poet.

Heber (and in different ways Blake) set the pattern for the majority of the play's later reception as a work of rationalist scepticism in which Cain and Lucifer share the role of hero-exile. Leslie Marchand, for instance, suggested that *Cain* is 'an outpouring, not wholly coherent or consistent, of Byron's revolt against conventional religious orthodoxy'.[6] Edward Bostetter, in an influential reading, takes the play in a more political direction, suggesting that Byron's 'God stands for the very real tyranny of a social and political hierarchy that justified its acts by appeal to divine authority'. Cain, in such a reading, is the 'rebellious intellect who insists upon questioning the justice of divine and therefore social decrees'.[7]

Bostetter's view of the play as staging a conflict between God as tyrant and Cain as hero in pursuit of 'emancipation of mind' seems eminently sensible in its recognition of Byron's God as a distant, authoritarian figure, and his cowed human subjects as having a strong whiff of the despot's yoke about them.[8] Cain, moreover, seems in many ways a sympathetic character: a rebellious spirit who, like other uncompromising Byronic heroes, is admirable for his courage and lack of self-interest. The play's eponymous 'hero', however, is susceptible of being read in very different terms, as frustratingly narrow-minded, chained to reason, and closed to the full range of possibilities that flit through (poetic) consciousness. Hoagwood, for instance, reads the character, in classical Pyrrhonist terms, as a 'counterexample of *ataraxia*'. Cain's 'relentless demanding of knowledge, of certainty, of an explanation', Hoagwood argues, 'consign him to the brutal incoherence of human tragedy, because his own demands for knowledge are not only frustrated but doomed. Chained to the conviction that one must *believe* something, and determined to forge or find an explanation of experience and the world, Cain dramatizes the deadliness of the wish for certainty'.[9] According to this reading Cain is less the hero of a political allegory and more a dogmatic philosopher who imposes an inadequately rigid understanding upon his world. Rather than fronting a sceptical assault on the establishment, his 'murmurs' are taken in reflection by the embracing scepticism of the work as a whole. Blake was right, from this point of view, to find in the play a morbid rationalism; his mistake was to identify this directly with the author rather than seeing it as the tragic flaw of the central character.

Classical Pyrrhonism, as we have seen, has a long association with orthodox Christianity, a fact exploited in Wolf Z. Hirst's reading of the play. Beginning from a similar position to Hoagwood, Hirst counter-intuitively argues for *Cain* as an expression of religious orthodoxy, finding in it a 'critique of unmitigated rationalism [which] invalidates the traditional view of the play's bias towards sacrilege'. *Cain* demonstrates, Hirst continues, 'the futility and danger of reason's rebellion, even in the name of justice, against the human condition and against the mystery of the cosmic order'. Rather than associating Byron's play with the tradition of nineteenth-century anti-establishment discourse, Hirst draws it more into line with the Book of Job or Montaigne's 'Apologie de Raimond Sebond' as a work that 'ultimately establishes the inscrutability of divine providence'.[10]

The fact that *Cain* has been associated with such radically different theoretical perspectives might be taken to suggest, in itself, that we are not dealing with a work of straightforward polemical intent but one that is more resistant to interpretation than has generally been allowed. In particular, the directly opposed readings of Bostetter and Hirst, when taken together, seem to call into question the very possibility of understanding the play from a single, overarching philosophical point of view. The latter's identification of Cain's 'unmitigated rationalism' as a potential object of sceptical critique is entirely plausible and tends to complicate the connection between rebellion and heroism assumed by the play's 'orthodox' readings. On the other hand, to go as far as to suggest that *Cain* is an expression of religious orthodoxy that 'facilitates the task of vindicating God' is to go too far.[11] Hirst's reading of Abel as one of the play's 'advocates of love', for instance, is unconvincing, whereas Bostetter's claim that he is one of the 'self-righteous supporters [...] of the tyrant God' fits the tones and emphases of the play far more closely.[12] As for why Byron would write a religiously orthodox play during a hiatus in the composition of *Don Juan*, Hirst's answer that *Cain* represents 'an extreme in the Byronic canon' and 'conveys a standpoint too absolute for Byron's philosophy of uncertainty' again fails to convince.[13] It is certainly the case that most established readings of *Cain* overstate or simplify Byron's rationalist and anti-establishment intentions, but I don't think the play licenses quite this much certainty at the other end of the spectrum either. Its sub-titular 'Mystery' is not so easily dispersed.

We might, given this apparent philosophical messiness, conclude that *Cain* is a muddled piece of thinking lacking any real intellectual coherence. We may even decide, with Philip W. Martin, that the work is 'as potent an affirmation of Byron's bankruptcy as a philosophical poet as we are likely to find'.[14] This seems undeniable if we understand 'philosophical poet' to mean a philosopher who has chosen to formulate his opinions in verse.[15] On the other hand, if we take such a poet to be a thinker interested in the philosophical implications of literary form as a distinct means of apprehension, then the case becomes more complex. If we understand poetry, that is, as being 'philosophical', not because it makes direct philosophical claims but because it is interested in the context of philosophy's emergence into epistemological privilege, then we will need to judge that poetry in less impoverished terms.

There is a bad habit in Byron criticism of deciding that the poet is not being serious when he says things that don't fit with the critic's reading of him. This leads to critics choosing what they listen to rather than listening. This is what Byron says in defence of *Cain* in letters to friends and associates:

> If "Cain" be "blasphemous" – Paradise lost is blasphemous – and the very words of the Oxford Gentleman [Byron is responding to a reviewer who signed himself 'Oxoniensis'] – 'Evil be thou my Good' are from that very poem – from the mouth of Satan, – and is there anything more in that of Lucifer in the Mystery? – – Cain is nothing more than a drama – not a piece of argument – if Lucifer and Cain speak as the first Murderer and the first Rebel may be supposed to speak – surely all the rest of the personages talk also according to their characters – and the stronger passions have ever been permitted to the drama. (*BLJ*, ix, 103)

> With respect to "Religion," can I never convince you that *I* have no such opinions as the characters in the drama, which seems to have frightened every body? [...] My ideas of a character may run away with me: like all imaginative men, I, of course, embody myself with the character while I *draw* it, but not a moment after the pen is from off the paper. (*BLJ*, ix, 118–9)

McGann claims that these 'remarks are [...], as *all* the early reactions to the play indicate, disingenuous'.[16] Certainly, Byron's attempt to hide behind Milton is difficult to take without a pinch of salt: although the latter can be and has been read in radically unorthodox terms, Byron's Lucifer ('bringer of light') seems far more clearly and subversively intended than the former's Satan ('adversary'). Lucifer's precipitous extrusion from his biblical context as well as his clear identification with the Byronic (not quite the same as Byron's) quest for liberty[17] might also suggest that Byron's claim to have written a 'drama' rather than an 'argument' is something of a red herring. On the other hand, it has not been easy for critics to agree about what precisely *Cain* is arguing. The play isn't as good as *Don Juan* at making the determined reducer of poetry look silly, but it also can't help being a literary work written by a poet who always struggles to accept the assumption that argument and thought are identical. This is partly to do with Byron's scepticism about the enthusiasms of liberal progress: he knew that the determined arguer who thinks that argument is everything can, for all his heroic potential, easily become the author of aftermath (the French Revolution made this clear enough, if it wasn't already). This is why Byron is very different to the Hunt brothers, even if he thought that they were broadly right in some of their key political convictions. The other side to this has more to do with poetry, and this is where I think the poet's insistence that he has written a work of literature rather than a manifesto should not be wafted off as just a smokescreen. I disagree with Hirst's distancing of *Cain* from *Don Juan*, because for all their stylistic differences the two works share important intellectual concerns. They are both interested in argument as something necessary, energetic and transformative, but also as a form of system, as something we should not mix up with truth. We can't escape the fact that *Cain* is full of philosophical and political purposiveness, and that it attacks things – the abuse of political power, the corruptions of State religion, the use of language to enslave. There is no need to argue any of this away or to say that Byron didn't believe it (he did, even if not in quite the way Shelley or Hunt did). What we can say, I think, is that conviction and belief in the play, while not undermined, are *thought about* in the very process of their articulation. *Cain* contains a critical and sceptical way of thinking about tyranny (through its appropriations of language), but it is not finally a work of scepticism because this initial critique is placed within a larger conditioning context of (literary) thought ('I doubt if doubt itself be doubting'). It is sceptical, that is, not just about the Establishment, but about the way in which we think we are supposed to think – we are supposed, for instance, to think about what kind of 'standpoint' a work of philosophical poetry takes. If we decide that it doesn't have a 'standpoint' then we are supposed to think that it is a work of 'scepticism' (and stand by that). What *Cain* does is register, at the level of form, Byron's scepticism about these assumptions concerning thought. It wonders about the deceptiveness of language as a prop for tyranny, but it also wonders if language has tricked us into misconstruing what our minds are for. What makes him wonder in this way is his acute sensitivity to the possibilities of literary cognition.

Thinking, that is, might happen differently when we are reading a poem compared to when we are reading an argument. *Cain*, I think, is (like *Don Juan*) deeply interested in this difference. It becomes a work of visionary poetics in the process of problematizing an argument it doesn't want to abandon.

One critic who recognized something of this is the critic who was closest to Byron's creative processes. Shortly after *Cain*'s publication, Mary Shelley wrote to her friend Maria Gisborne:

> Perhaps by this time you have seen Cain and will agree with us in thinking it his finest production – To me it sounds like a revelation – of some works one says – one has thought of such things though one could not have expressed it so well – It is not this with Cain – One has perhaps stood on the extreme verge of such ideas and from the midst of the darkness which has surrounded us the voice of the Poet now is heard telling a wondrous tale.[18]

Unlike the majority of the play's critics Mary does not read *Cain* with reference to specific philosophical and political aims but hears it as a voicing of 'the Poet' – as a 'wondrous tale' that does not break the cover of its own darkness. This voice does not speak according to the post-Lockean ideal of Augustan poetics;[19] its power does not derive from its conceptual clarity but from a capacity to intimate the precipitousness of poetic thought. Rather than realizing ideas, it places us on their 'extreme verge'.[20] Byron's wilderness, for Mary, is not one of reason and doubt as it was for Blake, but a place in which the indefinite energies of literary creation can be felt.

* * *

None of this is to suggest that critics have been wasting their time in seeking to identify the play's speculative and political content. Such content is clearly there, although its trajectories and circularities have not always been perceived. This is from Byron's serpentine, defensive prose Preface:

> THE following scenes are entitled 'a Mystery,' in conformity with the ancient title annexed to dramas upon similar subjects, which were styled 'Mysteries, or Moralities.' The author has by no means taken the same liberties with his subject which were common formerly, as may be seen by any reader curious enough to refer to those very profane productions, whether in English, French, Italian, or Spanish. The author has endeavoured to preserve the language adapted to his characters; and where it is (and this is but rarely) taken from actual *Scripture* [...] made as little alteration, even of words, as

the rhythm would permit. The reader will recollect that the book of Genesis does not state that Eve was tempted by a demon, but by 'the Serpent;' and that only because he was 'the most subtil of all the beasts of the field.' Whatever interpretation the Rabbins and the Fathers may have put upon this, I must take the words as I find them, and reply with Bishop Watson upon similar occasions, when the Fathers were quoted to him, as Moderator in the schools of Cambridge, 'Behold the Book!' – holding up the Scripture. (*CPW*, VI, 228)

Byron's literalist exegesis of scripture is provocative. By refusing to identify the serpent with a 'demon' he loosens conventionally fixed attributions of evil, thus opening up the moral territory he is about to enter. He also demonstrates the sort of rational questioning spirit that will characterize Cain himself, thereby encouraging the kinds of identification between protagonist and author that are common in the play's reception. Where Watson, an infamously pugnacious cleric Byron had read with little profit,[21] simply holds up his closed bible as if it were single and unquestionable, Byron suggests that intelligent reading and interpretation are crucial to any meaningful discussion of religion.[22]

Byron borrowed the point about the serpent and the demon from Bayle's *Dictionnaire historique et critique*, which he read in a huge ten-volume English translation of 1734.[23] Bayle's brilliant, clear-sighted interrogations of classical and Christian myth, which made him famous as an enemy to the forces of closed thought and bigotry, have thus naturally been proposed as a significant influence on *Cain*.[24] This is the Bayle whose writings have bequeathed an 'arsenal of sceptical weapons for use against religion',[25] who was admired by Gibbon and probably detected by Heber in his reading of *Cain* as a work of wide-wasting scepticism. But although Bayle, and especially in the eighteenth century, is typically associated with heterodox traditions, he remains a 'notoriously difficult philosopher to evaluate',[26] and, as a sceptic, has – like Byron – attracted widely different interpretations. While often viewed as the embodiment of enlightened reason, he can also, more like Montaigne,[27] be read as a Christian Pyrrhonist seeking to erect the 'edifice of faith on the ruins of reason'.[28] This is the Bayle who could write, in his defensive, and by no means reliable, third 'Clarification' that

By faith [man] will soar above those regions, where the storms of disputations prevail. He will stand on an eminence, whence he will hear, far beneath him, the thunder of argumentations and distinctions. An eminence which, with regard to him, will be the true Olympus of the Poets, and the true temple of the sages; whence he will behold, with a mind perfectly unruffled, the weakness of reason, and the mistakes of such mortals as follow no other guide.[29]

According to this the final aim of the sceptic is not to assert the primacy of human intelligence but to abolish its flawed productions, to rise above 'argumentations' in the 'unruffled' tranquillity of faith and to look down, from his poetic eminence, upon 'the weakness of reason'. Of course, this attempt, by an already exiled Bayle, to draw his method closer to orthodox acceptability might quite reasonably be doubted. On the other hand, the rifts evident in Bayle's reception resist his settling as a moment in the history of ideas.

The true literary writer is not unruffled, nor does he look down upon the disputant with contempt. He does, however, in turning us to the ironies and forms of the written page, locate argument within the broader contexts of the unarguable. He might do this by ironically overforcing the tones of a case, by peeling the voice away from straight-forward commitment as Byron does with his 'poetical commandments' in *Don Juan* (i, 204) and Bayle does with his mock-outraged attack on Jupiter and,[30] in different ways, with his fearless reassessment of King David (hugely controversial given the New Testament designation of Jesus as David's son).[31]

Bayle deplores David's treatment of Mephibosheth (the son of his friend Jonathan from whom David stripped his estate) which, when considered by any reasonable standard, was manifestly unjust.[32] Bayle's aim is polemical in that he wants to overturn orthodox apologists (such as Théophile Raynaud) who reason that since the 'holiness of [...] David is well known to us, and since he never ordered any reparation of the wrong which he had done to Mephibosheth, we are to conclude that the sentence was just'. This, Bayle points out, 'is to establish a very dangerous principle, [that] we must no longer examine the actions of the old Prophets by the ideas of Morality'.[33] As with Watson's holding up the book, Raynaud refuses to *read* in the interests of a pre-decided version of events. Bayle (like Byron) is not necessarily attacking religion, but he is attacking a refusal to accept the meliorative influences of intelligent reading.

The force of criticism here, however, cannot be trained upon a single target, nor can the critic presume his immunity to the spirit of his correction. Thus Bayle ends not with a neat conclusion, but with an opening up of critical perspective:

From all that has been said in the precedent Remarks, and in this, it may be easily inferred, that if the people of Syria had been as great Writers of Libels, as the Europeans are at this day, they would have strangely disfigured David's glory.[34]

A second possible object of criticism – the libellous, haranguing culture of Reformation polemic – is entered alongside David's own behaviour, which, from this newly relative point of view, might seem a target less worthy of pursuit. As a result the narrative voice slides down from the moralist's eminence to become implicated in the problem(s). As one who has himself disfigured 'David's glory', Bayle has participated in the strident righteousness characteristic of modern European polemical culture. Bayle's genius, as Voltaire recognized,[35] is not linear, but reflexive and dialogical; it lies in a capacity to demolish bigotry while remaining aware of how easily such reflexes atrophy into system.

* * *

The thinking of Bayle's *Dictionnaire* helps us with the difficulties of *Cain*. It also provides a context for the play's odd straightforwardness. The two converge in Byron's relentless interest in language as a staging of philosophical and political intention. *Cain* opens with a sequence of prayers:

> ADAM. GOD, the Eternal! Infinite! All-Wise! –
>   Who out of darkness on the deep didst make
>   Light on the waters with a word – all hail!
>   Jehovah, with returning light, all hail!
> EVE. God! Who didst name the day, and separate
>   Morning from night, till then divided never –
>   Who didst divide the wave from wave, and call
>   Part of thy work the firmament – all hail!

> > (*Cain*, I, i, 1–8)

Byron's claim that in his borrowings from Scripture he has 'made as little alteration, even of words, as the rhythm would permit' does not seem entirely outrageous if we consider his source:

> And the earth was without form, and void; and darkness *was* upon the face of the deep. And the spirit of God moved upon the face of the waters. And God said, Let there be light: and there was light. And God saw the light, that *it was* good: and God divided the light from the darkness. And God called the light Day, and the darkness he called Night.[36]

The changes that are made, however, are significant. By relocating the biblical text from its original third-person narrator to the mouths of Adam and Eve, Byron creates a sense that the first parents are nervously repeating their lines. The celebratory feel of the original is shaded by a sense of the dark reiterations upon which tyranny feeds. God's emphasized acts of division and naming, rather than being moments of incipience and liberation in the face of chaos, sound more like the proceedings of dominion, at least with respect to the modern political context in which Byron is working.

The opening of the play is pervasively concerned with language and its relationship to power. Where language for Adam is a 'returning light', an acknowledgement and celebration of God's luminary fiat, for Cain it is a tool to question established relations and to assert individual thought. The latter's first words, notably spoken before Lucifer's appearance, come in the form of a question that interrupts his family's flow of prayer: 'Why should I speak?' (*Cain*, I, i, 23). This withholding of officially legitimized language results in parental displeasure, Adam asking his son 'wherefore art thou silent' (*Cain*, I, i, 22) / 'thou [...] art silent still' (*Cain*, I, i, 26).

Cain's rebellion lies in his placing the question over the prayer:

CAIN [*solus*].   And this is
   Life! – Toil! and wherefore should I toil? – because
   My father could not keep his place in Eden.
   What had *I* done in this? – I was unborn,
   I sought not to be born; nor love the state
   To which that birth has brought me. Why did he
   Yield to the serpent and the woman? or,
   Yielding, why suffer? What was there in this?
   The tree was planted, and why not for him?
   If not, why place him near it, where it grew,
   The fairest in the centre? They have but
   One answer to all questions, ''twas *his* will,
   And *he* is good'. How know I that? Because
   He is all-powerful, must all-good, too, follow?
   I judge but by the fruits – and they are bitter –

(*Cain*, I, i, 64–77)

Where his family have 'One answer to all questions' – they regurgitate the book – Cain deploys his words to explore his predicament and its apparent injustices. Where they accept language as a means of marking a set of fixed, unquestionable relationships, he becomes the first (human) sceptic in asserting his freedom to decide for himself.

It would not be entirely wrong to end here, and there would be an appealing crispness to it. But even if we think that Byron only used dramatic form to stage and protect his argument, we cannot avoid the questions to which the drama's human contexts give rise. Is this really 'emancipation of mind' or just sullen, tiresome victimhood (or something between the two)?[37] Is Eve's 'Content thee with what *is*' (*Cain*, I, i, 45) the depressed coercion of the fellow subject, or is it the distillation of human wisdom in its incipient profundity? Cain's own questions may involve a form of self-realization, but questions can also become ways of avoiding other questions; they can become a mode of paralysis and an undermining of the basis of action. Cain certainly seems far from empowered by his sceptical re-visioning. He is in a rut, linear-minded, tyrannized over by 'why' and 'what'. He is also wildly unreflexive as a speaker. His 'I judge but by the fruits', although intended to assert independence of mind, seems, in the wake of Eve's well-crafted lines of regret – 'The fruit of our forbidden tree begins / To fall' (*Cain*, I, i, 30) – densely ironic and tied up in things Cain cannot see. Scepticism is an attempt to establish a form of mitigated control in the face of acknowledged disorder, but Cain remains all at sea amidst the inflections of his Byronic textual environment. His battle with apparent coercion may be genuine and courageous, but he lacks the intellectual fluidity that pulses through *Don Juan*. He may have grasped the rudiments of philosophical scepticism, but none of its subtleties or ironies.

Where both Hirst and Hoagwood take these problems to argue for a (Christian) Pyrrhonist reading of the play, I would suggest that Byron's pressurizing of doubt leads, as in *Don Juan*, to something less philosophically derivable but more poetically interesting. Lucifer's arrival on the scene changes the tack of Cain's aporetic musings; it also alters the manner of his voice:

> Whom have we here? – A shape like to the angels,
> Yet of a sterner and a sadder aspect
> Of spiritual essence: why do I quake?
> Why should I fear him more than other spirits,
> Whom I see daily wave their fiery swords
> Before the gates round which I linger oft,
> In twilight's hour, to catch a glimpse of those
> Gardens which are my just inheritance,
> Ere the night closes o'er the inhibited walls
> And the immortal trees which overtop
> The cherubim-defended battlements?
> If I shrink not from these, the fire-armed angels,

Why should I quail from him who now approaches?
Yet he seems mightier far than them, nor less
Beauteous, and yet not all as beautiful
As he hath been, and might be: sorrow seems
Half of his immortality. And is it
So? and can aught grieve save humanity?
He cometh.

(Cain, I, i, 80–98)

More questions, but these are of a different tenor: they respond not to apparent, external injustices, but to internal centres of emotional perception; and, while these unusual sensations are submitted to rational interrogation ('If I shrink not [...] Why should I quail'), no resolution is found. Where Cain's attempts to dissect his feelings are unproductive, however, his naive responses are latent with other possibilities. As a fresh if anxious sense of wonder comes over him, he becomes less the reasoner and more the man of Sensibility ('I linger oft, / In Twilight's hour'); he reveals a capacity to detect deep reserves of feeling, as well as an ability to reflect, with insight and no little power of expression, upon his intuitions ('sorrow seems / Half of his immortality'). There is a wonderfully obliterated mathematics to this.

Cain's choice is not simply between obedience and rebellion, but between knowledge and the world knowledge fails to contain. Lucifer even acknowledges something like this in demanding that his pupil 'Choose betwixt love and knowledge' *(Cain*, I, i, 429). By comparison we might think Adah's urging her brother to take the former option ('Oh, Cain! choose love.' *(Cain*, I, i, 431)) coercive, especially when she starts to sound like her parents: 'Alas! thou sinnest now, my Cain; thy words / Sound impious in mine ears' *(Cain*, III, i, 93–4). But Adah cannot be dismissed so easily. When Cain angrily exclaims 'Then leave me!' she replies not as Abel would – by reaffirming God's infallibility – but with a touchingly simple courage of her own: 'Never, / Though thy God left thee' *(Cain*, III, i, 94–5). Like Anah and Aholibamah, who defy God by loving the angels Samiasa and Azaziel in Byron's next 'Mystery' *Heaven and Earth*, Adah is a rebellious and passionate spirit rather than a compliant one. Cain may in the end choose 'knowledge', but the alternative remains vitally at stake in the ethical drama and poetical presences of the play. Adah may not be able to contend with Lucifer's power of argument ('I cannot answer this immortal thing / Which stands before me' *(Cain*, I, i, 406–7)), but this is to notice her profound difference from Lucifer rather than her irrelevance to the play.

Her silence does not award victory to reason. It resonates in the play's reflexive depths.

Drama continues to unsettle argument in the case of Lucifer himself. If we want to claim Byron's devil as the voice of enlightened reason then we also need to consider his opportunism and manipulative inconsistency. He appears on the scene at a high tide of dissatisfaction, just at the moment in which Cain is diagnosing the apparent bitterness of his existence. He also sounds, at first at least, more like a conventional Satanic stereotype than a liberating hero, demanding of Cain that he 'fall down and worship me – thy Lord' (*Cain*, I, i, 303). As if recognizing his miscalculation of Cain's proud, rebellious spirit, he then changes his approach to become a confederate in subjection.[38] It is God, not he, that would demand fealty: 'Believe – and sink not! doubt – and perish! thus / Would run the edict of the other God' (*Cain*, II, i, 5–6). Lucifer retracts his own demand and repositions himself in the shadow of his enemy's authoritarianism.

However we construe his intentions, Lucifer does not produce an independent, Enlightenment reasoner, but a murderer and an acolyte. The strategies of linguistic scepticism that run through Lucifer's words may offer liberation in a world where language has not yet developed a critical function, but are we truly liberated if we are merely mimicking a philosophical idea we do not fully understand? This is Lucifer defying God:

> LUCIFER. Ask the Destroyer.
> CAIN.   Who?
> LUCIFER. The Maker – call him
>   Which name thou wilt; he makes but to destroy.
>
> (*Cain*, I, i, 266–9)

This is Cain defying God via Abel:

> ABEL.   Why then commune with him? he may be
>   A foe to the Most High.
> CAIN.   And friend to man.
>   Has the Most High been so – if so you term him?
> ABEL. *Term him!* your words are strange to-day, my brother.
>
> (*Cain*, III, i, 168–71)

Abel may be awed into complicity by words that make him a subject, but is Cain's descent into irrational fury via scepticism necessarily to be preferred?[39] Eve's 'Oh! my son, / Blaspheme not: these are the serpent's words' (*Cain*, I, i, 34–5) may be in one sense an act of official censorship, but we might also read it as a charge of unoriginality, one echoed later by Adah: 'Thou hast not spoken well, nor is that thought / Thy own, but of the spirit who was with thee' (*Cain*, III, i, 77–8). We might also note that in the immediate aftermath of fratricide, Cain's questioning, which according to conventional readings of the play is the basis of emancipation, becomes confused and incoherent: 'Where am I? alone! Where's Abel? where / Cain? Can it be that I am he?' (*Cain*, III, i, 322–3). Cain's resistance to language-as-coercion, expressed in his initial withholding of prayer, is transformed into the silence of guilt and identity loss as the repeated imprecations of his family to 'Speak' (*Cain*, III, i, 393, 394, 396), rather than provoking just defiance, can now only be met by the flinching of one who has gone beyond reason.

These problems with Cain and Lucifer do not provide the basis of a counter-reading capable of supplanting established understandings of the play as a work of anti-establishment polemic. Such a reading would require us to ignore even more than the reading it seeks to overthrow. *Cain* has a profoundly straightforward aspect, especially (as McGann suggests) in Lucifer's final speeches where the processes of tyranny are subjected to a plangent critique grounded in linguistic scepticism. Where Milton's Satan forges his malice in acceptance, recognizing unequivocally that 'all good to me is lost' (*Paradise Lost*, iv, 109), Byron's Lucifer accepts only that he has lost the power to name abstract concepts:

> He as a conqueror will call the conquer'd
> *Evil*; but what will be the *good* he gives?
> Were I the victor, *his* works would be deem'd
> The only evil ones.
>
> (*Cain*, II, ii, 443–6)

Political action, construed in such terms, depends upon a reflexive capacity to apprehend the distortions created by official language. Lucifer's grasp of this sounds decidedly modern, notably in his complaint that his nemesis

> names me demon to his angels; they
> Echo the sound to miserable things,
> Which knowing nought beyond their shallow senses,
> Worship the word which strikes their ear, and deem
> Evil or good what is proclaim'd to them
> In their abasement.
>
> (*Cain*, II, i, 7–12)

Provocatively picking up Byron's (Bayle's) point about the biblical tempter not being named 'demon', Lucifer identifies the twin process through which ideology subsumes the real: the language of control is disseminated (echoed) by complicit forces, while education is denatured and reified in order to incapacitate dissent. To read this is to be jolted out of the fictive, especially when we come to the phrase 'tyrannous threats to force you into faith'. This is not really spoken by Lucifer to Cain (who can have no doubts about God's existence) but by the post-Waterloo (and post-Murray) Byron to his reader:

> Had Bonaparte won at Waterloo,
>   It had been firmness; now 'tis pertinacity:
> Must the event decide between the two?
>   I leave it to your people of sagacity
> To draw the line between the false and true,
>   If such can e'er be drawn by man's capacity:
>
> (*Don Juan*, xiv, 90)

Where 'event' rather than thought dictates our dominant economies of meaning then the Byronic hero of action must adapt to become a sceptic about language. This new kind of hero is identified in his refusal to be positioned within the flux of signification.[40] In the face of a hard, bullying language determined to bring down thought, to categorize, homogenize and control, we must forge our own meanings and codes. Lucifer in these terms is not goading Cain on to destruction, but urging him (or us) to create in defiance of those who would destroy:

> *One good* gift has the fatal apple given –
> Your *reason*: – let it not be over-sway'd
> By tyrannous threats to force you into faith
> 'Gainst all external sense and inward feeling:
> Think and endure, – and form an inner world
> In your own bosom – where the outward fails;
> So shall you nearer be the spiritual
> Nature, and war triumphant with your own.
>
> (*Cain*, II, ii, 459–66)

If Cain is being seduced here, then it is by the stirring, universal voice of Byronic heroism:

> Yet let us ponder boldly – 'tis a base
> Abandonment of reason to resign
> Our right of thought – our last and only place
> Of refuge; this, at least, shall still be mine:
>
> (*Childe Harold's Pilgrimage*, iv, 127)

If we can hold to anything of Byron's, then surely it is this.

The only reason not to end here (although in part we should) is that Byron didn't. Increasingly in his post-Harold works, and certainly by 1821, 'Our right of thought' resists the monopoly of 'reason' implied by these famous sentiments. The forming of our world was not, for Byron, something that could happen entirely according to the dictates of philosophy because 'she too much rejects'. Such acts of creation needed, rather, to open out into the less specifiable environments of imagination and literary form. This is not argued in *Cain*, but it is registered – often haphazardly – in the reshaping of argument by drama and also in the balancing of linguistic scepticism by visionary poetics. The play's critical stance on language-as-subjection runs into another sort of question, one concerned with language as a tentative claim upon the sublime. As we found with *Don Juan*, scepticism cedes to a more hopeful if less orderly poetics, something we will notice most clearly in Cain's transformation from failed sceptic to uncomprehending visionary. This shifting between textures of misapprehension will concern what remains.

* * *

In *Don Juan*, the anxieties of the question are offset by the energies of form. The poet's commitment to the word, always under pressure from a compelling linguistic scepticism, is revalidated in the act of poetry. I want to argue for a similar (and importantly different) shift from scepticism to poetics in *Cain*. To see this we will need to analyse the pedagogical contexts of Cain's journey with Lucifer through space and time.

The problem with Cain's response to mystery is that it is marked by a failure of imagination. This is not to say that he has a deficient mind or that he lacks the capacity for wonder (he is powerfully receptive to his surroundings), but that his insistence upon apprehending the world solely through reason inhibits as well as emancipates. Here he considers the spectral idea of death:

> Thoughts unspeakable
> Crowd in my breast to burning, when I hear
> Of this almighty Death, who is, it seems,
> Inevitable. Could I wrestle with him?
> I wrestled with the lion, when a boy,
> In play, till he ran roaring from my gripe.
>
> (*Cain*, I, i, 256–61)

Cain's question has more of the child than the Promethean sceptic. He wishes to comprehend the sublime mysteriousness of 'almighty Death', but instead of grappling with the idea as a philosopher might, he wonders if he could 'wrestle with him' as he 'wrestled with the lion'. He has unwittingly hit upon an appropriate metaphor for his predicament, but lacks any sense of the logic implicit in such substitutions. His 'ran roaring from my gripe' thus takes on an ironic charge in hinting at precisely what Cain fails to register – the limited grasp of reason.

Cain conceives of knowledge as 'being / The road to happiness' (*Cain*, II, ii, 230–1), as a direct, linear route to fulfilment. In this respect he has about him something of Pope's enthusiastic but inexperienced scholar:

> Fir'd at first Sight with what the *Muse* imparts,
> In *fearless Youth* we tempt the Heights of Arts,
> While from the bounded *Level* of our Mind,
> *Short Views* we take, nor see the *Lengths behind*,
> But *more advanc'd*, behold with strange Surprize
> New, *distant Scenes* of *endless* Science rise!
> So pleas'd at first, the towring *Alps* we try,
> Mount o'er the Vales, and seem to tread the Sky;
> Th' Eternal Snows appear already past,
> And the first *Clouds* and *Mountains* seem the last:
> But *those attain'd*, we tremble to survey
> The growing Labours of the lengthen'd Way,
> Th' *increasing* Prospect *tires* our wandering Eyes,
> Hills peep o'er Hills, and *Alps* on *Alps* arise!
>
> (*An Essay on Criticism*, 219–232)

Cain's cosmic education at the hands of Lucifer follows a similar trajectory, but the educative contexts established by Pope and Byron are very different. Where Pope's lesson is accompanied by the reassuring, narrative wisdom that marks the poem's solid couplets, Cain has only the untrustworthy Lucifer to shape his disappointment. Where Pope offers his reader a stable platform for comprehension by transferring the problem over to a navigable environment of metaphor ('What oft was *Thought*, but ne'er so well *Exprest*'), Cain is confronted directly with the wearying prospect of infinitude. Under Pope's guidance we are taught acceptance from one who has preceded us; under Lucifer's, Cain is immersed, as Mary Shelley recognized, in a reality that is subjected to a minimum of interpretation or rhetorical control. Philosophically this is disastrous for Cain because he has no capacity for absence; for the reader interested in poetics, however, we find ourselves drawn into an intriguing experiment.

Lucifer's pedagogy can claim very little in the way of eighteenth-century rectitude; it borrows its tricks, rather, from the discredited 'modes' of Aenesidemus.[41] Where the sun and the moon had been constants in Cain's experience they lose all distinctness as he is shifted rapidly away from them:

> Methinks they both, as we recede from them,
> Appear to join the innumerable stars
> Which are around us; and, as we move on,
> Increase their myriads.
>
> (*Cain*, II, i, 40–3)

The reverse effect occurs when Lucifer and Cain enter Hades where the latter is startled by his sudden close-up perspective:

> How silent and how vast are these dim worlds!
> For they seem more than one, and yet more peopled
> Than the huge brilliant luminous orbs which swung
> So thickly in the upper air, that I
> Had deem'd them rather the bright populace
> Of some all unimaginable Heaven
> Than things to be inhabited themselves,
> But on that drawing near them I beheld
> Their swelling into palpable immensity
> Of matter, which seem'd made for life to dwell on,
> Rather than life itself.
>
> (*Cain*, II, ii, 1–11)

While drawing a strong imaginative response, Lucifer's vast and rapid transitions successfully bewilder Cain's reason, leaving him desperate for something familiar to hold to:

> Can it be?
> Yon small blue circle, swinging in far ether,
> With an inferior circlet near it still,
> Which looks like that which lit our early nights?
> Is this our Paradise? Where are its walls,
> And they who guard them?
>
> (*Cain*, II, i, 28–33)

Byron found 'something sensible to grasp at' in the tangible presences of Catholic art. Cain, however, searches hopelessly for the walls that have determined the political geography of his life thus far.[42] Lucifer, knowing that his pupil's sense of wonder will always decay into the frustrations of reason, meanwhile seems to be revelling in his task, asking Cain to 'Point me out the site / Of Paradise' (*Cain*, II, i, 33–4) while knowing full well that Eden will no longer be distinguishable amidst the crowding myriads of space. Knowledge, we are subtly reminded, demolishes the prospect of bliss.

Cain pulses with the need for a reasoned, sophisticated response to the intellectual lockdown of tyranny. It also, in its testing and picking at Cain and Lucifer through the forms of drama, refuses to settle with the idea that reason might be sufficient. The play's heroism is constantly running into the unvanishing facts of Luciferian inheritance as well as Cain's tragically naive and suggestible framing of the mind's relation to its absolute contexts. The critical, conditioning awareness that generates this disjunction, however, also suggests a kind of synthesis. To be critical in these terms is inescapably to be creative as well. Thus, even as Lucifer is tearing up the remaining certainties of Cain's psycho-geography, the play's language is filling with a sense of why the tragedy we are witnessing need not have happened. Although he cannot make an argument out of it, Cain does intuit something of this visionary potential, telling Lucifer that 'Thou speak'st to me of things which long have swum / In visions through my thought' (*Cain*, I, i, 167–8). He also understands these 'visions' to be different in nature to the cognitive mapping of his 'Tamed down' (*Cain*, I, i, 180) parents who, he complains, 'talk to me / Of serpents, and of fruits and trees' (*Cain*, I, i, 170–1). But while Lucifer acknowledges Cain's visionary perspective ('thou now beholdest as / A vision that which is reality' (*Cain*, II, ii, 110–11)) he does not help him to understand the human and ethical contexts of his privileged but vulnerable predicament. Byron leaves out the reliable wisdom offered by Milton and Pope, or at least he has no narrator or character to voice such wisdom at the level of direct theorization.

Vision and prophecy for Lucifer are not objects for serious moral consideration; they are, rather, opportunities for some pointed Byronic mischief. Lucifer looks into the future (Byron's Baylean past) in order to multiply the ironies that work through his sceptical critique. He predicts, for instance, the unjustified interpretative tradition to which he will become subject:

> When thousand ages
> Have roll'd o'er your dead ashes, and your seed's,
> The seed of the then world may thus array
> Their earliest fault in fable, and attribute
> To me a shape I scorn [...]
>
> (*Cain*, I, i, 233–7)[43]

Lucifer rightly reiterates his proposal that the imposition of shape can be an act of hypocrisy and control. What he does not mention is the fact that the call to shape things, for all its inevitable inaccuracies, is not necessarily implicated in the immoral. Speculative activity will never get very far in a vacuum of form, and the genuine attempt to mitigate this in the act of shaping can be heroic as well as misleading. The fictive may be inherently unreliable, but it is not irrevocably so; we should not be too willing, then, to consign it over entirely to scepticism: 'Apologue, fable, poesy, and parable, / Are false, but may be render'd also true' (*Don Juan*, xv, 89).

The contrary impulse suggested here by the narrator of *Don Juan* is there in *Cain* for the reader who is attentive to the poetic and allusive textures into which he is being drawn.[44] This un-Luciferian idea of a truthful poetic shaping or rendering comes to Byron from the visionary poetics of Milton and is voiced by Raphael when asked by Adam to describe the proceedings of heaven:

> High matter thou enjoinst me, O prime of men,
> Sad task and hard, for how shall I relate
> To human sense the invisible exploits
> Of warring spirits; how without remorse
> The ruin of so many glorious once
> And perfect while they stood; how last unfold
> The secrets of another world, perhaps
> Not lawful to reveal? Yet for thy good
> This is dispensed, and what surmounts the reach
> Of human sense I shall delineate so,
> By lik'ning spiritual to corporal forms,
> As may express them best, though what if earth
> Be but the shadow of heav'n, and things therein
> Each to other like, more than on earth is thought?
>
> (*Paradise Lost*, v, 563–76)

Despite his archangelic eminence, Raphael is strikingly unsure of himself, caught up in questions that reflect Milton's own uncertainties about his role as divine interpreter. Such anxieties, which Byron feigns over in his Preface, circle around the central problem of all visionary and prophetic discourse, that of finding human words for that which 'surmounts the reach / Of human sense'. Raphael's solution, a form of compromise, is to employ figurative language to 'delineate' what exceeds the mind of man by 'lik'ning spiritual to corporal forms'. Not unlike Montaigne's solution to the problem of expressing his philosophical state of mind, Raphael's answer proposes metaphor as a form of resistance to the annihilation that lurks within every act of figuration.

Somewhere behind Raphael is Dante,[45] who is thus doubly behind *Cain* in that Byron, two years before composing his play, had written the lyric monologue *The Prophecy of Dante*. Speaking to us directly, an aged poet reflects upon the prophetic tradition to which he has contributed a life of thought:

> THE Spirit of the fervent days of Old,
>   When words were things that came to pass, and thought
>   Flash'd o'er the future, bidding men behold
> Their children's children's doom already brought
>   Forth from the abyss of time which is to be,
>   The chaos of events, where lie half-wrought
> Shapes that must undergo mortality;
>
> (The Prophecy of Dante, ii, 1–7)

The age of the great biblical prophets, when 'words were things that came to pass', was a time of exuberant spirit and inspiration. 'Dante's' own latter-day voyage into the 'abyss of time', however, has been more poignant than 'fervent': his vocation – to find words to approximate the 'half-wrought / Shapes' of prophetic experience – is, to recall Milton, a 'Sad task and hard'. He has not shaped events in the way complained of by Lucifer, but has sought some mitigation in poetry for the shapelessness of visionary truth. Rather as Mary Shelley describes Byron's own, his has been a 'voice from out the Wilderness' (*The Prophecy of Dante*, ii, 12), not only as a political exile, but as a poet excluded from divine centres of meaning. What presses upon him, even in the fullness of his prophetic power, is a moving sense of limitation:

> [...] I cannot all record
>   That crowds on my prophetic eye: the earth
>   And ocean written o'er would not afford
> Space for the annal, yet it shall go forth;
>   Yes, all, though not by human pen, is graven
>   There where the farthest suns and stars have birth.
>
> (The Prophecy of Dante, iii, 4–9)

Like the Harold poet, Byron's Dante cannot 'wreak [his] thoughts upon expression'. But where the former must 'live and die unheard, / With a most voiceless thought, sheathing it as a sword' (*Childe Harold's Pilgrimage*, iii, 97), Dante's voice, albeit from 'out the Wilderness', *will* be heard. Even if his 'human pen' can set down only a fraction of what flashes before him, his words 'shall go forth'. As with the narrator of *Don Juan* and his voyaging forth in his 'slight, trim, But *still* sea-worthy skiff' (*Don Juan*, x, 4), he accepts the fragmentary in preference to a cursed pursuit of identity.

Cain does not lack the Dantean or Miltonic capacity for visionary apprehension: where 'Dante's' 'prophetic eye' cannot 'record' all that 'crowds on' it, Cain finds, similarly, that 'Thoughts unspeakable / Crowd in my breast to burning'.[46] What he lacks is the pedagogical context in which to tone down this 'burning' into acceptance but also the capacity to mitigate an overhanging sense of loss in the energies of poetic shaping and creation. While vividly present to Byron, such wisdom is deliberately left out of the sceptical theorizations of Lucifer. Cain is not allowed to recognize his own voice as the universal voice of the poet and is left to construe his failure as personal, one relating to '*my* born faculties'. Where the Harold poet is attuned to the logic of curse and Dante and Raphael accept their struggle towards the partial, Cain is led fatally to misunderstand his predicament.

We need to understand *Cain*, then, not just as a work of philosophical scepticism or political critique (although we also shouldn't try to argue these things away), but as a unique intervention in the tradition of the reflexive visionary poem. Its uniqueness and experimental force derive from its eponymous 'hero' thinking like an (anachronistic) Enlightenment philosopher while occupying the position and bearing the raw aptitude of the vatic poet. In this sense the play's intelligence is concerned with the irrevocable difference between these two roles. *Cain* is about our rise and slide into the mind of modernity. The poet's reporting back reflects and tests this thinking in its odd, resistant emptiness. Visionary poetry wonders what it might look like when exiled from the pedagogical contexts of Dante and Milton:

> Oh ye interminable gloomy realms
> Of swimming shadows and enormous shapes,
> Some fully shown, some indistinct [...]
>
> (*Cain*, II, ii, 30–2)

The words on the page have not travelled very far from their origins. There has been no recollection in the Wordsworthian sense, nor is there any of Raphael's saddened but necessary control. Byron's lines have more in common with the radically defamiliarized, smashed up utterances of Shelley's Maniac, and, like Shelley's, open themselves to accusations of weakness. Poetry, in wondering about itself, is in danger of annihilating its own possibility. Unframed by theory, wisdom or even strong technique, the reader is thrown upon writing that tumbles about in visionary unknowing. He may sense a slight shaping of form in the way the thinness of the punctuation is subtly counteracted by the regular density of the long vowel sounds, but no clear way is opened to emerge from the 'midst of the darkness'.

Cain's first act is to question the sanctity of God's imposition of form upon chaos. He is encouraged throughout to see this simply as an act of tyranny. His ending as an exiled murderer is thus ironic because it depends upon his blindness to his own capacity to shape boundlessness. This suppressed wisdom is not set down in the play as an argument or rational proposition, but it is felt in the struggle of language with its own figurations:

> Oh, thou beautiful
> And unimaginable ether! and
> Ye multiplying masses of increased
> And still-increasing lights! what are ye? what
> Is this blue wilderness of interminable
> Air, where ye roll along, as I have seen
> The leaves along the limpid streams of Eden?
> Is your course measured for ye? Or do ye
> Sweep on in your unbounded revelry
> Through an aeriel universe of endless
> Expansion, at which my soul aches to think,
> Intoxicated with eternity?

(Cain, II, i, 98–109)

Any sense of Miltonic concreteness is tugged back into the vacuum of space by those echoing, untethering words: 'unimaginable', 'interminable', 'unbounded', 'endless', 'eternity'. They become an ironic stress pattern within a jumbled and fractured blank verse marked by ungainly clashes and jagged questioning pauses. The sculptured majesty of Milton's far-from-blank writing has lapsed into a boy throwing himself at words. Those rushed repetitions ('increased / And still-increasing') smack of desperation as Cain takes up an already emptied word and taps it on the side in the hope that more meaning will fall out.

One line stands out from this and thus suspends, briefly, the poetry of the abyss: 'The leaves along the limpid streams of Eden'. With its metrical regularity (apart from the final unstressed syllable), tethering metaphors and paced, euphonic vowels it might have come from another poem. As Cain is seized with a sudden, recollected apprehension of beauty his words break free from the logic of despair that haunts the play's philosophical contexts. We are shifted to a poetics of the path not taken. Cain's insistence upon the way of reason leads to an engulfing silence, broken only by stage direction ('*striking him with a brand, on the temples, which he snatches from the altar*'). But if he could only have listened (closely) to his own voice rather than becoming Lucifer's first un-nuanced reader, things might have been different:

> LUCIFER: Approach the things of Earth most beautiful,
>   And judge their beauty near.
> CAIN: I have done this –
>   The loveliest thing I know is loveliest nearest.
>   Lucifer: Then there must be delusion – What is that,
>   Which being nearest to thine eyes is still
>   More beautiful than beauteous things remote?
> CAIN: My sister Adah. – All the stars of heaven,
>   The deep blue noon of night, lit by an orb
>   Which looks a spirit, or a spirit's world –
>   The hues of twilight – the sun's gorgeous coming –
>   His setting indescribable, which fills
>   My eyes with pleasant tears as I behold
>   Him sink, and feel my heart float softly with him
>   Along that western paradise of clouds –
>   The forest shade – the green bough – the bird's voice –
>   The vesper bird's, which seems to sing of love,
>   And mingles with the song of cherubim,
>   As the day closes over Eden's walls; –
>   All these are nothing, to my eyes and heart,
>   Like Adah's face: I turn from earth and heaven
>   To gaze on it.
>
> (*Cain*, II, ii, 248–69)

Lucifer once more plays the sophist-sceptic with a touch of Swift's misogynistic deadness to beauty thrown in. It doesn't really work, however, because Cain is too alive amidst the poetry of his love. What he cannot do is construe the choosing of love as anything else than a betrayal of knowledge. The philosophical hero cannot 'turn from earth and heaven' because he is born to throw his mind at them. He can link the acceptance of the 'indescribable' with 'pleasant tears' (an emotional sublime) but he cannot link its address with meaningful philosophical (ethical) action. The choice, which many readers have failed to see, was never as clear-cut as Cain is led to believe. Turning towards Adah and life is only un-philosophical where philosophy is understood as being securely tied to reason and abstract truth. The alternative, present here in

Cain's brief turn as a love poet, cannot guide us clear of the wilderness but it might help us to re-vision such places as emblems of possibility rather than failure.

Notes

1 The reasons for this suspension (after completing five cantos) are complex, but seem to involve a mixture of *Don Juan*'s hostile reception back home, increasing tensions with Murray, and Byron's domestic instability in Italy. Byron had also recently lost both his daughter Allegra and his friend Shelley. Also see *CPW*, V, 716–18.

2 See M. K. Joseph, *Byron the Poet*, appendix C.

3 Byron thought the review 'extremely handsome & any thing but unkind or unfair' (*BLJ*, x, 68).

4 *Lord Byron: The Critical Heritage*, ed. Andrew Rutherford (London: Routledge, 1995), 243.

5 *Blake: The Complete Poems,* ed. W. H. Stevenson, 2nd edition (London: Longman, 1989), 869.

6 Leslie A. Marchand, *Byron's Poetry: A Critical Introduction* (London: John Murray, 1965), 84. Compare Bernard Blackstone, *Byron: A Survey* (London: Longman, 1975), 44.

7 Edward E. Bostetter, *The Romantic Ventriloquists: Wordsworth, Coleridge, Keats, Shelley, Byron* (Seattle: University of Washington Press, 1963), 287.

8 Bostetter, *The Romantic Ventriloquists*, 287.

9 Hoagwood, *Byron's Dialectic*, 106.

10 Wolf Z. Hirst, 'Byron's Lapse into Orthodoxy: An Unorthodox Reading of *Cain*', in *The Plays of Lord Byron*, ed. Robert Gleckner and Bernard Beatty (Liverpool: Liverpool University Press, 1997), 253–72 (257, 270–1, 258).

11 Hirst, 'Byron's Lapse into Orthodoxy', 270.

12 Hirst, 'Byron's Lapse into Orthodoxy', 256; Bostetter, *The Romantic Ventriloquists*, 288.

13 Hirst, 'Byron's Lapse into Orthodoxy', 272.

14 Philip W. Martin, *Byron: A Poet Before his Public* (Cambridge: Cambridge University Press, 1982), 148.

15 The most obvious reason for doing this is that it is harder for the authorities to suppress an apparently dramatic work of literature than an undisguised manifesto. It was, of course, precisely by reading *Cain* as the latter that the authorities did come to suppress the work. See Truman Guy Steffan, *Lord Byron's Cain: Twelve Essays and a Text with Variants and Annotations* (Austin: University of Texas Press, 1968), 13–18.

16 *BMW*, 1071. This is not quite correct. Heber, despite reading the play as an attack on orthodox religion, in fact also defended it in terms strikingly similar to Byron's own: the 'expressions of Cain and Lucifer', he claims, 'are not more offensive to the ears of piety than such discourses must necessarily be, or than Milton, without offence, has put into the mouths of beings similarly situated'. *Byron: The Critical Heritage*, ed. Rutherford, 243.

17 'Lucifer's final two speeches [...] declare a commitment to intellectual freedom that has never been surpassed in English verse' (*BMW*, 1072).

18 *The Letters of Mary Wollstonecraft Shelley*, ed. Betty T. Bennet, 3 vols (Baltimore: Johns Hopkins University Press, 1980–88), I, 212.

19 Mary alludes to Pope: '*True Wit* is *Nature* to Advantage drest, / What oft was *Thought*, but ne'er so well *Exprest*' (*An Essay on Criticism*, 297–8).

20 Compare Percy Shelley's *A Defence of Poetry*: 'We are on the verge where words abandon us, and what wonder if we grow dizzy to look down the dark abyss of – how little we know' (*Shelley's Poetry and Prose*, 508).

21 As early as 1811 (when Watson was Professor of Divinity at Cambridge) Byron wrote: 'I have read Watson to Gibbon. He proves nothing, so I am where I was, verging toward Spinoza; and yet it is a gloomy Creed, and I want a better, but there is something Pagan in me that I cannot shake off.' (*BLJ*, ii, 136). Byron also described Sir William Drummond's *Oedipus Judaicus* (1811) as 'worth fifty Watsons' (*BLJ*, ii, 140).

22 Compare Leigh Hunt's lively, ironic defence of *Cain* which attacks those who find in the bible 'nothing but morality, right reason and perfection' and who 'take the letter of the story for the very essence of the Divine Spirit'. *The Examiner*, no. 52 (Sunday, 2 June 1822), 337–52 (339).

23 See Roy E. Acock, 'Lord Byron and Bayle's Dictionary', *Yearbook of English Studies*, vol. 5 (1975), 142–52.

24 See Peter L. Thorslev, Jr., 'Byron and Bayle: Biblical Skepticism and Romantic Irony', in *Byron, the Bible and Religion: Essays from the Twelfth International Byron Seminar*, ed. Wolf Z. Hirst (Newark: University of Delaware Press, 1991), 58–76.

25 Harry M. Bracken, 'Bayle not a Sceptic?', *Journal of the History of Ideas*, vol. 25, no. 2 (April–June 1964), 169–80 (169).

26 Bracken, 'Bayle not a Sceptic?', 169.

27 See Craig B. Brush, *Montaigne and Bayle: Variations on the Theme of Skepticism*, International Archives of the History of Ideas, vol. 14 (The Hague: Nijhoff, 1966).

28 Bracken, 'Bayle not a Sceptic?', 170. See also Harry M. Bracken, 'Bayle's Attack on Natural Theology: The Case of Christian Pyrrhonism', in *Scepticism and Irreligion in the Seventeenth and Eighteenth Centuries*, 254–66.

29 *A General Dictionary, Historical and Critical: In which a New and Accurate Translation of that of the Celebrated Mr. Bayle is Included*, trans. Revd John Peter Bernard et al., 10 vols (London: G. Strachan et al., 1734–41), X, 413.

30 *A General Dictionary, Historical and Critical*, VI, 495–97).

31 See, for instance, Matthew 1.1 and Matthew 22.41–2.

32 II Samuel, 6 and 19.

33 *A General Dictionary, Historical and Critical*, IV, 536 (Remark I). The remarks of Raynaud are quoted by Bayle.

34 *A General Dictionary, Historical and Critical*, IV, 537 (Remark I).

35 In his *Poem on the Lisbon Disaster*: 'Bayle, great and wise, all systems overthrows / Then his own tenets labors to oppose'. Voltaire, *Candide and Related Texts*, trans. David Wootton (Indianapolis: Hackett Publishing, 2000), 106.

36 Genesis 1. 2–5 .

37 For an interesting account of Cain's complaint as 'partly [...] just' see David Eggenschweiler, 'Byron's *Cain* and the Antimythological Myth', in *The Plays of Lord Byron: Critical Essays*, ed. Robert Gleckner and Bernard Beatty (Liverpool: Liverpool University Press, 1997), 233–51 (238).

38 Byron wrote that 'Cain is a proud man – if Lucifer promised him kingdoms &c. – it would *elate* him – the object of the demon is to *depress* him still further in his own estimation than he was before – by showing him infinite things – & his own abasement – till he falls into the frame of mind – that leads to the Catastrophe – from mere *internal* irritation – *not* premeditation or envy – of Abel – (which would have made him contemptible) but from rage and fury against the inadequacy of his state to his Conceptions – & which discharges itself rather against Life – and the author of Life – than the mere living' (*BLJ*, ix, 53–4).

39 As the language of prayer echoes between Cain's family members the language of doubt echoes between Lucifer and Cain. The former's 'Amerced, for doubts beyond thy little life' (*Cain*, II, i, 15), for instance, is picked up later in Cain's 'thou shalt be amerced for sins unknown' (*Cain*, III, i, 24).

40 The Luciferian Stranger of *The Deformed Transformed*, for instance, proclaims that 'I have ten thousand names, and twice / As many attributes; but as I wear / A human shape, will take a human name (*The Deformed Transformed*, I, i, 533–5). Compare Byron's joke in the Preface to *Cain* about being 'accused of Manicheism – or some other hard name ending in '*ism*' which make[s] a formidable figure and awful sound in the eyes and ears of those who would be as much puzzled to explain the terms so bandied about as the liberal and pious Indulgers in such epithets' (*CPW*, VI, 229; compare *BLJ*, vii, 132). Goethe is somewhere behind this. When Faust asks Mephistopheles 'what is your name?' he receives the reply: 'The question is absurd, / Surely, in one who seeks to know / The inmost essence, not the outward show, / And has such deep contempt for the mere word'. Goethe, *Faust Part One*, trans. David Luke (Oxford: Oxford University Press, 1987), 41–2 (ll. 1327–30).

41 In particular the seventh 'mode', which denies that we can know the reality of something when its appearance varies according to perspective. As 'it is not possible to observe […] things apart from places and positions', as Diogenes Laertius puts it, 'their real nature is unknowable'. Diogenes Laertius, 'Life of Pyrrho', in *Lives of the Eminent Philosophers*, II, 499. For Hume's dismissal of this sophistry see *An Enquiry concerning Human Understanding*, ed. Beauchamp, 200.

42 Cain refers to these walls on a number of occasions (I, i, 88–90; II, ii, 139; II, ii, 266).

43 Compare his prediction of Christ's sacrifice (I, i, 163–6). On this aspect of the play's intelligence also see Eggenschweiler, 'Byron's *Cain* and the Antimythological Myth', 239.

44 Notably when Lucifer informs Cain that he is to bear witness to 'the history / Of past, and present, and of future worlds' (II, i, 24–5). Byron is remembering Milton's God looking down upon Satan: 'Him God beholding from his prospect high, / Wherein past, present, future he beholds' (*Paradise Lost*, iii, 77–8). The idea was clearly an important one for Byron who, six months before writing *Cain*, described poetry in his Ravenna Journal as the 'The feeling of a Former world and Future' (*BLJ*, viii, 37). Also see *Don Juan*, x, 61 and *The Vision of Judgment*, 53. Also compare Ian Balfour's observation that 'if prophecy is always oriented towards a future – even when it does not take the form of a prediction – it is also profoundly a thing of the past, an echo, a citation'. *The Rhetoric of Romantic Prophecy* (Stanford: Stanford University Press, 2002), 129.

45 'O how my speech falls short, how faint it is / For my conception! And for what I saw / It is not enough to say that I say little'. Dante Alighieri, *The Divine Comedy*, trans. C. H. Sisson, notes by David H. Higgins (Oxford: Oxford University Press, 1993), 499 (*Paradiso*, xxxiii, 121–3). Compare Cain: 'I know not what thou art: I see thy power, / And see thou show'st me things beyond *my* power, / Beyond all power of my born faculties, / Although inferior still to my desires / And my conceptions' (*Cain*, II, i, 79–83).

46 Compare Byron's early letter to his mother from Prevesa: 'I could tell you I know not how many incidents that I think would amuse you, but they crowd on my mind as much as would swell my paper, & I can neither arrange them in the one, or put them down on the other, except in the greatest confusion & in my usual horrible hand' (*BLJ*, i, 230).

PART 2

POETICS

The Need for 'all this'
Johnson, Bowles and the Forms of Prose

On 31 March 1821 Byron, by publishing the prose essay known as the
Letter to John Murray, publicly entered the controversy surrounding
William Lisle Bowles's provocative editing and subsequent pamphlet-
eering which queried Pope's status in the English canon.[1] Appalled by
what he saw as Bowles's modish but ill-considered depreciation of Pope,
Byron gave vent to his ire in an extended and uneven prose broadside.
He was the only major literary figure of the day to become so involved;
his prominent contemporaries, although they would have been aware of
the controversy through its dissemination in the literary press, tended
to be cautious about getting dragged into a grapple that was producing
more heat than light.[2]

Byron was probably not on his strongest ground when arguing in
prose and Hazlitt's sense of the poet's inadequacy in that regard has
not entirely disappeared.[3] In fact, Byron seems to have been wary
about expressing himself in prose at all because (as was not the case
with poetry) he found that it continually ran him into '*realities*'
and '*facts*'.[4] Prose is pulled strongly by the weight of its traditions
towards argument, and Byron was happier interrogating the notion of
argument than he was arguing himself. He seems on stronger ground,
for instance, in the first canto of *Don Juan* (published the same year
as Bowles's first pamphlet)[5] where he thinks about becoming a prose
controversialist but then nimbly holds off the idea amidst the ironic
enfoldings of the poetic text:

> If ever I should condescend to prose,
>   I'll write poetical commandments, which
> Shall supersede beyond all doubt all those
>   That went before; in these I shall enrich
> My text with many things that no one knows,
>   And carry precept to the highest pitch:
> I'll call the work 'Longinus o'er a Bottle,

Or, Every Poet his *own* Aristotle.'

Thou shalt believe in Milton, Dryden, Pope;
   Thou shalt not set up Wordsworth, Coleridge, Southey;
Because the first is crazed beyond all hope,
   The second drunk, the third so quaint and mouthey:
With Crabbe it may be difficult to cope,
   And Campbell's Hippocrene is somewhat drouthey:
Thou shalt not steal from Samuel Rogers, nor –
Commit – flirtation with the muse of Moore.

                           (*Don Juan*, i, 204–5)

By un-grounding his argument through the unstable and less accountable intelligence of his narrator, Byron evades the stasis he suspects of lying at the heart of all high-pitched polemic, be it brashly innovative or dourly conservative. He mocks the short-sightedness and arrogance of those (such as Bowles) who miss the irony inherent in any attempt to 'supersede beyond all doubt all those / That went before' while simultaneously recognizing that the incipient Romantic rule-making to which he objects cannot be rejected in kind: counterargument, that is, would only run counter to the kind of thinking Byron is dealing in here. He thus holds at bay both unthoughtful innovation and the kind of reactionary poetics that could lead only to 'drouthey' efforts such as those of Campbell and Crabbe. Byron stops short of taking full ownership of his words in a way that would be more difficult for the prose controversialist. He has, to some extent, rendered his thought 'Inform' (to recall Montaigne's word) in order to evade the encroachments of 'system' upon any settled opinion. Yet we also know that Byron means it – even if he does not quite mean his Mosaic rhetoric – when he writes that 'Thou shalt believe in Milton, Dryden, Pope; / Thou shalt not set up Wordsworth, Coleridge, Southey'. We also know that he *did* condescend to prose.

The question of how Byron negotiates these tensions between scepticism about argument and the wish to make claims about poetry is at the centre of what follows. Byron's critical prose, I want to suggest, comes to life in its staging and mulling over the moment in which theory begins to crumble into its own projecting language. Its shadings into its object mark an important and still unwritten recognition in the history of Romantic poetics.

                       * * *

Byron's main concern, in the *Letter to John Murray*, is not to defend Pope but to engage in a broader disagreement that spans and oversees the rise of British Romantic writing. The problem, as he saw it, was one of language and its relation to what we take it to describe. What was being said about literature in contemporary debate had become untethered from the truthfulness that distinguishes the literary in the first place. This dissociation, as far as Byron was concerned, was linked not only to the poetic poverty he diagnosed among his contemporaries, but to the dire political situation to which *Don Juan* responds. What Bowles was saying about (Pope's) poetry – and, crucially, *how* he was saying it – was for Byron inextricably linked to the kinds of linguistic dishonesty that expedite moral and political degeneration, and which he would address with particular energy in the siege of Ismail cantos of *Don Juan*.

In the *Letter to John Murray* Byron comprehends this delinquency of language in memorable terms:

> The truth is that in these days the grand "primum mobile" of England is *Cant* – Cant political – Cant poetical – Cant religious – Cant moral – but always *Cant* – multiplied through all the varieties of life. – It is the fashion – & while it lasts – will be too powerful for those who can only exist by taking the tone of the time. – I say *Cant* – because it is a thing of words – without the smallest influence upon human actions – the English being no wiser – no better – and much poorer – and more divided amongst themselves – as well as far less moral – than they were before the prevalence of this verbal decorum. (*CMP*, 128)

Cant, a disfiguring, pervasive betrayal of thought, is seen as especially pernicious in its effect upon 'those who can only exist by taking the tone of the time' – those, that is, who are unable to reflect upon the linguistic structures that constitute their narrowed and dislocated world. Public language, in its increasing removal from the scene of 'human actions', has become a force for moral and spiritual enervation, and thus, as Byron also recognizes in *Cain*, a facilitator of tyranny. Byron's urge to counteract this de-implication of language from morality helps to explain the forms and styles of *Don Juan* as a political poem; it also motivates the dashingly compendious casting about of his prose.

Dishonesty always wishes to fragment itself because an island is easier to defend than a continent. Bowles, in these terms, is not really defining poetry at all; he is participating in a self-obscuring conspiracy that works to enchain the collective mind of society. Byron's dashes ('Cant political – Cant poetical – Cant religious – Cant moral') resist this by scoring the links of the chain across the page; they cut into the paper to re-inscribe a truth that has filtered itself out of consciousness. The comma or the semicolon would not have done for this stark exposure of a particularly effective and thus particularly nasty co-opting of the normal.

'Cant' is part of a vocabulary that polices a post-Lockean world in which words and ideas are understood as being connected only by convention. Aware of the word's associations with religious enthusiasm,[6] Swift has his unhinged Hack eagerly defend a 'Language of the Spirit' in which *'Cant* and *Droning* supply the Place of *Sense* and *Reason'*.[7] It is this supplanting of thought by emotive but hollow language, something Swift would have associated with the horrors of religious civil war, which exercises the eighteenth-century moralist. Cant, however, gets everywhere; it has a habit of infecting the apparently harmless as with the silliness of our managerial talk or, for Johnson, the bland politeness of social discourse. As Johnson tells Boswell, however, these irritations need to be watched carefully lest they affect the mind:

> My dear friend, clear your *mind* of cant. You may *talk* as other people do: you may say to a man, 'Sir, I am your most humble servant.' You are *not* his most humble servant. [...] You tell a man, 'I am sorry you had such bad weather the last day of your journey, and were so much wet.' You don't care six-pence whether he was wet or dry. You may *talk* in this manner; it is a mode of talking in Society: but don't *think* foolishly.[8]

Cant needs to be kept out of serious business like moral reflection – or literary criticism – because it opens the door to those whose enthusiasm to get on and conclude things is not matched by their thoughtfulness about words. Byron inherits Johnson's sense of cant as a real problem in these terms (especially when it is turned to the purposes of defining poetry); he also sees its comic, sympathetic and subversive possibilities.[9]

Juan, upon arriving in Regency London, discovers a place in which signifier and signified are drastically at odds:

> Through Groves, so called as being void of trees,
>   (Like *lucus* from *no* light); through prospects named
> Mounts Pleasant, as containing nought to please,
>   Nor much to climb; through little boxes framed
> Of bricks, to let the dust in at your ease,
>   With 'To be let,' upon their doors proclaimed;
> Through 'Rows' most modestly called 'Paradise,'
> Which Eve might quit without much sacrifice; –
>
>   (*Don Juan*, xi, 21)

Byron is always concerned to trace the annihilations of Eden, and this regaining of 'Paradise' as purely 'a thing of words' suggests not only how far gone we are, but how complacently oblivious to the extremity of our lapse we have become. Concomitantly, cant (in this bureaucratic form at least) marks an absolute severance of language from poetry. Where the latter is concerned with glimpsing states of origin and recuperating fundamental truths, cant is involved in an act of extreme misdescription. Words, rather than tending towards 'Eternity', have become the raw material of a narrowed world in which, as Benjamin Disraeli put it rather well, 'all thoughts and things have assumed an aspect and a title contrary to their real quality and style'.[10] Instead of a referential and broadly sceptical function, language has taken on a role at once constitutive and delimiting. Bowles's cant, therefore, is for Byron an especial disaster because it signals the infection of the literary by the very forces it must be set against.

However, where cant is understood as meaning localized jargon or phraseology (especially where this involves unofficial language as with the whining or 'sing-song' canting of beggars) it becomes, in its natural challenge to legitimate language,[11] more interesting to a poet such as Byron. Here a trigger-happy Juan kills Tom, a Cockney highwayman, whose elegy is given by his own kind, in the cant of his place and social class:[12]

> Who in a row like Tom could lead the van,
>   Booze in the ken, or at the spellken hustle?
> Who queer a flat? Who (spite of Bow-street's ban)
>   On the high toby-spice so flash the muzzle?
> Who on a lark, with black-eyed Sal (his blowing)
> So prime, so swell, so nutty, and so knowing?
>
>   (*Don Juan*, xi, 19)

Mixed in with a never quite dominant sense of the ridiculous is the poet's attraction to a language of genuine energy and honesty. The cant of the lower classes did not interest Byron in quite the way it interested Wordsworth, but it is understood, by way of contrast to the empty signifiers of officialdom, as something closer to a direct apprehension of life. The language of these apparent criminals requires no policing because it is entirely straightforward in its attempts to grasp its physical and emotional environment. It expresses a culturally grounded and shared projection of experience, one that makes no attempt to dispute the reality it manifests. It has no stake in the 'tone of the time' and is thus crucially different to the cant Byron associates with Bowles.

* * *

Byron imagined his war on 'Cant poetical' as being in a direct line with the English Augustans, writing that 'As to Johnson and Pope [...] had they lived now – I would not have published a line of any thing I have ever written' (*BLJ*, ix, 68). Despite Pope's central importance to Byron, however, it was from Johnson that he drew most when thinking about the problems of contemporary literary criticism. Johnson's influence is widely apparent in the *Letter to John Murray*, where the critic is described as a 'great Moralist' (*CMP*, 125) and 'the noblest critical mind which our Country has produced' (*CMP*, 138). Medwin reports Byron to have said that 'I have been reading "Johnson's Lives," a book I am very fond of. I look upon him as the profoundest of critics, and had occasion to study him when I was writing to Bowles'.[13]

It would have been partly through Johnson that Byron came to know the history of the controversy about Pope in which he was becoming involved. We see this in a letter of April 1818 to John Murray from Venice, in which Byron describes the irritations that would eventually drive him to prose:

> but Pope quoad Pope the poet against the world – in the unjustifiable attempts at depreciation begun by Warton – & carried on to & at this day by the new School of Critics & Scribblers who think themselves poets because they do *not* write like Pope. – I have no patience with such cursed humbug – & bad taste – your whole generation are not worth a Canto of the Rape of the Lock – or the Essay on Man – or the Dunciad – or "anything that is his" but it is three in the matin & I must go to bed. (*BLJ*, vi, 31)

What Byron calls the 'depreciation' of Pope might be traced back even further than Joseph Warton, to early biographies of the poet by William Ayre and Robert Shiels, both of whom raised questions about the pre-eminence of Pope on the grounds of his perceived generic restrictions.[14] As Byron's letter suggests, however, the challenge to Pope's supremacy became serious in 1756 with the anonymous publication of the first volume of Joseph Warton's *An Essay on the Writings and Genius of Pope* (in subsequent editions *Genius* precedes *Writings*).[15]

Warton, who was headmaster of Winchester when Bowles was among its pupils, began, like many middling poets of his day, as an imitator of Pope's style. Around 1740, however, he seems to have had a change of heart. We get a sense of this from a letter to his father, in April of that year (just before he matriculated at Oriel College, Oxford), in which he declares 'I shall read Longinus as long as I live: it is impossible not to catch fire and raptures from his glowing style'.[16] The terms of this enrapturing, Warton would later conclude, required clear critical instantiation and were to be defined, at length and in prose, against the style and subject matter of Pope.[17]

Warton's *Essay* is a wide-ranging critical manifesto that puts forward its case in bold, uncompromising terms, arguing that 'the sublime and the pathetic are the two chief nerves of all genuine poetry' and that this 'genuine poetry' can be produced only by a 'creative and glowing IMAGINATION'.[18] Pope is applauded as a 'MAN OF WIT' and a 'MAN OF SENSE', but has no claim to the status of 'TRUE POET' (*Essay*, i, p.ii). It follows from this that Pope's works – which are hardly homogenous – should be divided up into qualitatively loaded categories:

> The reputation of POPE, as a Poet, among posterity, will be principally owing to his WINDSOR FOREST, his RAPE OF THE LOCK, and his ELOISA TO ABELARD; whilst the facts and characters alluded to and exposed in his later writings, will be forgotten and unknown, and their poignancy and propriety little relished. For WIT and SATIRE are transitory and perishable, but NATURE and PASSION are eternal. (*Essay*, i, 330)

Warton's shift from what M. H. Abrams terms a 'mimetic' or 'pragmatic' to an 'expressive' poetics has,[19] of course, been hugely influential; his voice is echoed by Matthew Arnold and persists into the twentieth century, where it sparked new (and very old) critical debates.[20]

Responses to Warton's criticism, however, begin rather closer to the *Essay*'s original publication. Johnson, an acquaintance and fellow Literary Club member of Warton,[21] reviewed the *Essay* for the *Literary Magazine*, describing it, in mutely thunderous terms, as a 'very curious and entertaining miscellany of critical remarks'.[22] Given the personal relationship between reviewer and reviewed it is perhaps not surprising that the review is restrained, but Johnson's real opinions are not hard to detect. He picks up in particular on Warton's ordering of the Pope canon, closely reproducing Warton's own terms in his response:

> He ventures to remark, that the reputation of *Pope*, as a poet, among posterity, will be principally founded to his *Windsor-Forest*, *Rape of the Lock*, and *Eloisa to Abelard*, while the facts and characters alluded to in his late writings will be forgotten and unknown, and their poignancy and propriety little relished; for wit and satire are transitory and perishable, but nature and passion are eternal.[23]

The skeleton of Warton's classificatory account is left in place, but Johnson intervenes to complicate the tone and thus undermine the logic of the original and its reliance upon strident rhetoric (and even typology). Warton's exclamatory final sentence, with its capitalized absolutes, is dampened to a rather tired-sounding final clause recalled as by one who has heard it all before. Johnson releases Warton's terms (such as 'poignancy' and 'propriety') from the coercive context of their rhetoric into a less confident and more questioning interpretative environment. He doesn't formulate a counterargument as such, but implies that language has been co-opted without due deference to the problems language use entails.

It was in the *Life of Pope* (1781) that Johnson delivered his most damning verdict on critics who were making Pope a scapegoat in the cause of cultural innovation:

> After all this it is surely superfluous to answer the question that has once been asked, Whether Pope was a poet? otherwise than by asking in return, If Pope be not a poet, where is poetry to be found? To circumscribe poetry by a definition will only shew the narrowness of the definer, though a definition which shall exclude Pope shall not easily be made.[24]

Johnson sets out the sceptical territory of his response by 'asking in return', by following one question with another, which is in turn left rhetorically open. Literary criticism must begin and end in awe of its object, not with a false sense of command drawn from wrong ideas about language. Warton's attempt to 'circumscribe poetry' is by comparison diagnosed as a failure of intelligence, as the assertion of a brash conviction that involves no sense of the shifting textures of poetic reflection. Warton imposes ego where he should acknowledge limitation; he misconstrues cultural baggage as existential travelling.

The 'shame' of Warton's *Essay*, as Johnson puts it in his similarly scathing review of Soame Jenyns's 'dogmatical limitations of omnipotence', is to 'impose words for ideas upon ourselves or others'. Warton writes 'with too much vivacity for the necessary caution';[25] he fails to see that 'Definition is [...] not the province of man' because 'everything is set above or below our faculties'.[26] Where Warton rushes into definition, for Johnson any attempt to use words to comprehend other words is an ironic, essayistic, tough, committed activity. It is to enter territory that is 'copious without order, and energetic without rules', to struggle to make choices within 'boundless variety'.[27] This struggle is sensed in the hard-won progress of the prose of Johnson's Preface, but also in the forms of the definitions themselves. His definition of 'definition' ('To circumscribe; to mark the limit; to bound'), to take one example, recalls the terms of his critique of

Warton's own definition of poetry; yet where the latter simply assumes its own success, the former is accompanied by an ironic sense of its own provisionality. This comes through the exemplary quotations which call into question the very enterprise for which they are being used. Locke's acknowledgement that 'there are some words that will not be defined' is set alongside some sceptical verses of Matthew Prior:

> Your God, forsooth, is found
> Incomprehensible and infinite;
> But is he therefore found? Vain searcher! no:
> Let your imperfect definition show,
> That nothing you, the weak definer, know.

Decided and strongly inscribed as it is, Johnson's definition, when taken as part of the entry as a whole, assumes a self-questioning tendency that distinguishes it from the formally unreflexive language, as Johnson understands it, of Warton or Jenyns.

Warton's failure, as a literary critic, to grasp the responsibilities that language bears towards thought is directly contrasted, for Johnson, by the vivacious literary criticism of Dryden's *Essay of Dramatic Poesy*:

> It will not be easy to find in all the opulence of our language a treatise so artfully variegated with successive representations of opposite probabilities, so enlivened with imagery, so brightened with illustrations. [...] the criticism of Dryden is the criticism of a poet; not a dull collection of theorems, nor a rude detection of faults, which perhaps the censor was not able to have committed; but a gay and vigorous dissertation, where delight is mingled with instruction, and where the author proves his right of judgement by his power of performance. (*Lives*, i, 412)

Johnson stresses the need for an alignment of critical and literary intelligence, arguing that without this an ossified and pedantic 'detection of faults', such as the kind he found in Warton, will take the place of a critical discourse that is 'variegated', 'enlivened' and 'brightened' by the mind of the poet. This performative aspect of critical practice, however, is more than decorative. It is seen as essential, rather, in authenticating the critic's 'right of judgement'. Johnson attributes to Dryden, in other words, a 'special critical authority',[28] one grounded in the critic's observance of continuities between the didactic and the aesthetic. A gloomier and tougher version of this authority is behind Johnson's 'after all this it is surely superfluous to answer'. Rather than answering Warton, that is, Johnson invokes the 'all this' of his own essayistic prose, the complex biographical and critical textures of the (soon to end) *Life of Pope*, a work which, unlike Warton's more intellectually linear and repercussive *Essay*, evades obvious master narratives. He does not turn out a competing theory or definition, but turns to the character of his own writing as a form of lived experience and as a form of argument where argument has been called into question.

* * *

Byron's study of Johnson provided not only a model for the riposte to Bowles, but a way of thinking about literary criticism that informs both the controversial prose and *Don Juan*. In distinguishing critically valid expression from the morally bankrupt claims of cant, Johnson helped Byron to a powerful and expansive recognition, one that cannot be wholly reconstituted as a theory or philosophical position, but which can be felt along the pulses of the poet's writing.

Although usually associated with the early 1820s, Byron's response to Bowles dates from as early as 1807. This was the year he started drafting his satire *English Bards and Scotch Reviewers*, which was published in 1811 but begun four years earlier under the title 'British Bards, A Satire'. *English Bards*, in this early form, was one of the first critical responses to the 1806 publication of Bowles's edition of Pope, which contains, in its notes and in an introductory biographical sketch, views (both on Pope's character and poetry) that would later be developed in the prose of the *Invariable Principles*. Bowles's edition (which Byron owned) was not, on the whole, well received. The *Edinburgh Review*, for instance, accused the editor of espousing 'principles of criticism by no means peculiar to himself, but which have obtained too great an influence over the public taste of our age'.[29]

Byron is more aggressively *ad hominem*, full of aristocratic prejudice, and more focused on the biographical aspects of the dispute:

> BOWLES! in thy memory let this precept dwell:
> Stick to thy Sonnets, man! at least they sell.
> But if some new-born whim, or larger bribe
> Prompt thy crude brain, and claim thee for a scribe,
> If 'chance some bard, though once by dunces fear'd,
> Now, prone in dust, can only be rever'd;
> If Pope, whose fame and genius from the first
> Have foil'd the best of critics, needs the worst,
> Do thou essay; each fault, each failing scan;
> The first of poets was, alas! but man!
> Rake from each ancient dunghill ev'ry pearl,

Consult Lord Fanny, and confide in CURLL;
Let all the scandals of a former age,
Perch on thy pen and flutter o'er thy page;
Affect a candour which thou can'st not feel,
Clothe envy in the garb of honest zeal;

(*English Bards and Scotch Reviewers*, 361–76)

Byron's claim that Bowles's critical 'candour' is inauthentic because it lacks the validation of personal experience is straight from Horace, probably via Johnson.[30] What isn't evident here is any sense of how such experience might be reasserted, as an act of (critical) form, beyond the limitations of basic satire.

After *English Bards*, discussion of Bowles seems to have lulled for more than a decade, before being stirred up again by Thomas Campbell in his 1819 *Specimens of the British Poets*, which was published by Murray and sent out to Byron in Italy. Campbell echoed Byron's distaste for Bowles's assessment of Pope's character, accusing the editor of a tendentious reorganization:

> The faults of Pope's private character have been industriously exposed by his latest editor and biographer, a gentleman whose talents and virtuous indignation were worthy of a better employment. In the moral portrait of Pope which he has drawn, all the agreeable traits of tender and faithful attachment in his nature have been thrown in the shade, while his deformities are brought out in the strongest, and sometimes exaggerated colours.[31]

Campbell's assessment is reasonable enough. Although at first Bowles is circumspect and proposes himself as arbitrator between Warton and Johnson, it becomes clear, as his biographical sketch proceeds, that his sympathies are almost entirely with his old headmaster. He retains and expands upon many of Warton's unflattering biographical observations and, while condensing Pope's laudable characteristics into three lines, lingers for many pages over the poet's jealousy, love of praise, animosity, and artfulness. He emphasizes Pope's fault in his disputes with Dennis, Philips, Addison, Cibber and Lady Mary Wortley Montagu, and highlights the Chandos affair and the publication of his own letters as instances of Pope's vanity, envy and scheming nature. Taken as individual details there was nothing here that Johnson hadn't already said, yet Bowles's manner of telling his story is very different in texture to the 'all this' of the *Life of Pope*.[32]

Bowles was incensed by Campbell's criticisms and threw himself into what would become a long line of pamphlets (beginning with *The Invariable Principles*) which set out to defend and expand upon the ideas set down in his edition. Byron was by this stage monitoring the debate with some interest and was so annoyed by Bowles's riposte to Campbell that he reached for his pen and dashed off 'Some Observations' in March 1820. He became distracted, however (most likely by the growing instability of his situation with Teresa Guiccioli in Italy), and the pamphlet remained on his desk. He did not, though, lose interest in the controversy, and early in February 1821, almost a year later, recorded in his Ravenna Journal that he had 'Read some of Bowles's dispute about Pope, with all the replies and rejoinders'. He goes on to note that 'my name has been lugged into the controversy, but have not time to state what I know of the subject' (*BLJ*, viii, 43). Two days later he wrote the *Letter to John Murray*.

By now Byron was somewhat embarrassed by *English Bards,* but makes a point of recalling his lines on Bowles as the part of the poem 'I regret the least' (*CMP*, 123). He maintains the view that Bowles was too inclined to 'omit the good qualities' (*CMP*, 152) of Pope's character and had thus produced an unbalanced biographical sketch. His response is not, however, to aim at the man, as he had in his earlier satirical poetry, but to raise questions about the nature of life writing and the responsibilities that attend any act of biographical reconstruction:

> Pope was the tolerant yet steady adherent of the most bigoted of sects – and Cowper the most bigoted and despondent Sectary that ever anticipated damnation to himself or others. – – Is this harsh? – I know it is – and I do not assert it as my opinion of Cowper – *personally* but to *show what might* be said – with just as great appearance of truth – and candour – as all the odium which has been accumulated upon Pope – in similar speculations. (*CMP*, 147)

Rather than opposing Bowles's depiction of Pope with a more positive account of his own, Byron returns it to the realm of '*what might* be said'. By identifying Bowles's biographical sketch as merely one possible construction among many, including his own deliberately 'harsh' reading, he makes the point that the totemic claims of the former (and 'similar speculations') depend upon the forcing of language against the truths of essayistic form.

Byron identifies Bowles's failure with a failure to read Johnson; Bowles, that is, is unwilling or unable to grasp the significance of the latter's 'all this':

> If the opinions cited by Mr. Bowles, of Dr. Johnson *against* Pope, are to be taken as decisive authority, they will also hold good against Gray, Swift,

Milton, Thomson, and Dryden: in that case what becomes of Gray's poetical, and Milton's moral character? even of Milton's *poetical* character, or indeed of *English* poetry in general? for Johnson strips many a leaf from every laurel. Still Johnson's is the finest critical work extant, and can never be read without instruction and delight.

(*CMP*, 150)

Johnson's criticism may be harsh (as Byron's is made to be above), littered with prejudice and even open to the very charges it brings against Warton (that it has more to do at times with its author than its apparent object). Despite this, Byron still claims Johnson's as the 'finest critical work extant', not necessarily because of its factual correctness but due to its self-understanding as a particular instance of '*what might be said*'. It recognizes, that is, its own constructedness as well as its subjection to history, language and the eccentricities of the individual mind. Johnson's equilaterally abrasive textures – he 'strips many a leaf from *every* laurel' – goes beyond the 'appearance of truth' to participate in a different form of truthfulness. This is not personal or cultural agenda but rigorous textuality.

* * *

As Richard Cronin has shown, Byron, in criticizing Bowles's biography, was operating within an environment where the line between what 'might be made public' and what 'must remain private' was 'unclear and rather fiercely disputed'.[33] Bowles's apparent impropriety in going through the bins of Pope's personal life was, however, only part of the problem. Byron objected to Bowles-as-biographer not only because of his tired scandal-mongering, but because of the connections he perceived between Bowles's biographical practice and his poetics. Both were firmly rooted in the moral wasteland of cant and were thus part of a much larger problem.

The most resonant cant-word – as Byron would see it – deployed by Bowles and his predecessors is 'Nature'. Bowles, in his edition, makes no original claims about poetry and acknowledges that 'criticism does not form part of my plan'.[34] He does, however, lift freely from Warton's edition of Pope, more than once without attribution.[35] In particular he reiterates his predecessor's case that Pope was not a poet of 'nature' and therefore cannot be considered as belonging to the highest 'order' of poets. If anything, Bowles hardens Warton's line: where the latter had found room in his 'eternal' category for *The Rape of the Lock*, presumably on the basis of its extraordinary imaginative qualities, Bowles tethers 'nature' more securely to the non-human, organic world, something Byron would mock towards the end of *Don Juan* in his quip that 'in-door life is less poetical' (*Don Juan*, xiv, 30). Bowles, in an attempt to claim the (Horatian) ground from which he would be assaulted by Byron, even links Pope's alleged deficiency as a nature poet to his physical limitations. As a poet of the natural world, 'Pope [...] must evidently fail', Bowles concludes, 'as he could not describe what his physical infirmities prevented him observing'.[36]

Campbell, responding to Bowles's edition, deplored what he saw as an implausible circumscription of what we mean when we use the word 'nature':

> Nature is the poet's goddess; but by nature, no one rightly understands her mere inanimate face – however charming it may be – or the simple landscape painting of trees, clouds, precipices and flowers. Why then try Pope, or any other poet, exclusively by his powers of describing inanimate phenomena? Nature, in the wide and proper sense of the word, means life in all its circumstances – nature moral as well as external.[37]

This rather Johnsonian reprimand – which widens and reattaches the word to 'life in all its circumstances' – helped to provoke the *Invariable Principles* in which Bowles expands upon and entrenches his opposition between 'natural' and 'artificial'. Given that the 'natural' acts more strongly on the reader than the 'artificial', Bowles argues, and that Pope is primarily concerned more with the latter than the former, it stands to reason that his poetry must be of secondary status. Bowles's certainty about this is reflected in the relentless forms of his prose: 'all images drawn from what is BEAUTIFUL or SUBLIME in the WORKS of NATURE, are MORE beautiful and sublime than images drawn from art, and are therefore more poetical'. Or: '*Works of nature*, speaking of those *more* beautiful and sublime, are *more* sublime and beautiful than works of art; therefore more poetical'.[38]

Among those annoyed by this was another Murray-circle acquaintance of Byron, Isaac D'Israeli. The *Quarterly Review* for November 1820, which Byron read belatedly in July of the following year, includes a review by D'Israeli of Spence's *Anecdotes*, in which space is found for a few swipes at Bowles's *Invariable Principles*.[39] Following Campbell, and with something of Johnson's tiredness, D'Israeli takes issue with Bowles's vocabulary: '"Nature", he quips, 'is a critical term which the Bowleses have been explaining for more than two thousand years'. In terms that strike a decidedly Byronic note, D'Israeli continues: 'We quarrel with Mr. Bowles for a kind of mysticism in the language of his criticism, nebulous as the dreams of a Muggletonian or a Swedenburghian'.[40] D'Israeli senses something incantatory and fetishitic, but also nebulously untethered, about a mode of critical practice that takes its stand in the word rather than in the poem, in a denatured 'nature' rather than amidst 'life in all its circumstances'.

As well as identifying with the tones of Byronic satire, D'Israeli invokes Johnson as critical precursor. If the 'Bowleses' are nothing new then neither is the method for flicking them away:

> It has frequently been attempted to raise up such arbitrary standards and such narrowing theories of art; and these 'criterions' and 'invariable principles' have usually been drawn from the habitual practices and individual tastes of the framers; there are a sort of concealed egotism, a stratagem of self-love.[41]

D'Israeli now immediately quotes, in full, the passage from the *Life of Pope* in which Johnson dismisses the 'narrowness of the definer'. In dealing with Warton, D'Israeli implies, Johnson had already dealt with Bowles. No new argument has been made and thus no new argument is required by way of refutation.

Byron, in part, inclined to this way of thinking ('had they lived now – I would not have published a line of anything I have ever written'), and shares D'Israeli's sense of the controversy as a series of repetitions in which egotistical innovation is to be corrected by tradition. Although he hadn't yet read him Byron sounds particularly like D'Israeli in 'Some Observations' where he stresses the lineage of Bowles's argument (and by implication its lack of originality) as well as its basis in ego rather than insight:

> The great cause of the present deplorable state of English Poetry is to be attributed – to that absurd and systematic depreciation of Pope, in which for the last few years there has been a king [sic] of Epidemical concurrence.– – Men of the most opposite opinions have united upon this topic.– Warton and Churchill began it, having borrowed the hint probably from the heroes of the Dunciad – and their own internal conviction that their proper reputation must be as nothing till the most perfect and harmonious of poets – he who having no fault – has had REASON made his reproach. (*CMP*, 104)

The critic, in these terms, is a custodian more than a controversialist. His job is to identify new outcroppings of critical 'system' and denounce them through alliances that connect present (D'Israeli, Byron) with past (Horace, Johnson).

Where for D'Israeli that is the end of matter, Byron's prose fizzes with energies that have too much of the moment about them to settle for anything like regurgitation. The past may ground us and protect us from absurdity but it cannot know everything about the present. To think otherwise, as *Don Juan* makes clear, is to go the way of the 'drouthey' Hippocrene, of Campbell, who saw the problems clearly enough but who had no ideas about where poetry was going and what it was to do. Moreover, Byron, unlike D'Israeli, has in mind the link between 'Cant Poetical' and 'Cant Political'. Bowles, as a literary critic, may require only a wearied reiteration of Johnson's already tired dismissal, but Byron is also thinking of a larger post-Waterloo situation in which the writtenness of political control calls for new forms of scrutiny.

However much Byron agreed with Campbell and D'Israeli, he makes a point of entering the controversy on his own (sceptical) terms: 'It is no affair of mine – but having once begun [...] I am like an Irishman in a "row" "any body's Customer"' (*CMP*, 129). As his name has been dragged into the controversy by others anyway, he may as well appear in his own right, but he is not, he is at pains to stress, here to take sides: 'Mr Campbell', he asserts, 'has no need of my alliance' (*CMP*, 129). Byron wants to be a Bayle and wade into the absurdities of category criticism; he also, however, wants to establish a set of preferences (as he does with his commandments in *Don Juan*) against which true poetry can be measured. Are 'we to be told', Byron asks in return, 'that Ethical poetry – or Didactic poetry – or by whatever name you term it [...] is not the *very first order* of poetry?' (*CMP*, 143). This is risky because 'Ethical' and 'Didactic' sound categorical and may be no easier to define than 'natural'; but while Byron doesn't have the ironic resources of *Don Juan* to hand here, he does still write himself an escape route with 'or by whatever name you term it'. While offering up something that might easily be taken (as it was by Hazlitt)[42] as a poetical commandment, he also undoes the totemic power of the critical word, thus leaving us not with an answer but with a reassertion of the question. 'Ethical' is a gesture or sketch; it registers due scepticism about contemporary vogues and asserts a bedrock connection between poetry and morality, but it also recognizes itself as a 'term', as a gesture within criticism rather than a final answer.

Byron's critical prose is at its richest where it intervenes in the territory contested between Campbell and Bowles. Campbell had attempted to refute Bowles by introducing instances of 'poetic' spectacles from 'artificial' life and stressing their inherent poetic quality; he gives examples, that is, which we may well call 'poetic' but which have little or nothing to do with what Bowles calls 'nature' (i.e. precisely what Hazlitt accuses Byron of doing). The example that generated most interest was a 'ship of the line' at sea which Campbell invokes as an instance of 'the sublime objects of artificial life'.[43] If the ship is both 'artificial' and 'sublime', Campbell reasons, then it follows that Bowles has drawn his line in the wrong place.

This was a red rag to Bowles, who replied that Campbell was mistaking the case entirely:

> Let us examine the ship which you have described so beautifully. On what does the poetical beauty depend? Not on *art*, but NATURE. Take away the *waves*, the *winds*, the *sun*, that, in association with the streamer and sails, make them look so beautiful! take all poetical associations away, ONE will become a strip of blue bunting, and the *other* a piece of coarse canvas on three tall poles!![44]

Byron's response to this was not to reassert Campbell's argument, but to poke fun at the quasi-scientific thinking on which both sides rest their case; he also, however, wants to make his own claims about the nature of aesthetic experience:

> Mr. B. asserts that Campbell's "Ship of the Line" derives all it's [sic] poetry not from "*art*" but from "*Nature.*" – – "Take away the waves – the winds – the Sun &c &c &c *one* will become a stripe of blue bunting – and the other a piece of coarse canvas on three tall poles." – – – Very true – take away the "waves" – "the winds" and there will be no ship at all – not only for poetical – but for any other purpose – & take away "the Sun" and we must read Mr. B's pamphlet by candle-light. – But the "poetry" of the "Ship" does *not* depend on the "waves &c." – on the contrary – the "Ship of the line" confers it's [sic] own poetry upon the waters – and heightens *theirs* […] the poetry is at least reciprocal. (*CMP*, 129–30)

The methodological problem noticed by Byron's jokes here is given clearer form in the later 'Observations upon Observations': 'If this is not "minute moral "anatomy"', Byron complains of Bowles's approach, 'I should be glad to know what is? – It is dissection in all it's [sic] branches' (*CMP*, 166). The image is recycled in *Don Juan*:

> The lawyer and the critic but behold
>   The baser sides of literature and life,
> And nought remains unseen, but much untold,
>   By those who scour those double vales of strife.
> While common men grow ignorantly old,
>   The lawyer's brief is like the surgeon's knife,
> Dissecting the whole inside of a question,
> And with it the whole process of digestion.
>
> (*Don Juan*, x, 14)

Where the envoy of 'Cant poetical' (again linked to 'Cant moral' in the despised figure of the lawyer) believes he is penetrating to the truth of his object he is fact wielding the knife over the very processes and reciprocities upon which poetry depends. Poetry's captureless incipience is unavailable to such brutal measures which, rather than participating in the subtleties of the poem, slice them up according to the dominant deceits of public discourse.

Byron may have Swift's delusional Hack in mind here,[45] but it is to Johnson that he turns to develop his point about reciprocity as an aesthetic virtue. 'What makes the poetry', Byron asks, 'in the image of the *"Marble waste of Tadmor* [sic]" in Grainger's "Ode to Solitude" so much admired by Johnson? – is the *"marble"* or the *"Waste"* the *artificial* or the *natural* object?' (*CMP*, 132). Byron refers to a passage from Boswell where the following lines are quoted along with Johnson's opinion ('very noble') of them:

O Solitude, romantick maid,
Whether by nodding towers you tread;
Or haunt the desart's trackless gloom,
Or hover o'er the yawning tomb;
Or climb the Andes' clifted side,
Or by the Nile's coy source abide;
Or, starting from your half-years sleep,
From Hecla view the thawing deep;
Or, at the purple dawn of day,
Tadnor's marble wastes survey.[46]

Johnson's approval of these lines, Byron suggests, has something to do with the co-presence of the different 'associations' that Bowles dissevers in his account of the ship. To put 'marble wastes' under the critical knife would be absurd because the effect of the image relies precisely on the conflation of the 'natural' and the 'artificial'. Such poetry might also be described as 'Ethical' in so far as it traces human presences in human absence. Without the symbolic heft or political edge, Grainger's imagery has something of Shelley's 'Ozymandias' and its interrogation of permanence as a human conceit. 'Trackless' both gestures towards and engulfs human endeavour.

Byron is thinking here not only of reciprocity as a poetic virtue, but of the necessarily reciprocal relation between poetic and critical practice. What Bowles gets wrong for Byron is his assumption that the claim to truth negates the critic's responsibility to participate in his object. Byron makes this point by showing Johnson not just as a judge ('very noble') of poetry but as a critic who is also a fine writer. He quotes, to this end, Johnson's famous praise for Gray's *Elegy*:

> He who reads those lines enjoys for a moment the powers of a poet; he feels what he remembers to have felt before, but he feels it with great increase of Sensibility; he recognizes a *familiar image*, but meets it again amplified & expanded, embellished with beauty – & enlarged with Majesty (Quoted by Byron, *CMP*, 138).

At its best, Johnson's criticism deserves the compliment it pays to Dryden by shaping itself to the contours of the experience with which it contends. Here Johnson revisits and generalizes his reading of the poem, not by placing it under the banner of a single word but by running his critical vocabulary – 'amplified', 'expanded', 'embellished', 'enlarged' – into a larger effect that captures something of the cultured expansion of sentiment he describes. Poetry occurs between sites of secure rational reflection and thus shakes off the words that locate such places. Johnson's writing, which extrapolates more than defines its object, is minded of this. His criticism, thus understood, lives out Byron's claim that poetry is a 'thing to be felt – more than explained' (*CMP*, 160).[47] The critic proves his 'right of judgement' in his 'power of performance'.

Byron is using Johnson to establish in prose some of the ideas that were driving the innovations of *Don Juan*. He also, however, risks creeping back towards the 'drouthey' Hippocrene problem. If Campbell (as poet or critic) and Crabbe are not the way to go – and Byron wasn't going anywhere near them with *Don Juan* – then neither, *a fortiori*, was Grainger. Such poetry may be useful in pointing to the failings of Bowles's logic, but it was hardly a model for poetic practice in the 1820s. Even Johnson, whose resilient integrity galvanizes Byron's prose effort, is too wedded to the rhetorical terms of Sensibility for Byron's purposes. Reciprocity in *Don Juan*, to put this in different terms, is far more immediate than the connectivities Byron the critic was pulling out of the eighteenth century. It responds, for one thing, to a more immediate threat of dissection. As well as the long-running attempt to cut Pope out of the picture for not being 'sublime' enough, Byron was also faced with the more pressing irritation of his own work being put under the knife. There were Murray's apprehensive editorial interventions to endure, his 'damned cutting & slashing' (*BLJ*, vi, 105) as Byron called it. There were also the critics, who had not greeted the first two cantos of *Don Juan* with much enthusiasm. They deplored, on the whole, not only the daring irreverence of Byron's poem, but its deliberate blurring of expected generic, tonal and experiential distinctions.[48] *Blackwood's Edinburgh Magazine*, for instance, although concerned more with the poet's behaviour towards Lady Byron than with *Don Juan*, wields the scalpel in remarking that it would have been better had the 'wickedness been less inextricably mingled with the beauty and the grace, and the strength of a most inimitable and incomprehensible muse'. 'It is indeed a sad and an humiliating thing to know', it continues, 'that in the same year there proceeded from the same pen two productions, in all things so different, as the Fourth Canto of Childe Harold and this loathsome Don Juan'.[49] This was the review that provoked Byron's 'Some Observations', largely because of its highly personal nature, but also because it flies in the face of everything Byron was trying to do with *Don Juan* and its deliberate swerve away from the style of *Childe Harold's Pilgrimage*.

The *Blackwood's* reviewer may have had in mind stanzas such as this, which describes Haidée's maternal tenderness for Juan:

> And she bent o'er him, and he lay beneath,
>   Hush'd as the babe upon its mother's breast,
> Droop'd as the willow when no winds can breathe,
>   Lull'd like the depth of ocean when at rest,
> Fair as the crowning rose of the whole wreath,
>   Soft as the callow cygnet in its nest;
> In short, he was a very pretty fellow,
> Although his woes had turn'd him rather yellow.
>
> (Don Juan, ii, 148)

Taken singly, the similes that precede the couplet might be sourced from any of Byron's most popular and approved poems. Taken together, their sincerity comes under pressure from the comic form of the list before being undermined more fully by the couplet. Is the poet really feeling his metaphors or just plucking them out of overstocked poetic ether? In a world full of cant the poet cannot behave as if style were a guarantee of feeling; any such claim, Byron thought, had become perilously bound up in the enthusiasms of cultural self-definition. This does not mean, however, that *Don Juan* is merely a wrecking ball for the poetic world according to Bowles. This would mean the poem was an act of system or argument.

If the prerogatives of recognized Byronic (Romantic) practice needed careful monitoring, this did not mean that they were necessarily false. They simply needed to be played within newly connective generic environments:

An infant when it gazes on a light,
  A child the moment when it drains the breast,
A devotee when soars the Host in sight,
  An Arab with a stranger for a guest,
A sailor when the prize has struck in fight,
  A miser filling his most hoarded chest,
Feel rapture; but not such true joy are reaping
As they who watch o'er what they love while sleeping.
(Don Juan, ii, 196)

Here the list begins in similar fashion to the one above, using naturalistic images typically associated with emotional sincerity; it quickly loses its tonal consistency, however, under the pressure of increasing internal incongruities. Byron's 'beauty' and 'grace', as the *Blackwood's* reviewer would see it, have been contaminated by lower quality poetic substances. Such strategies on Byron's part are entirely deliberate and stand against precisely the kinds of aesthetic assumption according to which they were condemned. They do not, however, represent anything as final as a decision about Romantic poetic culture. The couplet here, unlike the previous one, surprises us not with an assertion of wit over emotion, but with an attempt to recover the feeling with which the stanza begins. The 'romantic' is not simply overturned into the 'burlesque' (*Don Juan*, iv, 3) but is quested after along a pair of lingering, eleven-syllable lines that seem all the more authentic for not succumbing to the comic forces that surround them. The 'beauty' and 'grace' of the final line are not vocally or formally pure; they have been transplanted from the easier conditions of the Byronic Spenserian stanza and feel hard won. They have been tested and approved for a world in which the poetry of feeling can no longer assume automatic rights.

What was at stake in *Don Juan* was nothing less than the grounding if unpredictable connection between poetic writing and human experience,[50] something that was at risk not only from the theoretical enthusiasms of second-rate Romantic thought, but from a critical and political establishment that was too happy with the dominant idea of the Byronic. *Don Juan*, by way of riposte, insists that the 'reciprocal' and 'Ethical' are linked as poetic virtues; it is the poem's tracing of life beyond the authorized limits of culture that gives it moral compass. Such thinking is inherently critical and, for Byron, political, in its claim to discover, in its own reciprocities, an antidote to cant in all its forms. It is also, while very much of its moment, firmly rooted in the tradition of Horace, Pope and Johnson in sourcing its critical power from the decentred insights of literary form.

Byron's thinking here also pours into the textures of the critical prose where it finds itself untethered from the (liberating) confines of the *ottava rima*. 'I do hate that word "*invariable*"', he complains in the *Letter to John Murray*: 'What is there of *human* – be it poetry – philosophy – wit, wisdom – science – power – glory – mind – matter – life – or death – – which is "*invariable*"?' (*CMP*, 129). Byron, we imagine, was hard on his paper; his dashes become the perforations through which we glimpse the life beyond. Their clearing out of more considered schemes of punctuation hints at the hardwiring of things. They endlessly echo the hyphen in 'serio-comic'.

Take Byron's well-known response to Francis Cohen (a friend of Murray and frequent contributor to the *Quarterly* and *Edinburgh Review*) who followed the magazines in complaining of *Don Juan*'s 'quick succession of fun and gravity'. Byron's reciprocities are once more cast across the page:

> His metaphor [Cohen's] is that "we are never scorched and drenched at the same time!" – Blessings on his experience! – Ask him these questions about "scorching and drenching". – Did he never play at Cricket or walk a mile in hot weather? – did he never spill a dish of tea over his testicles in handing the cup to his charmer to the great shame of his nankeen breeches? – did he never swim in the sea at Noonday with the Sun in his eyes and on his head – which all the foam of ocean could not cool? did he never draw his foot out of a tub of too hot water damning his eyes and his valet's? did he never inject for a Gonorrhea? – or make water through an ulcerated Urethra? – was he ever in a Turkish bath – that marble paradise of sherbet and sodomy? (*BLJ*, vi, 207)

Byron's prose here is deeply mimetic in its recognition that experience is variable and simultaneous, that it incorporates opposites and exists in its own backwash. It captures a roughness and tumultuousness in this process that can be harder to find with the more controlled – if more sophisticated – reciprocities of *Don Juan*.

In recognizing the intellectual contexts of Byron's enriched carelessness in prose we glimpse something important about *Don Juan*. We also, I think, see a writer who was starting to break paths as a literary (self-) critic. Byron's prose seems incipiently aware of the period's need for fresh springs of critical thought and practice to match what was happening in verse. He did not, of course, see this or act upon it as comprehensively as Hazlitt did, but he does, in moments, seem powerfully immersed in the formal-critical possibilities of prose in ways Hazlitt refused to see. This is Byron's prose reunion with Venice in the *Letter to John Murray*:

There can be nothing more poetical in it's [sic] aspect than the City of Venice – does this depend upon the Sea or the canals? […] Is it the Canal which runs between the palace and the prison – or the "Bridge of Sighs" which connects them that render it poetical? – Is it the "Canal Grande" or the Rialto which arches it, – the Churches which tower over it? – the palaces which line and the Gondolas which glide over the waters – that render this city more poetical than Rome itself? (*CMP*, 134)

Byron echoes and recalls ('the palace and the prison') some of his most famous lines ('I stood in Venice, on the Bridge of Sighs; / A palace and a prison on each hand' (*Childe Harold's Pilgrimage*, iv, 1–2)). The recollection, however, is more critical than nostalgic. Harold's static 'stood' marks a darkened, resonant connection in human psychology and history, but his presiding over things lacks the generic quicksilver and critical edge of *Don Juan*. For all its power, Harold's procession over the imaginative depths of Italy does not possess the immediacy required by the provocations of cant. Byron's prose, while reasserting the reciprocities slashed by Bowles, is thus also informed by a re-visioning of poetry that had led to Harold being jettisoned from Byron's 'slight, trim, / But *still* sea-worthy skiff' (*Don Juan*, x, 1–4). In retracing Venice's imaginative bridgings and blurrings, Byron wants to pull their aesthetic power into the bustling immediate political moment that his prose is always bordering. In so doing he marks an important difference between his two most significant poems.

Compare the poet's vivid recollection of a storm in the spring of 1810 when his ship was anchored off Cape Sigeum. His immediate thoughts are with the 'ship of the line' problem, but in the background we sense the deep symbolism and (anti-Wordsworthian) critical intent of *Don Juan*'s 'Ocean of Eternity':

what seemed the most '*poetical*' of all – at the moment – were the numbers (about two hundred) of Greek and Turkish Craft – which were obliged to "cut and run" before the wind – from their unsafe anchorage – some for Tenedos – some for other isles – some for the Main – and some it may be for Eternity. – – The Sight of these little scudding vessels darting over the foam in the twilight – now appearing – and now disappearing between the waves in the cloud of night – with their peculiarly *white* sails (the Levant sails not being of '*coarse canvas*' but of white cotton) skimming along – as quickly – but less safely than the Sea-Mew which hovered over them – their evident distress – their reduction to fluttering specks in the distance – their crowded succession – their *littleness* as contending with the Giant element – which made our stout 44.'s *teak* timbers (she was built in India) creak again, – their aspect – and their motion – all struck me as something far more "poetical" than the mere broad – brawling – shipless Sea & the sullen winds could possibly have been without them. (*CMP*, 131–2)

Byron's listing, as Curtis elegantly puts it, 'enacts, rather than simply describes, variability' – it 'communicates the unspoken'.[51] This is also serio-comic writing in that its descriptive flow is punctuated by witty asides that express Byron's suspicions about uninterrupted emotional playback. These hard-shelled parenthetical injections insist that we might think in more ways than one and at the same time. To do this might, it is suggested, be the opening of a meaningful discussion about poetry. In one sense Byron is being anti-theoretical in refusing to allow this specific experience ('at the moment') to ground an objective theory of the '*poetical*' (a word he crosses out in writing it). The mimesis of form, in these terms, is always anxious as well as knowing because the writer is a craftsman working at one remove from his materials, especially in such places where the vagaries of memory are at their most pressing. On the other hand there is a prescriptive side to Byron's thinking, one related to his sense that scepticism's conclusions are often mere cleverness or brittle sophistry. Poetry, it is asserted, depends upon specific configurations of human and environmental reciprocity. One such is the encounter between the precariousness of human life and its final, demolishing, yet wondrous context – 'their *littleness* as contending with the Giant element'. As well as their critical force, then, Byron's dashes hint at the poet's sense of vision. While cutting into the presentness of the page they also have something of *Cain*'s experimental force in gesturing at what they confess to be beyond them. This agency in the face of a deeply metaphorical ocean – one that begins in the mediatory sketch, hint or outline – is the object of the partially emergent poetics voiced by the narrator of *Don Juan*. It is also the object of my next essay.

Notes

1 Although the *Letter to John Murray* was the only contribution to the controversy published at the time, Byron wrote three related prose pamphlets defending Pope and offering opinions on contemporary poetry. The others are 'Some Observations upon an Article in *Blackwood's Edinburgh Magazine*' (1820) and 'Observations upon Observations of the Revd. W. L. B.' (1821). In the notes to *CMP*, Nicholson provides a detailed and lucid account of the various pamphlet exchanges. I acknowledge a debt to Nicholson's fine scholarship.

2 Shelley wrote to Byron (in a letter dated 4 May 1821) of a 'dispute in taste, on which, until I understand it, I must profess myself neuter'. '[T]rue genius', Shelley proclaims, 'vindicates to itself an exemption from all regard to whatever has gone before'; he can, he adds, 'feel no interest', therefore, in a dispute about Pope's

importance (*The Letters of Percy Bysshe Shelley*, ed. Jones, II, 290). Hazlitt wrote a contemptuous review of the controversy that lampoons Byron as a brawling aristocrat out of his depth when it comes to points of serious intellectual concern. 'He doles out his opinions', Hazlitt quips, 'with a great deal of frankness and spleen, saying, "this I like, that I loathe;" but he does not trouble himself, or the reader, with his reasons, any more than he accounts to his servants for the directions he gives them'. Hazlitt's review appeared in the *London Magazine* (June 1821) and is reprinted in *The Complete Works of William Hazlitt*, ed. P. P. Howe, 21 vols (London: Dent, 1930–4), XIX, 62. Also of relevance is Hazlitt's essay 'On the question whether Pope was a Poet' (*Complete Works*, ed. Howe, XX, 89–92).

3 'Byron's famous letters on Pope [...] are not very interesting or distinguished documents, more preoccupied with a tedious and self-important wrangle with Bowles than with a genuine understanding of Pope'. Claude Rawson, 'Byron Augustan: Mutations of the Mock Heroic in *Don Juan* and Shelley's *Peter Bell the Third*', in *Byron: Augustan and Romantic*, ed. Andrew Rutherford (London: Macmillan, 1990), 82–116 (82–3). Others, however, have been more open to the interests, qualities and importance of Byron's critical prose. They include James Chandler, 'The Pope Controversy: Romantic Poetics and the English Canon', in *Critical Inquiry*, vol. 10, no. 3 (March 1984), 498–501; Paul M. Curtis, 'The Bowles–Pope Controversy: Polemics and Paradox', in *Byron and the Mediterranean World*, ed. Marius Byron Raizis (Athens: Hellenic Byron Society, 1995); Robert J. Griffin, *Wordsworth's Pope: A Study in Literary Historiography* (Cambridge: Cambridge University Press, 1995); Stabler, *Byron, Poetics and History*, Chapter 3; Richard Cronin, *Paper Pellets: British Literary Culture after Waterloo* (Oxford: Oxford University Press, 2010), esp. 39–58.

4 Andrew Nicholson, 'Byron's Prose', in *The Cambridge Companion to Byron*, ed. Drummond Bone (Cambridge: Cambridge University Press, 2004), 186–206 (186). Nicholson quotes from two of Byron's letters (*BLJ*, iii, 209, 217).

5 William Lisle Bowles, *The Invariable Principles of Poetry: In a Letter addressed to Thomas Campbell, Esq; Occasioned by some Critical Observations in his Specimens of British Poets, Particularly relating to the Poetical Character of POPE* (London: Longman, 1819).

6 According to Richard Steele, 'Cant is, by some People derived from one *Andrew Cant* who, they say, was a Presbyterian Minister in some illiterate part of *Scotland*, who by Exercise and Use had obtained the Faculty, *alias* Gift, of Talking in the Pulpit in such a Dialect, that it's said he was understood by none but his own Congregation, and not by all of them'. *The Spectator* (no. 147), ed. Donald F. Bond, 5 vols (Oxford: Clarendon Press, 1965), II, 80.

7 Jonathan Swift, *A Tale of a Tub, to which is added The Battle of the Books and the Mechanical Operation of the Spirit*, ed. A. C. Guthkelch and D. Nichol Smith, 2nd edition (Oxford: Clarendon Press, 1958), 278.

8 Boswell's *Life of Johnson: Together with Boswell's Journal of a Tour to the Hebrides and Johnson's Diary of a Journey into North Wales*, ed. George Birbeck Hill, rev. L. F. Powell, 6 vols (Oxford: Clarendon Press, 1934–64), IV, 221.

9 Christopher Ricks writes about Johnson, Byron and cant in *Allusion to the Poets* (Oxford: Oxford University Press, 2002), 121–2.

10 *Sybil* (1845); quoted in Philip Davis, *The Oxford English Literary History*, vol. 8: *1830–1880: The Victorians* (Oxford: Oxford University Press, 2002), 35.

11 See Pierre Bourdieu, 'The Production and Reproduction of Legitimate Language', in *Language and Symbolic Power*, trans. Gino Raymond and Matthew Adamson (Cambridge: Polity (1991), 2005), 43–65.

12 Every 'class of society', Johnson notes, 'has its cant of lamentation, which is understood or regarded by none but themselves'. Samuel Johnson, *Rambler*, 128. The *Yale Edition of the Works of Samuel Johnson*, vol. 4: *The Rambler*, ed. W. J. Bate and Albrecht B. Strauss (New Haven: Yale University Press, 1969), 317.

13 *Medwin's Conversations of Lord Byron*, ed. Ernest J. Lovell, Jr. (Princeton: Princeton University Press, 1966), 198.

14 See Upali Amarasinghe, *Dryden and Pope in the Early Nineteenth Century* (Cambridge: Cambridge University Press, 1962), 22 and Joan Pittock, *The Ascendancy of Taste: The Achievement of Joseph and Thomas Warton* (London: Routledge, 1973), 142.

15 Byron owned Warton's *Essay* (as well as his edition of Pope) and when he had finished with it he sent it to Leigh Hunt remarking that 'it is perhaps better as more condensed than his Notes to the formal Edition' (*BLJ*, x, 83).

16 Quoted in John Wooll, *Biographical Memoirs of the late Rev. Joseph Warton* (London: Cadell, 1806), 9. An example of this new style is the poem 'The Enthusiast or the Lover of Nature', in which 'Nature' is preferred to the 'artificial' (see *The Three Wartons: A Choice of Verse*, ed. Eric Partridge (London: Scholaris Press, 1927), 73.

17 In Warton's 'Ranelagh House: A Satire in Prose in the manner of Monsieur Le Sage' (1747), Pope receives a striking backhanded compliment: 'Mr. Pope took his place in the Elysian fields not among the Poets but the Philosophers, and that he was more fond of Socrates' company than Homer's' (Quoted in Wooll, *Biographical Memoirs*, 178).

18 Joseph Warton, *An Essay on the Genius and Writings of Pope*, 2 vols (London: W. J. and J. Richardson et al., 1806), I, vi, iii. Subsequent references to this edition are given in the text.

19 M. H. Abrams, *The Mirror and the Lamp: Romantic Theory and the Critical Tradition* (New York: Oxford University Press, 1953), 1–26.

20 Despite having 'a thousand gifts and merits', Pope, Arnold thought, 'never, or scarcely ever, attain[ed] the distinctive accent and utterance of the high and genuine poets'. *Complete Prose Works*, vol. 9: 'English Literature and Irish Politics', ed. R. H. Super (Ann Arbor: University of Michigan Press, 1973), 48. For a discussion and critique of Warton's twentieth-century legacy see Griffin, *Wordsworth's Pope*, 132 and *passim*.

21 For varying accounts of what was clearly a complex relationship see Wooll, *Biographical Memoirs*, 98 and John A. Vance, *Joseph and Thomas Warton* (Boston: Twayne, 1983), 6. According to Boswell, Johnson called Warton 'an enthusiast by rule' and was privately critical of the *Essay*. See Boswell, *Life of Johnson*, IV, 33; I, 448.

22 *The Literary Magazine* (1756–8), ed. Donald D. Eddy, 3 vols (New York: Garland, 1978), I, 35.

23 *The Literary Magazine*, I, 38.

24 *Lives of the English Poets*, ed. George Birkbeck Hill, 3 vols (Oxford: Clarendon Press, 1905), iii, 251. Hereafter referenced in the text.

25 Johnson's 1757 review of Jenyns's *A Free Inquiry into the Nature and Origin of Evil* appeared in *The Literary Magazine* (II, 534, 171, 301).

26 *Rambler*, 125 (*Yale Edition of the Works of Samuel Johnson*, iv, 300).

27 I quote from Johnson's Preface to his *Dictionary*. *The Oxford Authors: Samuel Johnson*, ed. Donald Greene (Oxford: Oxford University Press, 1992), 307.

28 I borrow the phrase from Robin Sowerby's discussion of Horace ('Pope and Horace', in *Horace Made New: Horatian Influences on British Writing from the Renaissance to the Twentieth Century*, ed. Charles Martindale and David Hopkins (Cambridge: Cambridge University Press, 1993), 159–83 (160). Pope had something like this in mind when he wrote of Horace that 'His precepts teach but what his works inspire' (*Essay on Criticism*, 660). Byron's farewell to Horace on Mount Soracte (*Childe Harold's Pilgrimage*, iv, 77) recognizes Horace both as 'Bard' and 'Moralist'. Horace is a 'Satirist' who can pierce the conscience; but also a poet of 'lyric flow' who awakens the heart.

29 *Edinburgh Review*, vol. xi, no. xxii (Jan. 1808), 399–413 (407).

30 'Before you can move me to tears / you must grieve yourself. Only then will your woes distress me'. Horace, *Ars Poetica*, 102–3. *Horace Satires and Epistles / Persius Satires*, trans. Niall Rudd (Harmondsworth: Penguin [1973], 2005), 124. Compare Johnson's *Life of Cowley*: 'the basis of all excellence is truth: he that professes love ought to feel its power' (*Lives*, i, 6) as well as his description of Matthew Prior's 'Amorous Effusions' as 'the dull exercises of a skilful versifier resolved at all adventures to write something about Chloe, and trying to be amorous by dint of study. [...] He talks not "like a man of the world"' (*Lives*, ii, 202). Byron's letters are littered with comparable remarks: 'I could not write upon any thing, without some personal experience and foundation' (*BLJ*, v, 14); there is also the amusing attack on Keats in the *Letter to John Murray*: 'a System-maker must receive all sorts of proselytes. – When they have really seen life – when they have felt it – when they have travelled beyond the far-distant boundaries of the wilds of Middlesex – when they have overpassed the Alps of High-gate – and traced to it's [sic] sources the Nile of the New River – then – & not till then – can it be properly permitted to them to despise Pope' (*CMP*, 157). Also see Stephen Cheeke's account of how 'the notion of *being there*' is a 'powerful and complex aspect' of Byron's writing. Stephen Cheeke, *Byron and Place: History, Translation, Nostalgia* (Basingstoke: Palgrave Macmillan, 2003), 6.

31 Thomas Campbell, *Specimens of the British Poets; with Biographical and Critical Notices, and an Essay on English Poetry*, 7 vols (London: John Murray, 1819), V, 110.

32 Although Johnson by no means gives a glowing character reference, he does not amass his evidence on one side, preferring to interlace positive and negative judgements. According to Johnson, Pope could be socially graceless (*Lives*, iii, 201) and gluttonous (*Lives*, iii, 199), yet had a potential for 'magnificence' (*Lives*, iii, 203); we are told 'he never flattered those whom he did not love' (*Lives*, iii, 205), but that he boasted of his acquaintances (*Lives*, iii, 204); he is accused of 'artifice' (*Lives*, iii, 200) and parsimony (*Lives*, iii, 203), yet praised for 'liberality, gratitude, constancy, and tenderness' (*Lives*, iii, 206); he was on occasion 'malign' (*Lives*, iii, 213) and self-important (*Lives*, iii, 211), but 'it does not appear that his [religious] principles were ever corrupted' (*Lives*, iii, 215).

33 Cronin, *Paper Pellets*, 48.

34 *The Works of Alexander Pope*, ed. William Lisle Bowles, 10 vols (London, 1806), I, xcix.

35 In his notes to *Windsor Forest*, for instance, Bowles keeps Warton's initial long note, his separate section outlining Pope's 'Imitations' and lack of originality, and

retains a further note on Somerville's purported superiority to Pope (Bowles, *The Works of Alexander Pope*, i, 132).

36 A similar low blow (perhaps with the *Life of Pope* in mind) is aimed at Johnson who, by virtue of his poor eyesight and general physical infirmity, is considered as 'not a proper judge of this sort of Poetry' (Bowles, *The Works of Alexander Pope*, I, 123–4).

37 Campbell, *Specimens of the British Poets*, I, 264.

38 Bowles, *The Invariable Principles of Poetry*, 6, 22. Compare Warton: the 'largest portion of [Pope's works are] of the didactic, moral, and satiric kind; and consequently, not of the most poetic species of Poetry'. *The Works of Alexander Pope*, ed. Joseph Warton, 9 vols (London, 1797), I, lxviii.

39 Byron dedicated 'Some Observations' to D'Israeli, although he hadn't at that point read the review in the *Quarterly*. When he did read it he guessed the anonymous author's identity, writing to Murray that 'D'Israeli wrote the article on Spence – I know him by the mark in his mouth – I'm glad that the Quarterly had so much Classical honesty and honour as to insert it – it is good & true.' (*BLJ*, vii, 223). He also described D'Israeli as 'the Bayle of literary speculation' (*BLJ*, viii, 237).

40 *Quarterly Review*, vol. 23, no. 46 (July 1820), 400–34 (409). Chandler suggests that D'Israeli's attack on Bowles 'probably owes a great deal to Byron's *Don Juan* [the 'Dedication' and cantos i–ii]'. Chandler, 'The Pope Controversy', 500.

41 *Quarterly Review* (July 1820), 410.

42 'You see, my dear Bowles', Hazlitt's Byron pontificates, 'the superiority of art over nature' (Howe, *The Complete Works of William Hazlitt*, XIX, 63).

43 Campbell, *Specimens of the British Poets*, II, 265.

44 Bowles, *The Invariable Principles of Poetry*, 11.

45 'I have some Time since, with a World of Pains and Art, dissected the Carcass of *Humane Nature*, and read many useful Lectures upon the several Parts, both *Containing* and *Contained*; till at last it *smelt* so strong, I could preserve it no longer. Upon which, I have been at great Expence to fit up all the Bones with exact Contexture, and in due Symmetry; so that I am ready to shew a very compleat Anatomy thereof to all curious *Gentlemen and others*' (Swift, *A Tale of a Tub*, 123).

46 Boswell, *Life of Johnson*, III, 197.

47 Compare Hume: 'Morality [...] is more properly felt than judg'd of'. David Hume, *A Treatise of Human Nature*, ed. L. A. Selby-Bigge (rev. P. H. Nidditch) (Oxford: Clarendon Press, 1978), 470.

48 We should bear in mind here Cronin's description of Byron's 'serio-comic' as the 'most characteristic expression of the distinctly modern aesthetic that characterized the period' (Cronin, *Paper Pellets*, 171). *Don Juan*, ironically, has much in common, stylistically speaking, with the very magazines that were falling over themselves to attack it.

49 *The Romantics Reviewed: Contemporary Reviews of British Romantic Writers*, ed. Donald Reiman, 9 vols (New York: Garland, 1972), Part B, *Byron and the Regency Society Poets*, 5 vols, I, 143, 146. Francis Jeffrey, writing in the *Edinburgh Review*, takes a similar line by describing it as poem in which 'pure affection and uncorrupted honour [...] have flowed, in all their sweetness, from the very lips that instantly open again to mock and blaspheme them' (Reiman, *The Romantics Reviewed*, 936).

50 '[Y]ou have so many "*divine*" poems', Byron grumbled to Murray in defence of his poem, 'is it nothing to have written a *Human* one?' (*BLJ*, vi, 105).

51 Curtis, 'The Bowles–Pope Controversy', 144. Compare Nicholson's description of how the dashes 'often enshrine or capture Byron's accretive mode of thinking or writing'; they 'reflect a desire to gather the scattered impression and to communicate its immediacy' (Nicholson, 'Byron's Prose', 192–3).

'I wish to do as much by Poesy' Amidst a Byronic Poetics

According to Peter Atkins

> poets may aspire to understanding, [but] their talents are more akin to entertaining self-deception. They may be able to emphasise delights in the world, but they are deluded if they and their admirers believe that their identification of the delights and their use of poignant language are enough for comprehension. Philosophers, too, I am afraid, have contributed to the understanding of the universe little more than poets [...]. They have not contributed much that is novel until after novelty has been discovered by scientists [...]. While poetry titillates and theology obfuscates, science liberates.[1]

Such diminutions of poetry are nothing new. In opposing 'poignant', 'entertaining' and 'delights' to the rather more solid-sounding 'comprehension' and 'understanding', Atkins stands in a long rhetorical tradition.[2] Locke's famous account of 'wit', for instance, although part of a broader and more thoughtful analysis of language and its representations, works along similar lines:

> Men who have a great deal of Wit, and prompt Memories, have not always the clearest Judgment, or deepest Reason. For *Wit* lying most in the assemblage of *Ideas*, and putting those together with quickness and variety, wherein can be found any resemblance or congruity, therby to make up pleasant Pictures, and agreeable Visions in the Fancy: *Judgment*, on the contrary, lies quite on the other side, in separating carefully, one from another, *Ideas*, wherein can be found the least difference, thereby to avoid being misled by Similitude, and by affinity to take one thing for another. This is a way of proceeding quite contrary to Metaphor and Allusion, wherein, for the most part, lies that entertainment and pleasantry of Wit, which strikes so lively on the fancy, and therefore so acceptable to all People; because its Beauty appears at first sight, and there is required no labour of thought, to examine what Truth or Reason there is in it.[3]

The tone and diction imply a hierarchy of mental modalities in which 'judgment' ('clearest', 'deepest') is characterized as more careful, reliable and searching than 'wit' ('entertainment', 'pleasantry', 'misled') as a means of understanding ourselves and our world.

Primarily, Locke's concern, part a larger Enlightenment effort to 'make language more exact for philosophical purposes',[4] is to banish weak thought and the cumbrous baggage of its expression from intellectual discourse:

> Many of the Books extant might be spared; many of the Controversies in Dispute would be at an end; several of those great Volumes, swollen with ambiguous words, now used in one sense, and by and by in another, would shrink into a very narrow compass; and many of the Philosophers (to mention no other,) as well as Poets Works, might be contained in a Nut-shell.[5]

Many of our disagreements, Locke recognizes, result from nothing more than a lack of discipline and consistency in our use of language. As well as criticizing this unnecessarily 'swollen' philosophical discourse, however, Locke also argues that devices typically associated with literary writing, and metaphor in particular, are inherently rather than selectively problematic because they interfere with the processes through which the mind seeks to align itself with the external world:

> similes always fail in some part, and come short of that exactness which our conceptions should have to things, if we would think aright [...]; if all our search has yet reached no farther than simile and metaphor, we may assure ourselves we rather fancy than know, and are not penetrated into the inside and reality of the thing, be it what it will, but content ourselves with what our imaginations, not things themselves, furnish us with.[6]

To think through metaphor is to activate the imagination – but this is only of secondary philosophical significance, something to be 'content' with; it is not to 'think aright' if our object is real knowledge of 'things themselves'.

These views on metaphor were taken up and in some cases hardened by later thinkers, including Dugald Stewart, whose *Elements of the Philosophy of the Human Mind* (1792) and *Outlines of Moral Philosophy* (1793) Byron owned.[7] Stewart, a disciple of Thomas Reid's 'Common Sense School',[8] was deeply indebted to Locke's writing on language, especially *Of the Conduct of the Understanding*, which he admired for its 'truth and good sense'.[9] For Stewart, the 'accidental circumstance' and 'ambiguity' of literary devices have 'no essential connexion with that process of the mind which is properly called reasoning'.[10] He is especially scathing of those who introduce 'fancy and imagination' into philosophical discourse, and thus produce what are contemptuously referred to as 'philosophical romances', works which are seen not only as intellectually corrupt, but as morally suspect; they are apt, as Stewart puts it, to 'mislead young and inexperienced understandings'.[11] Stewart rigorously polices the line of division and opposition which Locke's dichotomy helped to draw, and deplores any challenge to it through generic innovation.

As well as influencing aggressive, anti-literary arguments such as Stewart's, Locke also opened the door to more positive appreciations of literary language and its cognitive effects. He acknowledges (in his account of 'wit') that metaphors (his own 'Nut-shell' being an example) can possess an immediacy that gives them an advantage over the more arduous efforts of strict reasoning. Metaphor, he admits, can convey 'Truth or Reason', qualities that appear 'at first sight', without the need for 'labour of thought'. This mitigated appreciation of metaphor contains the seeds of an ethically grounded poetics of Sensibility,[12] something that was drawn out by Hume in the opening section of his *An Enquiry Concerning Human Understanding*, where a distinction is made between 'an easy and obvious' literary-philosophical style, and the 'accurate and abstruse' kind, of which Locke's style of philosophy is seen as the great modern example. The value of the former 'easy' style, which is exemplified by Addison, is that it 'moulds the heart and affections' and makes its reader '*feel* the difference between vice and virtue'.[13] We may sense something of a backhanded compliment here, but given the primary role afforded to emotion in Hume's moral philosophy, his claim on behalf of the literary remains an important one.

Also distinctly post-Lockean in similar terms is Burke's account of the sublime and its challenge to Locke's tacit privileging of clarity through a recuperation of heightened indistinctness as a marker of the profound:

> Let it be considered that hardly any thing can strike the mind with greatness, which does not make some sort of approach towards infinity; which nothing can do whilst we are able to perceive its bounds; but to see an object distinctly, and to perceive its bounds, is one and the same thing. A clear idea is therefore another name for a little idea.[14]

For Burke, Locke's 'judgment', which works by 'separating carefully' one idea from the next, misses something vital because it precludes the moments of loss that Burke sees as fundamental to sublime experience. 'Exactness in every detail', as Burke's precursor Longinus would have it, 'involves a risk of meanness; with grandeur, as with great wealth, there ought to be something overlooked'.[15]

Burke uses poetry, and particularly Milton's, to exemplify the cognitive states with which he is concerned. Death in *Paradise Lost*, for example, is said to affect us as follows:

> the mind is hurried out of itself, by a croud of great and confused images; which affect because they are crouded and confused. For separate them, and you lose much of the greatness, and join them, and you infallibly lose the clearness. The images raised by poetry are always of this obscure kind.[16]

Where Locke had despaired of ambiguity in 'Poets Works' as well as in philosophical discourse, Burke finds in the crowded confusions of poetry an affective capacity that is not available to the separating tendencies of 'judgment'. This is not merely, as Locke would have it, to 'fancy' rather than 'know', but to come into the proximity of a 'greatness' that ennobles human experience.

Burke, like Hume, establishes claims for the literary in the wake of Locke that deeply inform Romantic aesthetics. Yet while these theorizations offer to reclaim some ground for 'wit' in the face of its Enlightenment downgrading, they also perpetuate some of the assumptions that underpin Locke's isolation of the literary in the first place; they maintain a sense of sharp differentiation (Hume's 'easy' versus 'abstruse'; Burke's 'obscure' versus 'clearness') that echoes Locke's original dichotomy and thus accept the placement of literature within a larger framework that it inevitably becomes less able to challenge. Burke's 'images raised by poetry are *always* of this obscure kind' (my italics), for instance, although recovering a value for ambiguity, also totalizes it as evidence, and thus places it in the service of a larger theoretical structure that assumes responsibility for the discourse of poetics in its entirety.

If Burke's response to Locke is one of accommodation, others (including some of Byron's strongest precursors) were more inclined to propose rupture. Sterne, from whom Byron learned not only how to work at the fine intersections of comedy and sincerity, but also about the opportunities created when texts are placed in dialogue with their own strategies of artifice, took direct issue with Locke's account of 'wit', describing it as 'the *Magna Charta* of stupidity'.[17] Locke's categorical assertiveness, Sterne thought, rather than clarifying our understanding of the human, impoverishes and simplifies it by downgrading comedy, irony and literary density as modes of investigation and expression, as well as guarantors of an appropriate complexity. Sterne's parody counter-argument, which imagines 'wit' and 'judgment' as the two knobs on the back of his chair, is a rewriting of linearity as simultaneity, and of abstraction as immediacy; it is a deliberate opening out of the earnestly philosophical to the comically energetic:

> [...] lay your hands upon your hearts, and answer this plain question, Whether this one single knobb which now stands here like a blockhead by itself, can serve any purpose upon earth, but to put one in mind of the want of the other; —and let me further ask, in case the chair was your own, if you would not in your consciences think, rather than be as it is, that it would be ten times better without any knobb at all.[18]

Sterne argues, but he also thrusts the manner of his writing to the fore. He opposes the Lockean sidelining of the written by rejecting its evaluative framework, but also by refusing to conform to Locke's assumptions about what an argument is. He thus ends not with a conclusion but on a rhetorical question that prefers the reader's imaginative engagement of metaphor to objectivity and fact.

This anti-Lockean line was picked out in more theoretical detail by Matthew Prior, who, in one of his *Dialogues of the Dead* (1760), places Locke in philosophical debate with another key intelligence for *Don Juan*, Montaigne (much to the advantage of the latter). Prior's dialogue, which is both formally and intellectually indebted to the sceptical tradition,[19] is a canny parody and highly attentive to the problematic nature of Locke's account of metaphor as both a theoretical and a rhetorical proposition. Prior's 'Locke' announces of his own philosophical writing that 'I use these terms as instruments and means to Attain to Truth [...]; I searched my own head, and dissected my understanding, with so great Diligence and Accuracy, that I cannot but think the Study of many Years, very usefully bestowed upon that subject'.[20] 'Montaigne's' response – one that recalls Byron's attack on Bowles's 'dissection' – is that Locke is one of the 'System makers' and that his 'instruments' do not penetrate to the truth of things at all, but – pointedly extending the metaphor – mutilate them beyond recognition: 'Believe me, Mr. Lock, you Metaphysicians define your Object as some Naturalists divide it, *in infinitum*: But while you are doing so, the parts become so far Separated from each other, that You lose the sight of the thing in itself'.[21] 'Locke', not to be put down, censures his antagonist for his imprecise, overly metaphorical language – 'Simile upon Simile, no consequential proof, right Montaigne by my troth. Why Sir you catch at Similes as Swallows at Flies' – but in so doing reveals the extent to which he is reliant upon the very devices about which he seeks to raise our suspicions. 'Montaigne' is quick to pounce upon this dependence and accuses 'Locke' of procedural inconsistency before going on to outline a more positive case for the truthfulness of simile:

> And you make Simeles while you blame them. But be that as it will, Mr. Lock, Arguing by Simele is not so absurd as some of you dry Reasoners would make People believe. If your Simele be proper and good, it is at once a full proof, and a lively illustration of your Matter, and where it does not hold, the very disproportion gives you Occasion to reconsider it, and you set it in all its lights, if it be only to find at least how unlike it is. Egad Simile is the very Algebra of Discourse.[22]

Where Locke, in his *Essay*, accepts that the 'Beauty' of simile appears 'at first sight', 'Montaigne' enters the more ambitious claim that it can manifest a 'full proof'; he also makes a virtue of the very unreliability or 'disproportion' that motivates Locke's critique in the first place. Where a simile does not 'hold', the reader is required to 'reconsider' the imperfect relationship between language and what it is taken to describe, a process of readerly involvement ('you set it in all its lights') seen as having its own value even in admitting a broader economy of failure. What Locke sees as a misadventure of mind into the trackless territories of metaphor is rewritten by Prior as a necessary precondition of the search for human truth.

* * *

Finding Byron within this post-Lockean situation is not especially easy, and not only because the poet was disinclined to engage in extended theoretical speculation. We might, given the likelihood of his siding with Montaigne and Sterne, predict a cool reception of Locke. Yet he is seemingly one of the major Romantics least inclined to resist Lockean ideas about poetry. Unlike Blake, who thought of Locke's theory of mind as a dire attack on human potentiality, Byron appears to have admired the broad reasonableness and orderly elegance of mind of 'great Locke' (*Don Juan*, xv, 18). Moreover, although he must have been acquainted with polemics such as Stewart's, he nowhere appears to take exception to them; we might even conclude from some of the poet's letters that he was in agreement:

> I by no means rank poetry high in the scale of intellect— —this may look like Affectation—but it is my real opinion—it is the lava of the imagination whose eruption prevents an earth-quake. (*BLJ*, iii, 179)

The thing to notice here is that for all Byron's off-hand disenchantment (in this case for the benefit of the future Lady Byron) he manages, by the end of his sentence, to say something striking about the object of his dismissal. He makes no great Romantic claim for poetry, proposing it rather as a kind of personal safety feature, but his shift from argument to poetry's own metaphorical grounding has its own interests. The terrain of Byron's reflexive articulations demands a mode of travelling to which the reader of his poetry will be accustomed:

> I can never get people to understand that poetry is the expression of *excited passion*, and that there is no such thing as a life of passion any more than a continuous earthquake, or an eternal fever. Besides, who would ever *shave* themselves in such a state? (*BLJ*, viii, 146)

The first sentence places poetry in an emotive sphere seen as limited with respect to a larger, containing sense of life. This seems to be confirmed by the second sentence and its well-judged reference to the mundane. Yet Byron isn't quite separating poetry off in the way Locke does. He is also tapping his serio-comic reserves to escape the moribund theorization he initially appears to invite and dwell in. His final quip is thus not a closing down of the thought but an activation of the forces the writer can harness on writing's behalf.

Such letters suggest a mind lacking high poetic ideals, but they also reveal a mental environment in which we are returned, repeatedly, to the possibilities of the written. Byron, to an eminent degree enactive of the forces that potentiate literary otherness, projects an awareness of and inquisitiveness about what is theorized as poetics. In what follows I want to track some of this thinking and attempt to discriminate some of the ways in which Byron's writing articulates the value of its own happening. Bearing in mind Byron's proximity to Miltonic, Burkean and Shelleyan notions of the sublime, and learning from the previous study of Byron's prose, I want to move towards the narrator of *Don Juan* and his most direct utterances about his own art.

We might begin by grasping a connection between *Don Juan* and its theoretical contexts and then letting it go. This is part of the description, in the later sections of the poem, of Norman Abbey, a symbol of continuity set within a troublingly disserved past:

> Huge halls, long galleries, spacious chambers, join'd
>   By no quite lawful marriage of the Arts,
> Might shock a Connoisseur; but when combined,
>   Form'd a whole which, irregular in parts,
> Yet left a grand impression on the mind,

At least of those whose eyes are in their hearts.
We gaze upon a Giant for his stature,
Nor judge at first if all be true to Nature.

(Don Juan, xiii, 67)

In a world of desiccated perception, Byron champions those whose 'eyes are in their hearts', conferring upon them, as Hume or Burke might have done, privileged access to a 'grand impression' that escapes rational scrutiny. According to any strict law of appreciation the Abbey is a collection of fragments, yet for those able to perceive through their feelings it can be experienced as a 'whole'. In this sense it is a microcosm of its containing poem: both are fragments that allow the perceiver/reader to find his way beyond the patchy contingencies of immediate form to its supervening intimations of wholeness.

Whatever we see of Hume and Burke here, however, Byron is far from being their static inheritor. He was acutely aware of how easily such theoretical constellations could become faddish and, even in admiring their civilizing potential, questioned their pragmatism in the face of what he saw as an irremediable human nature. He was also far less ready than Hume to take the promptings of feeling as certain indicators of moral truth. His Sardanapalus attempts to rule his people by principles of generosity and sympathy, but finds his ideals overturned by greed and interest; as his empire collapses around him, the ironic and tragic recognition thrust upon him (through Salemenes) is that "Tis now too late to feel' (*Sardanapalus*, iv, i, 543). The play's staging of its most potent moments beyond this brutal cessation of emotion registers Byron's pessimism about the robustness of any proposed meliorative culture of feeling, and is in turn related to the poet's complicated scepticism about the potential of art to sink into its own dedicated experiential categories. Transcending *Don Juan*'s jagged provisionality, moreover, can never be in any sense (to recall Hume's word) 'easy'. Theories of emotive immediacy may run through the stanza but nothing is clinched in such terms. The relation between the stanza's body and couplet, in particular, is oddly summative and generative at once; the juxtaposition of Abbey and Giant, although the two are apparently placed in a straightforwardly comparative relation, is more paratactic than the cursory reading encouraged by Byron's grammar suggests. There is enough interpretative give between the two to preclude the kinds of easy immediacy associated with metaphor by Locke and Hume; for all the snappiness of Byron's couplet, nothing here is given 'at first sight'. Rather than being ushered to full understanding we are dragged back into the problems of the text.

The Byronic sublime knows its sources and can be blunt in confessing them, but it is also restless, misfitting. It is always searching for, but never quite finding, theoretical settlement. As well as the Abbey's 'grand impression', Byron ranges through the looming Burkean shadowiness of 'Darkness' and *Cain*, the dramatically alliterative 'dim desolate deep' (ii, 49) against which the shipwreck scene of *Don Juan* is played out, and the Christian sublime of St Peter's in Rome:

> Enter: its grandeur overwhelms thee not;
> And why? it is not lessened; but thy mind,
> Expanded by the genius of the spot,
> Has grown colossal, and can only find
> A fit abode wherein appear enshrined
> Thy hopes of immortality; and thou
> Shalt one day, if found worthy, so defined,
> See thy God face to face, as thou dost now
> His Holy of Holies, nor be blasted by his brow.
>
> *(Childe Harold's Pilgrimage*, iv, 155)

Byron would have had limited exposure to Kant, although he would have known Madame de Staël's bipartite paraphrase of the Kantian sublime: the 'first effect of the sublime is to overwhelm a man, and the second to exalt him'.[23] But where Byron's logic certainly tends towards a form of exaltation, this is not generated (not here at least) in anything as uncontrolled as an overwhelming of mind. Consciousness is instead 'Expanded' in what sounds a more gradual and guided process. The mind may become 'colossal', but it is not fearfully overrun or translated out of itself. Unlike Burke's heightened blurrings the experience described is one in which lucid realization remains in play; the subject is 'defined', brought into a distinct understanding predictive of an ultimate 'face-to-face' encounter with God. The Byronic sublime, in these terms, can be distinguished from, or even construed as a critique of, what Bernard Beatty terms the 'new cult of the untethered Sublime'.[24]

If the experience is tethered, however, it is far from complacently so. The bristling complexities of Byron's sentence structure, and even his rather forced and formal second-person address – which has something of the guide book about it – suggest a mind more than aware of the forces that loom up against the possibility of vision. Compare the description of the ocean in the same canto:

> Thou glorious mirror, where the Almighty's form
> Glasses itself in tempests; in all time,
> Calm or convuls'd – in breeze, or gale, or storm,

Icing the pole, or in the torrid clime
Dark-heaving; – boundless, endless, and sublime –
The image of Eternity – the throne
Of the Invisible; even from out thy slime
The monsters of the deep are made; each zone
Obeys thee; thou goest forth, dread, fathomless, alone.

(*Childe Harold's Pilgrimage*, iv, 183)

Amidst the tensions of running iambic phrases and striving trochaic inversions, Byron dramatizes rather than stabilizes the theological context of his scene, thus enfolding the staggering potential of the experience within its extreme precariousness. Those triple constructions that end the third, fifth and final lines seem to be pushing against the control of the stanza's form, scratching at the white space that Byron's alexandrines so often bring into play. Again Byron proposes something more realized than Burke's shadow melding – a distinct 'image' – but rather than being abstracted, it is immersed in an environment of 'fathomless' and monstrous fecundity.

There is nothing here of Addison's 'sense of our own safety',[25] none of the confidence, that is, of his generalized, first-person theological sublime:

> A troubled Ocean, to a man who sails upon it, is, I think, the biggest Object that he can see in Motion, and consequently gives his Imagination one of the highest Kinds of Pleasure that can arise from Greatness. I must confess, it is impossible for me to survey this World of fluid Matter, without thinking on the Hand that first poured it out, and made a proper Channel for its Reception. Such an Object naturally raises in my Thoughts the idea of an Almighty being, and convinces me of his Existence, as much as a Metaphysical Demonstration. The Imagination prompts the Understanding, and by the Greatness of the sensible Object, produces in it the Idea of a Being who is neither circumscribed by Time nor Space.[26]

This gentlemanly, contemplative experience has more of the coffee shop than the perils of the high seas. Byron, although he does, like Addison, posit an 'Almighty' presence, can find no easy transition from 'troubled' to 'pleasure' and from there to 'Metaphysical Demonstration'. For him, clarity and instability – as in that fine phrase 'Glasses itself in tempests' – are compacted, simultaneous, unresolved. If Byron's poem quests after distinct, religiously invested sublime experiences then it does so against the grain of poetic textures that are all stormy tumultuousness. Where for Addison the imagination prompts the understanding, for Byron the two have blurred in the moment of form.

When Byron returns, towards the end of *Don Juan*, to the ocean as sublime object, his writing is far more descriptively subdued. We still don't get Addison's fast track to philosophical certainty, but we do get an odd kind of clipped serenity:

> That Watery Outline of Eternity,
>   Or miniature at least, as is my notion,
> Which ministers unto the soul's delight,
> In seeing matters which are out of sight.
>
> (*Don Juan*, xv, 2)

The stark 'image of Eternity' of *Childe Harold's Pilgrimage* is replaced by a more evanescent 'miniature' or 'Watery Outline of Eternity'. At the same time the mirror image of the religiously dreadful 'Almighty' is toned down to a sustaining, subtly religious process ('ministers') that works between human subject and that which is 'out of sight'. Rather than striving for distinctness and clarity, the poet seems content to accept the ocean as a site of mediation, as the beginning of an as yet undetermined imaginative journey. Correspondingly, we find none of the warping collisions that mark the Spenserian stanzas of *Childe Harold's Pilgrimage*. Where the act of poetry in the earlier poem is dramatically and simultaneously lucid and chaotic, here it is calmed into a moment of reflection and opportunity. Byron still cannot invest his intuition with a definite value by bringing it into the purview of rational demonstration, but he can offset some of its threat against a 'notion' which comes with the promise of hope.

Like the trope of (in)digestion, Byron's notion of the 'Outline' is one of *Don Juan*'s submerged but persistent poetic ideas; it is a sporadic outcropping of thought that has all the force but none of the organization or linearity of argument. Where digestion becomes a way of talking about and transforming epistemology, however, the latter is aligned with the visionary and with ideas of form (Byron's critical prose, as we have seen, is structured by a relentless outlining of the unsaid). Byron seems to have had such ideas in mind, in particular, during (the pivotal) canto six of *Don Juan*, as in this description of the imperial sublimity of Gulbeyaz:

> Her head hung down, and her long hair in stooping
>   Concealed her features better than a veil;
> And one hand o'er the Ottoman lay drooping,
>   White, waxen, and as alabaster pale:
> Would that I were a painter! to be grouping
>   All that a poet drags into detail!

Oh that my words were colours! But their tints
May serve perhaps as outlines or slight hints.

(Don Juan, vi, 109)

Poetry is not, as the poetics of Sensibility would have it, a site of immediate intuition that is other to rational effort; it is, rather, an arduous and imprecise process: the poet 'drags into detail' his resistant object and, unlike the painter, must despair of anything like verisimilitude. The threat of total scepticism, however, finds mitigation in poetry's 'outlines' or 'hints', which, in the absence of accurate reproduction, offer an unspecified hope. Although his veiled object cannot be stripped of its obscurity, it can be brought into a form of imaginative illumination that depends upon the unpredictable re-uptake of its transmission.

Compare another passage from the same canto:

Meantime Gulbeyaz, when her king was gone,
    Retired into her boudoir, a sweet place
For love or breakfast; private, pleasing, lone,
    And rich with all contrivances which grace
Those gay recesses: – many a precious stone
    Sparkled along its roof, and many a vase
Of porcelain held in the fettered flowers,
Those captive soothers of a captive's hours.

Mother of pearl, and porphyry, and marble,
    Vied with each other on this costly spot;
And singing birds without were heard to warble;
    And the stained glass which lighted this fair grot
Varied each ray; – but all descriptions garble
    The true effect, and so we had better not
Be too minute; an outline is the best, –
A lively reader's fancy does the rest.

(Don Juan, vi, 97–8)

The varying – but beautiful – effects of the 'stained glass' bring to mind the garbling effects of language and its grounding in 'Doubt', that 'sole prism / Of the Truth's rays'. Pressed by the poem's endlessly suggested scepticism the narrator acknowledges the limitations of his tools and brings a halt to descriptive proceedings. He then, however, moves quickly to mitigate his brief breakdown by finding a value for writing in its role as 'outline' or point of departure for the 'lively reader's fancy'. Achieving the 'true effect' in these terms depends not so much on accuracy of description as a capacity to engage and activate the imagination of the reader. The 'disproportion' of language, to recall Prior once again, invokes the reader who is required to 'set' the object of description 'in all its lights'. This can be construed not simply as a compromise but as a clear (political) gain in its activation of collective interpretative imagination. It suggests, moreover, that poetry's doing must never become overdoing as this would be to close down the space that determines the possibilities of its dissemination. In line with this Byron's own poetry, for all its loquacity, has a whisked through quality; it is at most half committed to the symphonics of verbal sensuousness. There is no Keatsian lingering here, no opportunities for readerly indulgence or indolence. There is only a sense of dashing on amidst the desires of narrative to hint at the silent visions beyond what must be said.

The clustering of these ideas behind this part of *Don Juan* may not be entirely coincidental. Byron had been writing *Cain* with its submerged poetics of silence and vision. It may also be significant that not long after Byron resumed his poem with a new Preface (inserted before the sixth canto) he was visited in Ravenna, in August 1821, by Shelley. The latter, in February and March of the same year, had written *A Defence of Poetry*, a work formed in its repeated striking out from the linguistic scepticism in which it is grounded. For Shelley, the act of poetics is fated to occur 'on the verge where words abandon us'. The encounter of poetry itself, however, 'defeats the curse which binds us to be subjected to the accident of surrounding impressions'; it 'purges from our inward sight the film of familiarity which obscures from us the wonder of our being' and 'withdraws life's dark veil from before the scene of things'.[27] Where the efforts of direct description conduct to frustration ('how vain are words', Shelley exclaims), poetry's cognitive possibilities suggest a hope that for Shelley is emancipative and collective.

Byron's poetry is less certain about what is being held in reserve ('The One remains, the many change and pass' (*Adonais*, 52)) than Shelley's; it is thus less mournful and less directly hopeful in the face of what lies beyond. Although quick to test the trajectories of what Shelley calls 'the scene of things', it lacks Shelley's pervasive sense of yearning beyond words and is quicker to rebound on its ironies into the moment. Byron's words are also more radically split by the prism, more evasive in their serio-comic tracings. While gesturing at theory his 'better not / Be too minute' also suggests a mock-chivalrous joke about not looking too minutely into this intimate female scene of 'love or breakfast'. Byron is also refusing to commit to what is understood, finally, as a mode of enriched captivity. A pall of enslavement hangs over Gulbeyaz, infecting and defamiliarizing the conventionally decorative; even the flowers ('Those captive soothers of a captive's hours') are 'fettered' in their porcelain vases. Pulling up short of Keatsian luxuriance, in these terms, becomes an act of political awareness.

These differences acknowledged, there remain Shelleyan presences in Byron's idea of the 'outline' that are harder to detect in earlier sections of the poem.[28] The point of connection is the proposition that poetry's cognitive impact – its engagement of the reader as locus of imaginative production – works to offset the apparently insurmountable difficulties incurred by the descriptive urge. In these terms the poetry of *Don Juan* comes to theorize itself, at least partially, as a site of cognitive renewal and initiation.

* * *

Between the two oceans of *Childe Harold's Pilgrimage* and *Don Juan* we see a shift in focus from ultimate goal to middle distance, from mirror image to outline or sketch. Some of the pressure has been taken off; the energies that worked the language of the earlier poem have been redistributed. This alteration mitigates the risk of egotistical trauma and unblocks the conduits between poet and reader; it also involves, according to the prerogatives of mimesis, a loss of written presence. Form is no longer thrust into the face of the sublime because form has been emptied, reshaped and (ironically) refilled according to a different and humanly more extensive and hopeful dynamic. I think this has something to do with Shelley. I also think we are touching here on the root of Byron's difference with himself. If we want to understand the poetics of *Don Juan*, then, we need to think about the poem's emergence from *Childe Harold's Pilgrimage*.

Don Juan revels in it discovery of new serio-comic energies, but it also refuses to bury the fact that it has hurtled beyond the visions of youth. If we want to place the poem at the end of a narrative of poetic development then we should bear in mind that Byron did not quite see it that way:

> Now my sere fancy 'falls into the yellow
>   Leaf,' and imagination droops her pinion,
> And the sad truth which hovers o'er my desk
> Turns what was once romantic to burlesque.
>
>   (*Don Juan*, iv, 3)

This is a poem in the process of transformation, not the product of such a process. The 'romantic' is placed not in the past but the present continuous ('Turns'). While always fresh in its reciprocities for the

(new or old) reader it is also poetry on the turn, a massive structure
for predicting the death of its author. The individual life of the poet, as
Auden recognizes so powerfully in his elegy for Yeats, must be given up
to the poem's ungovernable afterlife. Amidst these Shandean tracings
any gains in self-comprehension and symbolic reach are to be gleaned
through sacrifice.

In this sense *Don Juan* is not so much a clean break from or
abandonment of earlier 'romantic' Byronic texts as a haunting of their
problematic possibilities. We see this most where Juan's wanderings fall
into the tracks of Harold's pilgrimage, as they do, for instance, along
the course of the Rhine. This is from the earlier journey:

> Away with these! true Wisdom's world will be
> Within its own creation, or in thine,
> Maternal Nature! for who teems like thee,
> Thus on the banks of thy majestic Rhine?
> There Harold gazes on a work divine,
> A blending of all beauties; streams and dells,
> Fruit, foliage, crag, wood, cornfield, mountain, vine,
> And chiefless castles breathing stern farewells
> From gray but leafy walls, where ruin greenly dwells.
>
> And there they stand, as stands a lofty mind,
> Worn, but unstooping to the baser crowd,
> All tenantless, save to the crannying wind,
> Or holding dark communion with the cloud.
> There was a day when they were young and proud,
> Banners on high, and battles pass'd below;
> But they who fought are in a bloody shroud,
> And those which waved are shredless dust ere now,
> And the bleak battlements shall bear no future blow.
>
> (*Childe Harold's Pilgrimage*, iii, 46–7)

This is Juan's rather different experience of the same place:

> From Poland they came on through Prussia Proper,
>   And Konigsberg the capital, whose vaunt,
> Besides some veins of iron, lead, or copper,
>   Has lately been the great Professor Kant.
> Juan, who cared not a tobacco-stopper
>   About philosophy, pursued his jaunt
> To Germany, whose somewhat tardy millions
> Have princes who spur more than their postillions.

And thence through Berlin, Dresden, and the like,
    Until he reached the castellated Rhine: –
Ye glorious Gothic scenes! How much ye strike
    All phantasies, not even excepting mine:
A grey wall, a green ruin, rusty pike,
    Make my soul pass the equinoctial line
Between the present and past worlds, and hover
Upon their airy confine, half-seas-over.

(Don Juan, x, 60–1)

This is not just a geographical revisiting but a stylistic reconfiguration. By returning to the 'grey but leafy walls, where ruin greenly dwells' of the earlier poem in the much sketchier 'grey wall' and 'green ruin' of the later Byron reveals how closely he was thinking of Harold when writing of Juan. What has changed, aside from the narrator's tone and focus, is the extent and emotional emphasis of the descriptive poetry. Within the quasi-Wordsworthian framework of the earlier poem, the teeming description of 'Maternal Nature' is a 'divine', Burke-ish 'blending of all beauties'. The whole, to recall Byron's own description of his poem, is a 'fine indistinct piece of poetical desolation' (*BLJ*, v, 165). What seems particularly fine, although not quite 'indistinct', is the extraordinary sense of compressed vastness in the second stanza. That detail 'shredless dust' is both imaginatively precise and evocative of the graded historical sublime that distinguishes the poem. The dust contains no shreds to indicate its origin (the banners that once fluttered 'on high') yet the reminder of 'shred' in 'shredless' serves to comprehend the gradualness of decay nonetheless. Although blurred at the edges, this is a scene centred in dense economies of meaning.

The narrator of *Don Juan*, on the other hand, offers a much barer sense of the surrounding 'glorious Gothic scenes'. There is no retenanting of the 'chiefless castles' by the Byronic 'lofty mind', no merger of ruin and ruined ego in their concurrent 'holding' of 'dark communion', and only the briefest of glances at a 'castellated Rhine' that has already received its descriptive dues. These losses are compensated by a broader tenanting of a serio-comic existence that contains the sublime moment while remaining critical of the contemporary culture of the sublime. The poetry's descriptive sketchiness – its acceptance of outline where Harold grasps and blurs at the whole – conducts, finally, to a fuller sense of a world glimpsed in the disfiguring of acculturation. Not being 'too minute' is 'best' in asserting a scene of things that engulfs and redetermines the Romantic while dismissing any claims upon it from a critic such as Bowles. The 'burlesque', rather than being distinct from the 'romantic', becomes a guarantee of the latter's authenticity in marking what the sketch must omit. This compacting of visionary and comic is most visible in the final couplet: to 'hover / Upon their airy confine, half-seas-over' scrambles its own vatic resonance ('half-seas-over' is slang for drunk), but it does so for more important reasons than those of simple parody.

One of the reasons why the Shelleyan sublime must tear up the Addisonian is that the latter is so politically uninteresting. It depoliticizes our most radical way of seeing. A similar but more nuanced and troubled version (certainly not a tearing up) of this dynamic is going on between *Don Juan* and *Childe Harold's Pilgrimage*. The latter is a strongly political poem as those with interests in orientalism and the Napoleonic Wars will tell us. What it doesn't see as clearly as *Don Juan* is that modern poetry is not needed to tell us about the Convention of Cintra (such things frame and prompt and inform poetic intelligence, but the future will breed more efficient modes of reportage and commentary). The Harold poet sees the reclamations offered by imaginative life, but he cannot extricate these sufficiently from the mire of ego to grasp the full political significance of form.

The reader of *Childe Harold's Pilgrimage* is a compelled witness to the firework display of Byronic psychodrama; he is also shut out from the poem's sublime egotistical ground, a problem Byron is pressed to acknowledge:

> Could I embody and unbosom now
> That which is most within me, – could I wreak
> My thoughts upon expression, and thus throw
> Soul, heart, mind, passions, feelings, strong or weak,
> All that I would have sought, and all I seek,
> Bear, know, feel, and yet breathe – into *one* word,
> And that one word were Lightning, I would speak;
> But as it is, I live and die unheard,
> With a most voiceless thought, sheathing it as a sword.
> (*Childe Harold's Pilgrimage*, iii, 97)

Where Milton's Raphael ponders how to describe to Adam what 'surmounts the reach / Of human sense', here the arch-Romantic despairs of communicating 'That which is most within me'. Milton's angel, in the face of an intensely present but reserved divine other, establishes a poetics of constructive mitigation. By contrast, Byron looks stymied amidst the decay of self and is forced to concede that his efforts may be little more than a scattering of words across the void. But some hope remains. If interiority is incommunicable it can at least be recuperated and extended, albeit in gloomy, spectral ways:

> 'Tis to create, and in creating live
> A being more intense, that we endow
> With form our fancy, gaining as we give
> The life we image, even as I do now.
> What am I? Nothing; but not so art thou,
> Soul of my thought! With whom I traverse earth,
> Invisible but gazing, as I glow
> Mix'd with thy spirit, blended with thy birth,
> And feeling still with thee in my crush'd feelings' dearth.
>
> *(Childe Harold's Pilgrimage*, iii, 6)

The prominently central 'Nothing', while exerting its pull on Byron's various personal pronouns, is offset by the 'life we image', a vital and primary mode of existence that contrasts the spent force of the poet's 'I'. What is gained in the act of giving – in reaching out to the imagination of audience – is a recharging of self in the 'birth' of poetry.

Such gains, of course, remain poignant in their reliance upon the logic of testament:

> But I have lived, and have not lived in vain:
> My mind may lose its force, my blood its fire,
> And my frame perish even in conquering pain,
> But there is that within me which shall tire
> Torture and Time, and breathe when I expire;
> Something unearthly, which they deem not of,
> Like the remembered tone of a mute lyre,
> Shall on their softened spirits sink, and move
> In hearts all rocky now the late remorse of love.
>
> *(Childe Harold's Pilgrimage*, iv, 137)

These sentiments, which do now form a permanent witnessing of the poet (in Westminster Abbey) are revisited in *Don Juan* in terms that seem less fraught with the anxieties of ego and less gloomily tethered to Byronic autobiography. Those 'hearts all rocky' – the disaffected, immediate audience of Byron's personal life – are replaced by a less specifiable but potentially more extensive and politically meaningful readership:

> But words are things, and a small drop of ink,
>   Falling like dew, upon a thought, produces
> That which makes thousands, perhaps millions, think;
>   'Tis strange, the shortest letter which man uses

Instead of speech, may form a lasting link
    Of ages; to what straits old Time reduces
Frail man, when paper – even a rag like this,
Survives himself, his tomb, and all that's his.

                                        (*Don Juan*, iii, 88)

Byron is still concerned with the poem as self-epitaph, but his focus is
less on the compensatory gains of the individual (the 'I' that proliferates
above has disappeared), than the possibilities of poetry's dissemination
amidst a collective consciousness yet to be.[29] The Harold narrator's
discourse of personal damnation and salvation shades into a more
politically suggestive idea of community: the entrapped 'voiceless
thought' of *Childe Harold's Pilgrimage* is succeeded by an uncluttered
and intransitive 'think'. Isolated at the end of its line the word is striking
in its unadorned simplicity, but it is also strongly drawn, through
bold rhyming links, into the formal weave of the stanza. Rather than
being attributed with a specific democratic value, the act of thought is
associated with the bonds of poetic form and the informing wealth of
tradition.[30] The political moment, so often discovered on the outskirts
of the literary, wants to divest itself of the mundane and occupy the
ever-yet-to-be of literary thought.

                              * * *

If the symbolic territory of the ocean is adapted to accommodate
the reflexiveness of *Don Juan*, it also stands in direct critical contrast
to the poetics of 'narrowness' which Byron, as Johnson's inheritor,
associated with a contemporary Romantic culture that had grown out
of (as Johnson and Byron thought them) the misshaped ideas of Joseph
Warton. At the centre of this problem – or perhaps an emblem of it –
was Wordsworth. Byron's 'war' against the 'Lake School', as McGann
notes, was fought 'under the twin banner of the traduced genius
of Pope and the betrayal of enlightened political ideals'.[31] It is also
concerned with the possibilities of poetic vision and the relationship
of style and form to thought. It was at the door of the 'Lake School',
therefore, that Byron placed Johnson's accusation of a narrow, theory-
engendered mistaking of poetry:

You, Gentlemen! by dint of long seclusion
    From better company have kept your own
At Keswick, and through still continued fusion
    Of one another's minds at last have grown

To deem as a most logical conclusion
　　That Poesy has wreaths for you alone;
There is a narrowness in such a notion
Which makes me wish you'd change your lakes for ocean.
　　　　　　　　　　　　　　(*Don Juan*, 'Dedication, 5')

Disinformed by tradition and excessively subject to the coerciveness of theory, the Lake Poets, according to Byron, are not innovators but prisoners of an immediate culture they have conspired to overdefine on their own behalf. Wordsworth, in some respects, was for Byron what Locke was for Matthew Prior: an optimist whose language, rather than probing the extent of human possibility as it thinks, has retracted into an unengaged sphere of self-admiration which is both too narrow and too complete. His organicist rhetoric – 'still *con*tinued *fusion* / Of one another's minds' – represents for Byron a basic confusion about the relation of poetic language to experience. Its undoing, within the more expansive serio-comic environment of *Don Juan*, is a reassertion of poetry's right to range through language in all its modulations. Byron claims a visionary poetry that cannot be guaranteed by visionary-sounding language.

The oceanic counterclaim of *Don Juan*, and its radicalization of vision, begins in an encounter between Romantic rhetoric and the prodigious verbiage of comedy and digression. Byron reinvents silence. What remains unspoken in so many words can be glimpsed here in the poem's drowning of philosophical thought:

WHEN Newton saw an apple fall, he found
　　In that slight startle from his contemplation –
'Tis *said* (for I'll not answer above ground
　　For any sage's creed or calculation) –
A mode of proving that the earth turned round
　　In a most natural whirl called 'Gravitation;'
And this is the sole mortal who could grapple,
Since Adam, with a fall, or with an apple.

Man fell with apples, and with apples rose,
　　If this be true; for we must deem the mode
In which Sir Isaac Newton could disclose
　　Through the then unpaved stars the turnpike road,
A thing to counterbalance human woes;
　　For ever since immortal man hath glowed
With all kinds of mechanics, and full soon
Steam-engines will conduct him to the Moon.

And wherefore this exordium? – Why, just now,
   In taking up this paltry sheet of paper,
My bosom underwent a glorious glow,
   And my internal Spirit cut a caper:
And though so much inferior, as I know,
   To those who, by the dint of glass and vapour,
Discover stars, and sail in the wind's eye,
I wish to do as much by Poesy.

In the Wind's Eye I have sailed, and sail; but for
   The stars, I own my telescope is dim;
But at the least I have shunned the common shore,
   And leaving land far out of sight, would skim
The Ocean of Eternity: the roar
   Of breakers has not daunted my slight, trim
But *still* sea-worthy skiff; and she may float
Where ships have foundered, as doth many a boat.

                            (*Don Juan*, x, 1–4)

Anne Mellor paraphrases this remarkable articulation as follows:

> Unlike Newton, who by his own admission has been content merely to pick up pebbles on the seashore, the narrator's imagination has ventured out into the ocean of eternity. His creative wit has thus been able to apprehend and to communicate the ultimate incomprehensibility of the universe. In this sense, the imagination provides a surer road to truth, whatever the toll in self-deception, than Newton's more cautious mechanics.[32]

Byron, it is suggested, makes the case for 'creative wit' as a 'surer road to truth' in preference to the more scientific methods of comprehension associated with Newton. Where the latter, in a famous moment of humility, compares the ocean to the vastness of his ignorance,[33] Byron's narrator, with uncertain haughtiness, shuns the 'common shore' that establishes the limits of Newton's 'mechanics' and sets sail, however precariously, upon the poet's true element, the boundless 'Ocean of Eternity'.[34] Byron's scorn in these terms would put him somewhere near Blake and his attack on Newton as the mechanical scourge of spiritual possibility, with the difference that where the latter is full of visionary confidence, the former can only confirm his scepticism, his fixed sense of the 'ultimate incomprehensibility of the universe'.

   Such a reading runs into problems when we pay attention to the intricacies of what Byron has written. The language of the first three stanzas in particular, rather than supporting a sceptical, anti-Enlightenment reading, is in fact strikingly non-antagonistic; it tends rather towards inclusiveness and an imaginative breaking down of the dichotomies upon which oppositional readings depend. The poetry conjures an act of negotiation and enlargement that both depends upon and celebrates the plasticity of words. Clearly, the narrator of *Don Juan* has his doubts about scientific progress – 'This is the patent-age of new inventions / For killing bodies, and for saving souls' (*Don Juan*, i, 132) – but his inclination here is not to distance poetry from science, but to hold the two together under the sign of linguistic accommodation; he matches up the 'glorious glow' of his poetic insight with the 'mechanics' that 'glowed' in the previous stanza, as well as uniting poetry and science in the figure of the telescope.[35] Newton's own discoveries, similarly, do not result from the laborious processes that Locke and Hume associate with scientific method, but from a 'slight startle', a sudden interruption (of thought and rhythm) that seems closer to the poet's inspiration than the scientist's toil.

Byron, like Shelley, was gripped by the imaginative and mythic suggestiveness of new technologies,[36] and presents Newton, that 'Proverb of the Mind' (*Don Juan*, vii, 5), not as a figurehead of the Enlightenment, but as a character of primal significance positioned within, rather than against, the depth of literary and biblical meaning stirred up in these stanzas. He is a second Adam, a new rising ('fell with apples, and with apples rose') in the undulating rhythms of post-lapsarian human perception. He is also, however, that very different progenitor, Milton's Satan, moving through the 'unpaved stars' with Sin and Death in his wake. Like Plato earlier in the poem he has reconceptualized knowledge and created the world afresh, but he has also 'paved the way' for lesser minds – like the 'poets and romancers' following in Plato's wake – to extend, in their obliviousness to the vital mimesis of creativity, the sway of 'system' over the 'controlless core' of human truth.

Rather than taking sides with a Romantic version of 'wit' over 'judgment', Byron seems more concerned to distinguish and mythologize a tradition of genius and originary creation that is seen to pre-exist (and implicitly critique) any such divisive conception of mind. If he is being sceptical here then his scepticism is directed not towards the possibility of knowledge *per se*, but towards historical and cultural processes that have conspired to diminish the vitality of thought and language through acts of controlling categorization and narrowed circumscription. As a Romantic, Byron wants to trace poetry to its source, but he does this against the grain of determined Romantic styles – the Wordsworthian, the Harold-Byronic, and anything argued for by Bowles. Poetry, in such deep places, is chaotic, undecided, uncontrolled; it lurches into definition, lucidity and ideation. It happens along the hyphen of 'serio-comic'. Anything more homogenized and endorsed will take us away from such primal energies towards the deceits of ego and the flatteries of immediate culture.

Notes

1 Quoted in Mary Midgley, *Science and Poetry* (London: Routledge, 2001), 21.

2 See Janet Soskice, *Metaphor and Religious Language* (Oxford: Clarendon Press, 1987), 67–71.

3 John Locke, *An Essay Concerning Human Understanding*, ed. Peter H. Nidditch (Oxford: Clarendon Press, 1975), 156.

4 Hans Aarsleff, 'Leibnitz on Locke and Language', in *From Locke to Saussure: Essays on the Study of Language and Intellectual History* (London: Athlone, 1982), 43.

5 Locke, *An Essay Concerning Human Understanding*, 523.

6 John Locke, *Of the Conduct of the Understanding* ([1706], facsimile Bristol: Thoemmes, 1993), 209–10.

7 See the 1816 sale catalogue of Byron's books (reprinted in *CMP*, 242).

8 Byron allegedly claimed (in conversation) that 'the philosophy of common sense is the truest and the best' (*HVSV*, 275), although how far we can associate this with the 'Common Sense School' is another question.

9 *The Collected Works of Dugald Stewart*, ed. Sir William Hamilton, 11 vols (Edinburgh: Constable, 1854–60), iv, 228.

10 Stewart, *Collected Works*, ii, 180.

11 Stewart, *Collected Works*, iv, 225.

12 For a broader account of Locke's eighteenth-century reception see Kenneth MacLean, *John Locke and English Literature of the Eighteenth Century* (New York: Russell, 1962).

13 Hume, *An Enquiry Concerning Human Understanding*, 87–8. Also see Hume's essay 'On the Standard of Taste': David Hume, *Essays: Moral, Political, and Literary*, ed. Eugene F. Miller, rev. edn. (Indianapolis: Liberty, 1987), 300–30 and John Richetti, *Philosophical Writings: Locke, Berkeley, Hume* (Cambridge, MA: Harvard University Press, 1983).

14 *The Writings and Speeches of Edmund Burke*, vol. 1: *The Early Writings*, ed. T. O. McLoughlin and James T. Boulton (Oxford: Clarendon Press, 1997), 235.

15 *Classical Literary Criticism*, Oxford World's Classics, ed. D. A. Russell and Michael Winterbottom (Oxford: Oxford University Press, 1998), 175.

16 Burke, *The Early Writings*, 234. Burke refers to *Paradise Lost*, i, 589–99.

17 *Tristram Shandy*, II, 238.

18 *Tristram Shandy*, II, 236.

19 Where Prior takes sides, Pope is more radical in his untethering: 'Sworn to no Master, of no Sect am I: / As drives the storm, at any door I knock, / And house with Montagne now, or now with Locke' ('The First Epistle of the First Book of Horace Imitated', 24–6).

20 Matthew Prior, *Dialogues of the Dead and Other Works in Prose and Verse*, ed. A. R. Waller (Cambridge: Cambridge University Press, 1907), 225, 224.

21 Prior, *Dialogues of the Dead*, 241, 228.

22 Prior, *Dialogues of the Dead*, 223.

23 Baroness Staël Holstein, *Germany* (translated from the French), 3 vols (London: John Murray, 1813), III, 91. For a more accurate, tripartite account of the Kantian sublime see Thomas Weiskel, *The Romantic Sublime: Studies in the Psychology of Transcendence* (Baltimore: Johns Hopkins University Press, 1976), 23–25.

24 Bernard Beatty, '"An Awful Wish to Plunge Within it": Byron's Critique of the Sublime', in *Revue de l'Universiténde Moncton: Des actes sèlectionnés du 30ᵉ Congrès international sur Byron*, 'Byron and the Romantic Sublime', ed. Paul M. Curtis (Moncton: Université de Moncton, 2005), 265–76 (269).

25 Quoted in Tom Furniss, *Edmund Burke's Aesthetic Ideology: Language, Gender and Political Economy in Revolution* (Cambridge: Cambridge University Press, 1993), 23.

26 Steele, *The Spectator*, IV, 234.

27 *Shelley's Poetry and Prose*, 508, 533. Compare William Keach: 'Shelley's style [...] is the work of an artist whose sense of the unique and unrealized potential in language was held in unstable suspension with his sense of its resistances and limitations'. William Keach, *Shelley's Style* (New York: Methuen, 1984), xvi.

28 Compare, for instance, the initial description of Julia in canto i (55), which, although ironically aware of its own struggling attempts at description ('But this last simile is trite and stupid'), lacks the philosophical suggestiveness of the descriptions of Gulbeyaz.

29 We need to bear in mind here the rising 'tension between Byron and his readership' that characterizes the post-Harold period (Stabler, *Byron, Poetics and History*, 99).

30 Byron has Shakespeare in mind: 'Nor marble, nor the gilded monuments / Of princes shall outlive this powerful rhyme' (Sonnet 55). *The Sonnets and A Lover's Complaint*, ed. John Kerrigan (Harmondsworth: Penguin, 1995), 104.

31 'Byron and Wordsworth'; reprinted in Jerome McGann, *Byron and Romanticism*, ed. James Soderholm (Cambridge: Cambridge University Press), 173–201 (175).

32 Anne K. Mellor, *English Romantic Irony* (Cambridge, MA: Harvard University Press, 1980), 70.

33 Byron refers to the following alleged remark: 'I don't know what I may seem to the world, but as to myself, I seem to have been only like a boy playing on the sea shore, and diverting myself in now and then finding a smoother pebble or a prettier shell than ordinary, whilst the great ocean of truth lay all undisclosed before me'. Spence, *Anecdotes, Observations, and Characters*, 54. Byron also alludes to the anecdote at *Don Juan*, vii, 5 and ix, 17.

34 Compare Shelley's anxious sense of superiority in *Adonais*: 'my spirit's bark is driven / Far from the shore, far from the trembling throng / Whose sails were never to the tempest given' (488–90).

35 Byron also uses the image in 'The Dream', 177–83 and *The Vision of Judgment*, 106.

36 Thomas Medwin records Byron asking 'Where shall we set bounds to the power of steam? [...] Might not the fable of Prometheus, and his stealing the fire, and of Briareus and his earth-born brothers, be but traditions of steam and its machinery? (*Medwin's Conversations of Lord Byron*, 188). A similar compression occurs in Shelley's *Letter to Maria Gisborne*, when the poet imagines himself as a 'mighty mechanist, / Bent with sublime Archimedean art' (16–17).

PART 3

OUTLINES

The Flower and the Gem
Narrative Form and the Traces of Eden

Byron's 'wish to do as much by Poesy' remains partially and crucially submerged in poetry itself. Its incompleteness as a moment of poetics is its first claim. Its second, perhaps surprisingly, is on behalf of theory, although not of the kind Byron associates with Bowles or Wordsworth. The narrator of *Don Juan* is always keenly susceptible to the advances of doubt, but he resists the sceptic's satisfaction and conclusiveness; there is a restless search for origin with Byron that has something of Shelley but nothing of the Pyrrhonist. While sneering at 'system', Byron commits to theory where it recognizes itself as a process shaped both by knowledge of its own limits and the poet's right to judge. Byron's skiff and telescope are markers of this commitment, as is the notion of the 'outline' with its proposal of the poem as site of imaginative mediation and political possibility. As in the sketching, dashing critical prose, theory is both held off and pursued through an intellectual vitality that will not settle for a name. Byron's 'wish' is to write a critical and wary visionary poetry that throws off Romantic acculturation and its post-Enlightenment scene of division to touch upon 'Eternity'.

So far I've approached these ideas mainly through the narrator of *Don Juan* as digressive 'philosopher' and weaver of reflexive images. Byron's poetics, however, can also be seen in the poet's work as a narrative artist, in the forms and symbolic characters that shape Juan's experience. As well as telling stories, *Don Juan* is fundamentally concerned with how stories are told; it is a poem preoccupied with the ethics of fictionality. Narratives are in their very nature selective, and their meaning depends upon their inclusions, exclusions and emphases. They are necessarily outlines of an implied whole that cannot be presented in its totality; as such they must assume (or evade) responsibility for the unrepresented. Much of this selectiveness is a form of disinterested and necessary filtering and a precondition for the production of plausible narrative

art; it may also, however, be bound up in ideological or other agendas
that seek to reproduce the world through an act of bad faith. Narrative,
thus understood, might be compared to argument (as both Byron and
Keats understood it) in plotting its way through a sprawling range of
experience and possibility. Locke was accused by his detractors of an
implausible tidiness on such grounds, and Byron attacked Wordsworth
and Bowles for establishing circumscribed narratives on poetry's behalf.
As if minded of this, the narratives of *Don Juan* are sharply sensitized
to their own constructedness. They become self-comprehending and
critically charged in confessing the extent of their emergence from origin.
Their probing for cracks in the walls of Eden tells of the plight of the
Romantic in an age of fallen words.

Paradise becomes a serious concern of *Don Juan* in the section of
narrative that begins with Juan's awakening into the world of Haidée
after surviving the shipwreck, and ends with Lambro's unceremonious
hurling of Juan back into the poem's containing narrative flow. Haidée,
the beautiful inhabitant of an Edenic island, discovers a barely alive
Juan, restores him to health, and the pair fall in love:

> And thus they wander'd forth, and hand in hand,
>   Over the shining pebbles and the shells,
> Glided along the smooth and harden'd sand,
>   And in the worn and wild receptacles
> Work'd by the storms, yet work'd as it were plann'd,
>   In hollow halls, with sparry roofs and cells,
> They turn'd to rest; and, each clasp'd by an arm,
> Yielded to the deep twilight's purple charm.
>
> They look'd up to the sky, whose floating glow
>   Spread like a rosy ocean, vast and bright;
> They gazed upon the glittering sea below,
>   Whence the broad moon rose circling into sight;
> They heard the wave's splash, and the wind so low,
>   And saw each other's dark eyes darting light
> Into each other – and, beholding this,
> Their lips drew near, and clung into a kiss;
>
> A long, long kiss, a kiss of youth and love,
>   And beauty, all concentrating like rays
> Into one focus, kindled from above;
>   Such kisses belong to early days,
> Where heart, and soul, and sense, in concert move,
>   And the blood's lava, and the pulse a blaze,

Each kiss a heart-quake, – for a kiss's strength,
I think, it must be reckon'd by its length.

(Don Juan, ii, 184–6)

As well as including some fine descriptive poetry, these stanzas involve a complex act of placement. The lovers, we are told, 'look'd up' to the sky, which is likened to a 'rosy ocean', and also 'gazed upon the glittering sea below'. They are located between sublime bodies that reflect upon each other in crosscurrents of literal and metaphorical exchange. Placed between these energies the lovers themselves seem faintly supernatural as they move over the surface of the earth ('Glided along the smooth and harden'd sand'). In this charged environment of incanted rhythms, their kiss acts as a conductor, a site of concentration where understanding, unshackled from reason, is perfectly realized. Unlike 'Doubt', the 'sole prism / Of the Truth's rays', the lovers are a 'focus' for a truth that is taken directly from 'above'. This is no 'common shore', but a privileged space suffused by the perfection of young love.

Although Byron recognizes the fragile truth of this 'romantic' bliss, it cannot and does not dictate the limits of poetic consciousness. Paradise is marked out by the wisdom of tradition as susceptible and doomed.[1] The lovers' fall is also predicted by the part-comic rhyme patterns of Byron's *ottava rima* which draw towards the inapposite 'I think' of a witty and deeply lapsarian narrator. Contrary to usual structurings of the sublime, a known, defined and all-too-human presence marks the limit of an immediate scene of transcendence and ineffability.

Where Juan is carried along by the picaresque momentum of the narrative, the poem's female characters are generally fixed to their initial settings. Within these environments they act as transmitters and receivers of the sustaining and destructive energies that are carefully traced through the poem. Haidée's sustaining life force, as well as preserving Juan, prevents the total moral demise of her vice-riddled father, the pirate Lambro:

But whatsoe'er he had of love reposed
   On that beloved daughter; she had been
The only thing which kept his heart unclosed
   Amidst the savage deeds he had done and seen;
A lonely pure affection unopposed:
   There wanted but the loss of this to wean
His feelings from all milk of human kindness,
And turn him like the Cyclops mad with blindness.

(Don Juan, iii, 57)

Lambro is positioned 'Amidst' a world of savagery, but remains 'unclosed' – not quite open – but not quite finally cut off from all hope either. Haidée prevents his final descent into madness by being herself 'unopposed'; her 'pure affection', unlike the flawed efforts of reason and argument, is impervious to contradiction. She acts as a conduit between the origin from which Lambro risks absolute alienation and the energetic but deadly sphere of 'deeds' into which he has emerged.

If Haidée's 'affection' is redemptive, however, it is also 'lonely'; it is bound up in the very human frailty it promises to counter. Although she revives Juan from his 'doubt' and 'despair' (*Don Juan*, ii, 112), there is something desperate and consuming about this 'lovely female face' (*Don Juan*, ii, 112) that 'Seem'd almost prying into his for breath' (*Don Juan*, ii, 13).[2] With a name that evokes the underworld and eyes as 'black as death' (*Don Juan*, ii, 117), Haidée is far from straightforward as a symbol of melioration. The giver of sustenance, like the narrative she inhabits, cannot be self-sufficient and must be sustained from elsewhere, a role performed in the poem by the maidservant Zoe (a name linked to Eve and meaning 'life'), who helps Haidée move the feeble Juan to a nearby cave:

> And lifting him with care into the cave,
>   The gentle girl, and her attendant, – one
> Young, yet her elder, and of brow less grave,
>   And more robust of figure, – then begun
> To kindle fire, and as the new flames gave
>   Light to the rocks that roof'd them, which the sun
> Had never seen, the maid, or whatsoe'er
> She was, appear'd distinct, and tall, and fair.
>
> (*Don Juan*, ii, 115)

While the vampiric Haidée is positioned over Juan 'still as death / Bent, with hush'd lips, that drank his scarce-drawn breath', Zoe 'the meantime some eggs was frying' (*Don Juan*, ii, 144). In the end it is the latter's worldliness (she knows 'by tradition, for she ne'er had read' (*Don Juan*, ii, 158)) rather than Haidée's purer energy that saves Juan's life. Rather than a simple affirmation of transcendence in the face of a fallen world Byron's narrative looks to bring Haidée's dark-pristine energies into balance. Her redemptive function is framed by complex comic forces represented in different ways by both the narrator and Zoe. Byron's poem conjures a strong sense of what lies beyond the narrowed frame of the 'romantic' story.

The narrator's observation that 'love must be sustain'd like flesh and blood' (*Don Juan*, ii, 170) also bears a critical force. Zoe's 'most superior mess of broth', we are told, is a 'thing which poesy but seldom mentions' (*Don Juan*, ii, 123), a reference to Homer that activates Byron's larger satire about the limitations of contemporary writing. Poetry, the narrator opines, has become infected with an 'air / Of clap-trap, which your recent poets prize' (*Don Juan*, ii, 124). Its language, under the influence of poets such as Wordsworth, has become stuck in a rut, something *Don Juan* challenges through its generic and rhetorical scramblings:

> And Juan, too, was help'd out from his dream,
>   Or sleep, or whatsoe'er it was, by feeling
> A most prodigious appetite: the steam
>   Of Zoe's cookery no doubt was stealing
> Upon his senses, and the kindling beam
>   Of the new fire, which Zoe kept up, kneeling,
> To stir her viands, made him quite awake
> And long for food, but chiefly a beef-steak
>
> (*Don Juan*, ii, 153)

The bliss of young love may be 'kindled from above', but here a similar phrase – the 'kindling beam' of Zoe's cooking fire – is placed in a very different register and with reference to a very different sphere of experience. The word's doubleness, its radical serio-comic reciprocity, is mobilized by the poem's critical intelligence; it registers consciousness in transition and in so doing cuts against the mono-registers of cultural self-sufficiency (Bowles's 'Nature'). The unfamiliar realism proposed in giving us both Haidée and Zoe is present in the very words of the poem and their multiple inhabitation of experience.

As Haidée's story nears its dissolution, the narrator's broadly sympathetic framing of paradise becomes increasingly infiltrated by less controllable forces:

> They fear'd no eyes nor ears on that lone beach,
>   They felt no terrors from the night, they were
> All in all to each other: though their speech
>   Was broken words, they *thought* a language there, –
> And all the burning tongues the passions teach
>   Found in one sigh the best interpreter
> Of nature's oracle – first love, – that all
> Which Eve has left her daughters since her fall.
>
> (*Don Juan*, ii, 189)

Unlike Harold's more Wordsworthian 'mutual language, clearer than the tome / Of his land's tongue' (*Childe Harold's Pilgrimage*, iii, 13), this supra-linguistic, Edenic communication is understood as doomed by a narrator who cannot shake Eve from his thoughts.[3] He is not writing about what happens to Haidée but about what has already happened to her. The lovers may fear neither 'eyes nor ears on that lone beach', but they have been seen many times before, and their ignorance of this will not defend them. Neither, in the end, can the narrator's nostalgia, which must share its worldly purview with the world's boundless capacity for disenchantment:

> The gentle pressure, and the thrilling touch,
>   The least glance better understood than words,
> Which still said all, and ne'er could say too much;
>   A language, too, but like to that of birds,
> Known but to them, at least appearing such
>   As but to lovers a true sense affords;
> Sweet playful phrases, which would seem absurd
> To those who have ceased to hear such, or ne'er heard:
>
> (*Don Juan*, iv, 14)

Again, it is the couplet that stages the incursion of knowledge into a paradise oblivious to its own permeability. Here, however, the likes of the narrator who have 'ceased to hear such' are accompanied by more threatening and unknown presences who have 'ne'er heard'. Byron may invest in the (future) reader as site of imaginative mediation, but he also knew that much of his readership was locked up in a language that expressed its lack of self-comprehension as envy. As the poet knows only too well, the story of Adam and Eve is a story about the fall of words.

It is the forces of misunderstanding that finally overrun the lovers' sphere of charged silence when it is broken apart by Lambro after a brief balancing of sublime and carnivalesque energies. Severed from Juan, Haidée is left at the mercy of an inrushing world:

> She look'd on many a face with vacant eye,
>   On many a token without knowing what;
> She saw them watch her without asking why,
>   And reck'd not who around her pillow sat;
> Not speechless though she spoke not; not a sigh
>   Relieved her thoughts; dull silence and quick chat
> Were tried in vain by those who served; she gave
> No sign, save breath, of having left the grave.
>
> (*Don Juan*, iv, 63)

Haidée is 'Not speechless though she spoke not': her unspoken language of thought continues, but without Juan it has no receiver and thus she is given over to the fatal misunderstanding of the surrounding throng.

In an exquisite moment just prior to her death she hears the music of a harpist, the beauty of which reverberates with her profound speechlessness and elicits a response. As she hears the music 'her thin wan fingers beat the wall / In time to his old tune' (*Don Juan*, iv, 66). This final act of connection with the 'old tune' acknowledges an informing world of song and tradition but also hints, amidst tragedy, at the energies of renewal that drive the comic progress of Byron's poem. Haidée is not obliterated any more than Eve was; she is, rather, reimplicated in the tasks of the beyond.

* * *

Haidée's 'romantic' energies, which keep in mind the culture of Byronic orientalism, are returned to a containing poem that in its own narrative journey is heading towards Regency England. It is there, in the poem's final major narrative sequence, that these energies are most obviously recollected and redeployed. Instead of awakening into a blissful scene defined by the complimentary energies of Zoe and Haidée, Juan, in *Don Juan*'s English cantos, enters a busy social sphere in which two new female characters, Lady Adeline Amundeville and Aurora Raby, establish the erotic and existential framework within which the poem's intelligence moves. Juan's position between these two very different women is made explicit at the feast, where by 'some odd chance [he] was placed between / Aurora and the Lady Adeline' (*Don Juan*, xv, 75).

Lady Adeline Amundeville, a name suggesting a devilish urban worldliness, is a creature of society and her element is the 'hetero-geneous mass' (*Don Juan*, xiii, 94) of guests assembled at her country home, Norman Abbey. Adeline is first encountered 'amidst the gay world's hum' (*Don Juan*, xiii, 13), tuned to the low-level noise of social bustle. This immersive state – 'amidst' is an important word in the poem – glances back to Lambro, but also forward to the narrator's own semi-careful self-positioning:

> I perch upon an humbler promontory,
> > Amidst life's infinite variety:
> With no great care for what is nicknamed glory,
> > But speculating as I cast mine eye
> On what may suit or may not suit my story
>
> > > > (*Don Juan*, xv, 19)

The state of plenitude that is also a state of oppression is an ambiguous one in *Don Juan*. To be amidst things can signal a proximity to origin as it does here for the narrator as he selects the materials for his 'story' out of 'infinite variety'. His reflexive 'amidst', however, is very different to those that govern Lambro and Adeline. Where the narrator understands the relation between 'infinite variety' and 'story', between 'Eternity' and 'miniature', his characters are unaware of their miring in immersive abstractions.

The narrative that sees nothing beyond itself must concoct its own internal sublime. Thus Wordsworth gives us lakes not ocean. Adeline's urban, spiritless world, in these terms, can only muster the lavishly proliferating, mock-sublime banquet at the centre of the English cantos. Unlike the nurturing sustenance provided by Zoe, the banquet bespeaks a world utterly disserved from origin. Poetry, by way of ironic sympathy, becomes a 'conundrum of a dish' (*Don Juan*, xv, 21), one restricted in its ingredients to the mock heroic ('Great things were now to be achieved at table, / With massy plate for armour' (*Don Juan*, xv, 62)) and Louis Ude's famous *The French Cook* (1813), the latter supplying many of the fashionable dishes served up by the Amundevilles. Instead of being 'Amidst life's infinite variety' the poet finds himself 'Amidst this tumult of fish, flesh, and fowl' (*Don Juan*, xv, 74).

The straining poet of vision is reduced to something more like an overworked food writer:

> Alas! I must leave undescribed the gibier,
>   The salmi, the consommé, the purée,
> All which I can use to make my rhymes run glibber
>   Than could roast beef in our rough John Bull way:
> I must not introduce even a spare rib here,
>   'Bubble and squeak' would spoil my liquid lay;
> But I have dined, and must forego, alas!
> The chaste description even of a 'Becasse',
>
> (*Don Juan*, xv, 71)

In such a place the poet's exclusion from Eden seems absolute. Where *Paradise Lost* resounds with divine creation, the nineteenth-century poet cannot 'introduce even a spare rib'. The very idea of higher creation seems to have been cancelled amidst the linguistically dismal, cant-ridden sphere of the Amundevilles:

> The mind is lost in mighty contemplation
>   Of intellect expended on two courses;
> And indigestion's grand multiplication
>   Requires arithmetic beyond my forces.
> Who would suppose, from Adam's simple ration,
>   That cookery could have call'd forth such resources,

As form a science and a nomenclature
From out the commonest demands of nature?

(Don Juan, xv, 69)

Adeline's world is abstracted from nature, debarred, through the categorizing effort of 'science' and its 'nomenclature', from Haidée's supra-linguistic paradise. Hers is a spirit weighed down amidst the uncreative aftermath of Enlightenment. Similarly mired in this post-Adamic (and post-Lockean) situation, the poet is confronted with a language that seems dead to the potentiality of human life. Where Adam named the animals with ontologically vital words of origin, the modern poet lives in a world of 'dictionaries, / Which encyclopedize both flesh and fish' (Don Juan, xv, 68). Something has been lost behind Shelley's (Coleridgean) 'film of familiarity'; category has replaced apprehension at the ground of linguistic function.

What hope remains here certainly has nothing to do with Bowles's 'Nature' but does seem to involve the frozen-out yet unextinguished human (female) spirit. Byron does, after all, find a spare rib from somewhere. Adeline, with her 'two transcendant [sic] eyes' (Don Juan, xv, 75), is more the victim of her world than its contemptible emanation. Far from being a simple object of satire, she is identified with the poet himself as sharing that characteristic Byronic quality of 'mobility' or 'an excessive susceptibility of immediate impressions'.[4] Her fascinating spiritual compression is also a prompt to poetic creativity:

But Adeline was not indifferent: for
   (Now for a common place!) beneath that snow,
As a Volcano holds the lava more
   Within – et caetera. Shall I go on? – No!
I hate to hunt down a tired metaphor:
   So let the often used volcano go.
Poor thing! How frequently, by me and others,
It hath been stirred up till its smoke quite smothers.

I'll have another figure in a trice: –
   What say you to a bottle of champagne?
Frozen into a very vinous ice,
   Which leaves few drops of that immortal rain,
Yet in the very centre, past all price,
   About a liquid glassful will remain;
And this is stronger than the strongest grape
Could e'er express in its expanded shape:

(Don Juan, xiii, 36–7)

The comparison of a passionate but suppressed interiority and a volcano, a simile to which Byron admits being no stranger ('the lava of the imagination whose eruption prevents an earthquake'), is now recognized as 'tired'; it has become part of the 'clap-trap' that spoils contemporary poetry. It is not so much that the volcano is inapposite as that it has lost its spark as a moment of creation. It has become more like the stuff of the encyclopedias than the language of Adam. Adeline's 'quintessence' (*Don Juan*, xiii, 38) thus requires a more original figure, which it becomes the task of the poet to hunt down.

This questing for identity takes us to the verge of nihilism as metaphor becomes an act of energetic staving off:

> The evaporation of a joyous day
>   Is like the last glass of champagne, without
> The foam which made its virgin bumper gay;
>   Or like a system coupled with a doubt;
> Or like a soda bottle when its spray
>   Has sparkled and let half its spirit out;
> Or like a billow left by storms behind,
> Without the animation of the wind;
>
> Or like an opiate which brings troubled rest,
>   Or none; or like – like nothing that I know
> Except itself; – such is the human breast;
>   A thing, of which similitudes can show
> No real likeness, – like the old Tyrian vest
>   Dyed purple, none at present can tell how,
> If from a shell-fish or from cochineal.
> So perish every tyrant's robe piece-meal!
>
> (*Don Juan*, xvi, 9–10)

The telling moment here is the redirecting stutter in the second stanza ('or like – like nothing'). Byron's dash represents a tiny stretch of the infinite quietness predicted by any quest for figurative identity. Indeed, it is only through sleight of hand (by using the failure of simile as a simile itself) that the narrator is able to continue at all. The poet has verve and range – he ends by flicking out his couplet politically – but his energies, nonetheless, seem hectic and unsustainable. He has found an answer of sorts to Harold's 'voiceless thought', but one that comes with the suspicion that we have merely exchanged despair for textuality.

We might set against this Prior's ('Montaigne's') claim that where a simile 'does not hold, the very disproportion gives you Occasion to reconsider [the apparently unknowable object], and you set it in all its lights'. Prompted imaginative activity generates illumination (however dim) in scenes the sceptic wants to tell us are covered over with irrevocable pitch black. In these terms we can reconstrue Byron's brilliantly shifting and integrally human lines as activations of human imagination that glimpse the very thing (the 'human breast') acknowledged to be indescribable. It is important to note here, however, that Byron's lists don't all operate in the same way (they don't *all* annihilate knowledge claims, nor do they *all* seek to replace them); they may suggest patterns, but they never overwrite the particularized moment. The 'bottle of champagne', unlike the 'last glass of champagne', is not carried off upon a tide of signification; it appears, in Prior's terms, to 'hold'. It may not rank with the perfect significations of Adam's language, but neither is it the stuff of the encyclopedias. In Shelley's terms, Byron has exchanged language that is 'dead to all the nobler purposes of human intercourse' with language that 'marks the before unapprehended relations between things'.[5] Reality, in however small a way, has been re-exposed.

Byron's poetry thinks a great deal about what it is doing in these places. Its characters, images and narrative forms are all worked by an intelligence deeply concerned with the questions that motivate poetics. With Haidée, poetry is investigated through the fall it has already endured. Paradise is not mocked off the stage but accepted as unavailable in any direct sense. What Byron does attack is the secular Romantic claim to have rediscovered origin in the rhetoric of Nature. The narrator's role in this gradually shifts from storyteller to reluctant conduit for offstage forces that are preparing rupture. When Juan enters the very different isolation of Regency England the poet is retasked as his primal 'amidst' shrinks to a mock one. He becomes trapped at the centre of his own (comic) tragedy and must do what he can to write himself – and his reader – an escape. This he does, with Adeline, through a return to human essence as a prompt to and regrounding of metaphor. He takes a different and altogether more ambitious path with Juan's other love interest.

Aurora Raby, who signals a more direct return to Haidée than Adeline, is Byron's most resplendent symbol of poetic possibility. Rather than Haidée's fragile Romantic and pantheistic associations, Aurora is tangibly religious and specifically Roman Catholic.[6] She is 'pure as sanctity itself from vice' (*Don Juan*, xv, 52) and her beyondness, unlike Haidée's, is full of self-possession: her 'spirit seem'd as seated on a throne / Apart from the surrounding world' (*Don Juan*, xv, 47). She is like

Haidée in being 'unopposed', but her transcendence seems more secure, knowing and untroubled:

> The dashing and proud air of Adeline
>   Imposed not upon her: she saw her blaze
> Much as she would have seen a glowworm shine,
>   Then turn'd unto the stars for loftier rays.
>
> (Don Juan, xv, 56)

Where Haidée depends upon Zoe, Aurora's soul is 'strong / In its own strength' (*Don Juan*, xv, 47). The differences between the two are developed in detail:

> Juan knew naught of such a character –
>   High, yet resembling not his lost Haidée;
> Yet each was radiant in her proper sphere:
>   The Island girl, bred up by the lone sea,
> More warm, as lovely, and not less sincere,
>   Was Nature's all: Aurora could not be
> Nor would be thus; – the difference in them
> Was such as lies between a flower and a gem.
>
> (Don Juan, xv, 58)

Unlike Pope, who places the gem above the flower,[7] Byron establishes a more nuanced contrast. Aurora lacks Haidée's natural warmth but does, like the poet himself, have self-knowledge. Aurora 'could not' in any case be 'Nature's all', but she also 'would not' even if she were given the choice. It is as if she knows the tragedy of her ancestry in her DNA and has evolved away from its errors.

Where Haidée is engulfed by miscomprehension and Adeline is compressed by vulgarity, Aurora is liberated and powerfully interstitial:

> Radiant and grave – as pitying man's decline;
>   Mournful – but mournful of another's crime,
> She look'd as if she sat by Eden's door,
> And grieved for those who could return no more.
>
> (Don Juan, xv, 45)

Aurora's 'throne' occupies the margin of paradise and the fallen world, commanding views over both. Part sentry, part conduit, she draws together the spheres of Adam and the encyclopedias. She also possesses depths of compassion that have a distinctly visionary feel:

> The worlds beyond this world's perplexing waste
>   Had more of her existence, for in her

There was a depth of feeling to embrace
Thoughts, boundless, deep, but silent too as Space.

(Don Juan, xvi, 48)

Cain seeks to comprehend the boundlessness of space with reason and
falls into tragic perplexity. Like other mistakers of poetry he misses
the true poetic logic of the 'outline'. Aurora, however, seems to exceed
any such compromises in her 'embrace' of 'Thoughts, boundless, deep,
but silent too as Space'. She presides over a paradox by containing
(embracing) that which can permit no bounds. For all her surface
intellectual coldness she is marked by depths of angelic feeling: 'In
figure, she had something of sublime / In eyes which sadly shone, as
seraphs' shine' *(Don Juan*, xv, 45). This sublime simultaneity of thought
and feeling has something of the pre-Enlightenment scene conjured by
the narrator, a place in which Newton can be numbered among the
poets. Where the narrator tentatively navigates the 'Ocean of Eternity',
however, Aurora's embrace (her face was 'always clear, / As deep seas in
a Sunny Atmosphere' *(Don Juan*, xvi, 94) implies a supernaturally lucid
poetics of origin.

Aurora gazes out over the severe fragmentariness of Byron's life. We
can only speculate about what might have followed the suggestions
made by her powerful symbolism. What seems likely is that Byron
would have continued to create remarkably reflexive poetry of a kind
that remains underestimated within the canons of Romantic thought.
We cannot, without slicing up Byron's poetic textures, turn Aurora into
a philosophical or theological position on Byron's behalf (or a political
or feminist one against him). We can, however, notice the forms of her
thoughtfulness. We can notice that her gaze is fixed upon the written
word:

Aurora, who look'd more on books than faces,
    Was very young, although so very sage,
Admiring more Minerva than the Graces,
    Especially upon a printed page.

(Don Juan, xv, 85)

This reminder of the 'printed page', which has more to it than bluestocking
satire, in turn generates one of the narrator's most revealing philosophical
digressions:

If people contradict themselves, can I
    Help contradicting them, and every body,
Even my veracious self? – But that's a lie;

I never did so, never will – how should I?
He who doubts all things, nothing can deny;
    Truth's fountains may be clear – her streams are muddy,
And cut through such canals of contradiction,
That she must often navigate o'er fiction.

Apologue, fable, poesy, and parable,
    Are false, but may be render'd also true
By those that sow them in a land that's arable.
    'Tis wonderful what fable will not do!
'Tis said it makes reality more bearable:
    But what's reality? Who has its clue?
Philosophy? No; she too much rejects.
Religion? *Yes*; but which of all her sects?

                                        (*Don Juan*, xv, 88–9)

Aurora may have access to 'Truth's fountains', but this only serves to remind the poet of his own far muddier sceptical mire. He quickly, however, scrambles up again through his usual trick of undoing doubt into endless possibility ('He who doubts all things, nothing can deny'), an epistemological state that is, however, inherently unstable and drawn back to the looming questions that overrun the final lines. Philosophy offers no anchorage here. Religion – in Aurora's presence – does offer a 'clue' but is also, from Byron's fallen position, unable to shake off scepticism. He can't get beyond the 'sects' to the real thing. Another source of hope lies with 'fiction', a word that hinges the stanzas in a shift of meaning: it begins as a synonym for 'falsehood' but then brings to mind 'Apologue, fable, poesy, and parable', which may be 'false' but which can be 'render'd also true'. What is required for this quasi-mystical transformation is 'a land that's arable'. This is the 'lively reader's fancy', an object of great anxiety but also of great hope. This takes us back to Byron's 'wish' and its unique contribution to Romantic poetics. It also reminds us that in *Don Juan* poetic reflex and political intent are simultaneous, a claim I now want to pursue.

Notes

1 Byron's 'they wander'd forth, and hand in hand' recalls the final lines of *Paradise Lost*: 'They hand in hand with wandering steps and slow, / Through Eden took their solitary way' (xii, 648–9).
2 On the issue of Haidée's power (and powerlessness) see Malcolm Kelsall, 'Byron and the Romantic Heroine', in *Byron: Augustan and Romantic*, ed. Andrew Rutherford (London: Macmillan, 1990), 52–62 (56).

3 There is also perhaps something of Pope's Eloisa here: 'Ev'n thought meets thought, ere from the lips it part, / And each warm wish springs mutual from the heart. / This sure is bliss (if bliss on earth there be)' (*Eloisa to Abelard*, 95–7).

4 See *CPW*, V, 769; for Byron's own 'mobility' see *HVSV*, 241–2.

5 *Shelley's Poetry and Prose*, 512 (*A Defence of Poetry*).

6 Aurora is identified as a Catholic at xv, 46.

7 'We prize the stronger effort of his pow'r / And justly set the Gem above the Flow'r' (*Epistle to Cobham*, 99–100).

'Glory's dream Unriddled'
Politics and the Forms of War

Byron's participation in the Bowles controversy coincided with an increasing involvement in revolutionary politics, prompted by the poet's relationship with the Gamba family in Italy and his consciousness of revolutions in Spain and Portugal in the summer of 1820. It is perhaps not surprising then that Byron's defence, via Pope, of the sustaining values of literary tradition is charged with a political awareness that is very much of its moment. The polemical energies generated by the controversy, in turn, flowed into *Don Juan*, a poem that takes on a new philosophical and political directness from its new beginning with the Preface to canto vi. Overseen by his new publishers, the radical Hunt brothers, Byron was also no longer threatened by Murray's conservative 'cutting and slashing'.

The terms of Byron's newfound political intent are suggested by a letter to Thomas Moore of August 1822 in which the poet discusses, among other things, the war poetry of *Don Juan*: 'it is necessary', Byron writes, 'in the present clash of philosophy and tyranny, to throw away the scabbard. I know it is against fearful odds; but the battle must be fought' (*BLJ*, ix, 191). Although the image is similar, Byron is saying something very different to Shelley's (in *A Defence of Poetry*) 'Poetry is a sword of lightning, ever unsheathed, which consumes the scabbard that would contain it'.[1] Where Shelley vitally metaphorizes poetics to suggest its real political function, Byron sounds ready to give up on the whole business, to get on the next boat to Greece, dust off his pistols, and forget about metaphors entirely. The will to action threatens to eclipse the purposiveness of the written. As Byron knew, however, tyranny is bound up in cant and thus requires a response of mind as well as body. He would, of course, get on the boat to Greece, but before doing so he would re-vision war poetry as something essential to the fight. In a world of 'Cant Political' the biggest battlefield is the public mind, and any thought of victory depends upon its shaping.

Although characteristically Byron chose to stick with *Don Juan* rather than starting a fresh poem, it is clear that the siege of Ismail cantos, which tell of Juan's involvement (on the side of the invading Russian forces), represent a new departure. Byron signals this most clearly by writing a new Preface that is inserted before canto vi. The Preface centres in a vitriolic attack on Castlereagh, the British Foreign Secretary, who had recently cut his own throat, probably after being set up and then blackmailed on the grounds of homosexuality.[2] Byron's prose is drawn between liberal political anger and a fascination with the gory details of the suicide. The imaginative pull of the grim demise of 'Carotid-artery-cutting Castlereagh' (*Don Juan*, x, 59) brings Byron's prose to life, but also threatens to upset its political concentration. On the other hand, the compound adjective, which Byron requires us to chew our way through, has its own political force. It stands in stark contrast to the dishonest writing that, according to Byron, characterizes the public response to Castlereagh's death.

The official reading of Castlereagh's legacy is accused of exploiting public sentiment to distract from political realities:

> That he was an amiable man in *private* life, may or may not be true; but with this the Public have nothing to do; and as to lamenting his death, it will be time enough when Ireland has ceased to mourn for his birth. As a Minister, I, for one of millions, looked upon him as the most despotic in intention and the weakest in intellect that ever tyrannized over a country. It is the first time too indeed since the Normans, that England has been insulted by a *Minister* (at least) who could not speak English, and that Parliament permitted itself to be dictated to in the language of Mrs Malaprop.
>
> Of the manner of his death little need be said, except that if a poor radical devil such as Waddington or Watson had cut his throat, he would have been buried in a cross-road, with the usual appurtenances of the stake and mallet. But the Minister was an elegant Lunatic – a sentimental Suicide – he merely cut the 'carotid artery' (blessings on their learning) and lo! – the Pageant – and the Abbey! and 'the Syllables of Dolour yelled forth' by the Newspapers – and the harangue of the Coroner in an eulogy over the bleeding body of the deceased – (an Anthony worthy of such a Caesar) – and the nauseous and atrocious cant of a degraded Crew of Conspirators against all that is sincere and honourable. (*CPW*, 295–6)

Whether or not we agree with Kelsall that Byron's is a 'simplistic solution to political problems' will likely depend on how we feel about the tradition of Paine and Shelley that Byron here approximates.[3] As well as recalling the attacks on Bowles, the accusation of an official conspiracy of 'nauseous and atrocious cant' has a similar logic to Paine's famous riposte to Burke's eulogy for Marie Antoinette: 'We pity the plumage, but forget the dying bird'. Where Paine had pointed out that Burke's mourning of the French Queen, while not inherently objectionable, is a distraction from the political realities of revolutionary France, Byron deplores the disingenuous and irrelevantly personal eulogizing of the newspapers. As Shelley puts it in *An Address to the People on the Death of Princess Charlotte* (1817), the 'appeal to the feelings of men should not be made lightly, or in any manner that tends to waste, on inadequate objects, those fertilizing streams of sympathy which a public mourning should be the occasion of pouring forth'. Eulogy, as a public concern, has a duty not to allow personal sentiment to obscure the significance of public events, especially, as Byron implies, where this is done for dishonourable political ends. Its 'character', as Shelley puts it, 'ought to be universal, not particular'.[4]

Byron's commitment to abstract or 'universal' politics, not to mention the 'poor radical devil', does not match Shelley's. He was also one of Princess Charlotte's most prominent literary mourners (see *Childe Harold's Pilgrimage*, iv, 169–70) and, while he is happy to show his distaste for the '"the Syllables of Dolour yelled forth" by the Newspapers', would have been less ready to dismiss fine rhetoric such as Burke's on the grounds of its implicit political content. Indeed, it is Castlereagh's alleged lack of flair as a speaker rather than his apparently despotic intent that seems to annoy Byron most. This 'Orator of such set trash of phrase' (*Don Juan*, 'Dedication', 13), who cannot 'speak English', is an insult to an establishment that Burke had graced.[5]

Byron's pleasure in rhetoric distances him from Paine, but they clearly share an interest in the (corrupt) power structures of public discourse, an issue also at the heart of several of Byron's later plays, including *Sardanapalus*, *Marino Faliero* and, as we have seen, *Cain*. These concerns are brought to the centre of the Preface via two quotations from Voltaire: 'La pudeur s'est enfuite des couers, et s'est refugiée sur les lèvres' and 'Plus les moeurs sont dépravés, plus les expressions deviennent mesurées; on croit regagner en langage ce qu'on a perdu en vertu'.[6] Thus understood, language is not a forum for honest communication and discussion, but a way of reacquiring, in debased form, the virtue we have lost through our actions. It becomes, by implication, a means of normalizing the immoral.

Byron usually, in attacking this most egregious form of cant, has one eye on the figure of the contemporary poet, as he does in this unflattering invocation of Wellington:

> Though Britain owes (and pays you too) so much,
>> Yet Europe doubtless owes you greatly more:
> You have repaired Legitimacy's crutch, –
>> A prop not quite so certain as before:
> The Spanish, and the French, as well as Dutch,
>> Have seen, and felt, how strongly you *restore*;
> And Waterloo has made the world your debtor –
> (I wish your bards would sing it rather better).
>
> (*Don Juan*, ix, 3)

The authority of the European *ancien régime*, although it has been 'repaired' through military action, has nonetheless been called into question to an irreversible extent. This enervation of traditional power structures, however, is being offset by the poetically weak but politically coercive poets of the establishment – including, for Byron, the turncoats Wordsworth and Southey. The bottom line (literally here) is not martial action or moral truth but the conscience of the writer.

Byron's siege cantos comprehend and oppose this complicity between corrupt politics and unreflective writing. They make a case, in the process, for the human importance of poetry as a means of (re)connecting virtue with expression and action. They urge, perhaps more clear-sightedly than any other section of the poem, their reader to *think* – not just about the immediate consequences of war, but about its connection with written culture: 'Cockneys of London! Muscadins of Paris! / Just ponder what a pious pastime war is / Think how the joys of reading a Gazette / Are purchased by all agonies and crimes' (*Don Juan*, viii, 124–5). Thinking here isn't easy because it requires us to distinguish between propaganda and poetry. What we have to help us is a poem that is rigorously honest about its own status as 'outline'.

* * *

Byron's responses to war are remarkably diverse and shaped by a series of not always consistent factors. These include his self-identifying hero worship of Napoleon; his desire, one he acted upon, to become a military hero; his reformist, even radical, political leanings; his self-conscious membership of the English ruling class; his Whig inheritance; his keen sensitivity to unnecessary suffering; his detestation of imperial expansionism, and his sheer enthusiasm for history. This psychological complexity is matched by Byron's formal, thematic and stylistic diversity as a war writer. The Oriental Tales, which supplanted Scott's more domestic military romances as the most popular fictional works of their day, are populated by guerrilla heroes and chivalrous, mysterious freedom fighters. It was a form Byron never quite abandoned, taking it through to *The Island* (1823), a poem that although based in the heroic action of earlier narratives is also touched by the comic modes of *Don Juan*. *Childe Harold's Pilgrimage*, while emerging from the romance tradition, is also an edgily modern political poem that assesses Britain's role in the Peninsula War (in canto i) and analyses the career of Napoleon and the climactic event of Waterloo (in canto iii) – a subject Byron would return to in *The Age of Bronze* (1823). The former also includes, in its final canto, a powerful vision of the battle of Thrasimene. Byron's obvious interest in siege warfare is also explored in *The Siege of Corinth* (1816) and *The Deformed Transformed* (1824). The majority of his historical plays have military action and its political contexts at their centre.

One of Byron's earliest poetic responses to war comes in the first canto of *Childe Harold's Pilgrimage*, which was published in 1812 on Byron's return from his tour of Portugal, Spain and the Levant. Echoing what had been a general outcry back in England, Byron laments the Convention of Cintra (1808)[7] which allowed the French army to retreat largely unscathed following their defeat by British forces at Vimiero. Reporting on location (the treaty was signed at the Palace of Queluz), Byron's narrator scorns decisions that were not, it would appear, in the national interest: 'Behold the hall where chiefs were late conven'd! / Oh! Dome displeasing unto British eye!' (*Childe Harold's Pilgrimage*, i, 24).

Perhaps the most displeasing thing for Byron was not Cintra's apparent failure of British interests, but its betrayal of the heroic tradition that inhabits his poem's Spenserian stanzas:

> Convention is the dwarfish demon styl'd
> That foil'd the knights in Marialva's dome:
> Of brains (if brains they had) he them beguil'd,
> And turn'd a nation's shallow joy to gloom.
> Here Folly dash'd to earth the victor's plume,
> And Policy regain'd what arms had lost:
> For chiefs like ours in vain may laurels bloom!
> Woe to the conqu'ring, not the conquer'd host,
> Since baffled Triumph droops on Lusitania's coast!
>
> (*Childe Harold's Pilgrimage*, i, 25)

Byron's lines are fairly uncontroversial and there is no sympathy for

Napoleon, who appears in this context as the invader of independent countries, and as driving a project of imperialist expansion. What has been failed here is not the cause of liberty in a modern political sense but the ideals of an imagined past set ringing by the rhymes 'victor's plume' and 'laurel's bloom'. 'Policy' has reversed the rightful and honourable outcomes of military conflict ('Woe to the conqu'ring, not the conquer'd host') and 'Triumph' has been 'baffled' into a corner.

Byron's chivalric sense of things, however, coexists with a more modern and critical response to armed conflict. Where the traditions he mourns are designed to celebrate the qualities and achievements of the glorious individual, the reality is that in modern warfare, with its long-range weaponry and leaders who do not lead from the front, such heroes are not readily available. It was a problem that would generate the initiating irony of *Don Juan*:

> I WANT a hero: an uncommon want,
>> When every year and month sends forth a new one,
> Till, after cloying the gazettes with cant,
>> The age discovers he is not the true one
>
>> (*Don Juan*, i, 1)

Don Juan's textually sophisticated recognition that the scene of heroism has been emptied of truth and refilled with cant is anticipated by the simpler analysis of the Cintra poetry:

> Enough of Battle's minions! let them play
> Their games of lives, and barter breath for fame:
> Fame that will scarce reanimate their clay,
> Though thousands fall to deck some single name.
>> (*Childe Harold's Pilgrimage*, i, 44)

'Fame', which in the later poem would morph into the cant of the gazettes, is recognized as a bloodthirsty and deeply undemocratic mistress as the price, in human life, for decking a 'single name' can run into the thousands. Byron's longing for the past – and its rhetorical presence – is juxtaposed with suspicions about the textual conventions of elegy.

Byron's strong sense of heroic continuity endured another crisis in 1814 when Napoleon was exiled to Elba. Later that year he wrote *Lara*, a poem set in a country bristling with revolutionary anger at its oppressive and corrupt ruling elite. Byron's politics, however, are by no means straightforwardly the politics of revolution: 'Within that land was many a malcontent, / Who cursed the tyranny to which he bent' (*Lara*, ii, 57–8).[8] The pejoratives are balanced across both sides of the couplet: Byron anticipates Dickens's sense, in *A Tale of Two Cities*, that the 'malcontent' is not uncritically to be preferred to the tyrant who breeds him. Heroism, moreover, which is embodied by the returning figure of Lara himself, is clearly dissociated from democratic interests: 'What cared he for the freedom of the crowd? / He raised the humble but to bend the proud' (*Lara*, ii, 252–3). Heroic action appears to have retreated into the sphere of personal whim and the fatalism of Byronic gloom.

The disappointments of *Lara* flow into Byron's *Ode to Napoleon Buonaparte* (1814), which deals directly with the poet's disillusionment at Napoleon's abdication. Part evocation of Ecclesiastes, part self-dramatization, Byron's ode is notable for its fine turns of political thought and complex tapestry of allusions. Its 'meditation on flawed heroism results in a poem of fractured tones and feelings'.[9] Key to the poem's intertextual manoeuvring is Shakespeare, through whom, as Simon Bainbridge suggests, Byron is able to 'recast Napoleon in the role of the Shakespearean hero'. This recasting mitigates Byron's disappointment that in his abdication 'Napoleon had failed to play the part of the Shakespearean tragic hero that [Byron] had scripted for him'.[10] The intricate and abundant literary life of the *Ode*, that is, helps to offset a reality in which heroic ideals have been let down by their most promising recent aspirant. Classical honour, as at Cintra, has been betrayed by modernity, and Byron's response is to invoke the sanctity of literary tradition in one of its most elite forms.

If Byron has one eye on Shakespeare, then the other is on Johnson, specifically *The Vanity of Human Wishes*, which provides the *Ode* both with its high moral tone and its model (Johnson's Charles XII) for the depiction of Napoleon's demise. Where Charles, after his fall from the heights of ambition, is 'Condemn'd a needy Supplicant to wait / While Ladies interpose, and Slaves debate' (*The Vanity of Human Wishes*, 213–14),[11] Byron's Napoleon, where he had been 'The Arbiter of other's fate' is now reduced to being 'A Suppliant for his own!' (*Ode to Napoleon Buonaparte*, 39–40). Johnson's famously decisive conclusion – 'He left the Name, at which the World grew pale, / To point a Moral, or adorn a Tale' (*The Vanity of Human Wishes*, 221–2) – is also present in Byron's 'Oh! ne'er may tyrant leave behind / A brighter name to lure mankind!' (*Ode to Napoleon Buonaparte*, 89–90). Where Johnson's stately couplet is glacially calm, however, Byron's accusatory exclamation is far less steady.[12] For all his morality his response remains in part that of the reader of romances who feels he has not got his money's worth. He has been taken in, 'lured' by a bright name that has turned out to be an *ignis fatuus*. Heroic narrative may be dismissed by Johnson ('adorn a Tale'), but for Byron it is too pressingly real to abandon. If Johnson's Charles fulfils his moral purpose by leaving a name, Byron's Napoleon will never be forgiven for *losing* his:

> 'Tis done – but yesterday a King!
>   And arm'd with Kings to strive –
> And now thou art a nameless thing
>   So abject – yet alive!
>
> *(Ode to Napoleon Buonaparte, 1–4)*

By failing to provide appropriate narrative closure for his spectacular career, Napoleon has compromised the tradition he was born to extend and glorify. He has also failed his poet in not affording him suitable materials.

Byron's response to Napoleon is marked by contrary thrusts, one coming from his partial subscription to the anti-war sentiments represented by Johnson, the other from his cherished belief in literary heroism. This is the poet's journal entry on hearing of Napoleon's abdication:

> I don't know – but I think *I*, even *I* (an insect compared with this creature), have set my life on casts not a millionth part of this man's. But, after all, a crown may not be worth dying for. Yet to outlive *Lodi* for this!!! Oh that Juvenal or Johnson could rise from the dead! [...] Alas! this imperial diamond hath a flaw in it, and is now hardly fit to stick in a glazier's pencil: – the pen of the historian won't rate it worth a ducat. (*BLJ*, iii, 256–7)

The shift from 'imperial diamond' through 'glazier's pencil' to 'the pen of the historian' is slick, but its peevishness is also telling. As in the *Ode*, Byron's disappointment leads him to consign Napoleon over to the morality of Johnson. The problem, however, is that he isn't thinking about Napoleon as Johnson would have, as an exemplar of unsustainable ambition. Nor is he thinking – for that matter – of Napoleon the reformer or liberal administrator. His imagination lights instead upon the battle of Lodi, one of the brilliant early victories that highlighted Napoleon's heroic resourcefulness, spirit and sheer will. Where the historian's pen seems obliged to record Napoleon as a failure, the poet struggles to transcend linear narrative and its promise of decline. He is searching for something that the poet of the siege cantos will find on the other side of analysis.

Byron's poetic interest in siege warfare begins amidst the bleakness of *The Siege of Corinth*. Based loosely around a Turkish assault of

1715, the poem describes a grimly ironic rather than a heroic sequence of events: the repulsed Turkish invaders are suddenly decimated by the accidental explosion of their own powder magazine; this drives them on to fury and slaughter where parley and compromise had looked more likely. Rather than being dictated by extraordinary acts of individual will, the narrative is shaped by the sheer blankness of circumstance. Even the poem's hero figure Alp seems spare and dispirited, as much a passive observer of events as a determining partaker.

Through Alp's eyes we see little of the laurel and plume side of war, the poem's interests being more with the ghoulish aftermath of the siege:

> And he saw the lean dogs beneath the wall
> Hold o'er the dead their carnival,
> Gorging and growling o'er carcass and limb;
> They were too busy to bark at him!
> From a Tartar's skull they had stripp'd the flesh,
> As ye peel the fig when the fruit is fresh;
> And their white tusks crunch'd o'er the whiter skull,
> As it slipp'd through their jaws, when their edge grew dull,
> As they lazily mumbled the bones of the dead,
>
> (*The Siege of Corinth*, 409–17)

Alp's stillness, his lack of heroic energy, makes his numb witnessing of the scene all the more effective. This is poetry where vigorous action ('had stripp'd') is in a past tense that has lapsed into a present of hideous enervation ('lazily mumbled'). More uncomfortable still, at least for John Murray's leisured reader,[13] is that quick shift into the second person ('ye peel the fig') that leaves us just one quick metaphor away from a dog stripping the flesh from a dead soldier's skull. Byron's poetry here is anti-voyeuristic even in the midst of its voyeurism; it is charged with criticism and anticipates, in less direct terms, the emphasis on readerly thought in the siege poetry of *Don Juan*. It is also, however, poetry devoid of hope, not just in modern warfare but in itself as a means of reconciling action with virtue.

The *Siege of Corinth* was the first of Byron's poems to be published after the event of Waterloo, a fact which may help to explain its pervasive gloom. A more direct response to the iconic battle of the age comes in the third canto of *Childe Harold's Pilgrimage*, written later the same year. Shortly after leaving England for the final time, Byron visited Brussels where he stayed with some old friends of his mother. He was keen to visit the nearby battlefield at Waterloo, although when he arrived he was observed to view the scene in a sombre mood, after which he galloped over the field, probably re-enacting some of the cavalry charges.[14]

Compared to his account of Cintra (published almost four years after the fact), Byron was now writing much closer to the event, his stanzas emerging amidst a flurry of Waterloo pamphlets and poems, the bulk of which are notable for their celebratory bombast and unreflecting patriotism. At the more thoughtful end of the spectrum was Scott, who, like Byron, was one of the first Waterloo tourists. His *The Field of Waterloo*, written to raise a subscription for the battle's many widows, mixes quiet wariness with conventional chivalric eulogy:

> Period of honour as of woes,
> What bright careers 'twas thine to close!
> Mark'd on thy roll of blood what names
> To Briton's memory, and to Fame's,
> Laid there their last immortal claims!
> Thou saw'st in seas of gore expire
> Redoubted Picton's soul of fire,
> Saw'st in the mingled carnage lie
> All that of Ponsonby could die,
> De Lancey change Love's bridal-wreath
> For laurels from the hand of Death,
> Saw'st gallant Miller's failing eye
> Still bent where Albion's banners fly,
> And Cameron in the shock of steel
> Die like the offspring of Lochiel;
> And generous Gordon, 'mid the strife
> Fall while he watched his leader's life.[15]

Scott begins by balancing war's twin outcomes, 'honour' and 'woes', but it is the former, through his emphasis on 'bright careers' and 'names' that comes to dominate our experience of his lines. The heroic officers stand out from an aestheticized and de-individuated backdrop made up of phrases such as 'roll of blood', 'seas of gore', 'mingled carnage' and 'shock of steel'. Scott's rhetorical geography has the effect of eliding the experience of the rank and file soldiery, an unintended outcome, but, looked at from Paine's point of view at least, an inescapably political one.[16]

Byron's response to Waterloo, which deplores the Congress of Vienna and is far from orthodox in its take on the vanquished Napoleon, is very different to Scott's. There are, however, some similarities. Like Scott, Byron uses archaic poetic diction to describe the British commanders, including the Duke of Brunswick (George III's nephew, who was killed at Quatre Bras), or 'Brunswick's fated chieftain' (*Childe Harold's Pilgrimage*, iii, 23). Byron also, like Scott, uses the weight of his rhetoric to distinguish particular individuals, as when he singles out Frederick Howard, who was killed at Waterloo:

> Their praise is hymn'd by loftier harps than mine;
> Yet one I would select from that proud throng,
> Partly because they blend me with his line,
> And partly that I did his sire some wrong,
> And partly that bright names will hallow song;
> And his was of the bravest, and when shower'd
> The death-bolts deadliest the thinn'd files along,
> Even where the thickest of war's tempest lower'd,
> They reach'd no nobler breast than thine, young, gallant Howard!
>
>   (*Childe Harold's Pilgrimage*, iii, 29)

Howard is brought forth from a 'throng' that is acknowledged but then pushed to the background in phrases such as 'thinn'd files' and 'war's tempest'. Where similar acts of selectiveness in Scott's poem are broadly untroubled, however, Byron is far more self-conscious about narrowing his focus. He talks his reader through his reasons, clearly feeling a need to justify himself. Partly his motives are personal (Howard was Byron's cousin); partly they come from a perceived obligation to tradition ('bright names will hallow song'). Byron seems uneasy, however, about turning the spotlight on his own family where thousands have perished – he may also be recalling past problems with 'bright names' (Napoleon's 'brighter name') and his attempts to establish them in 'song'. The stanza seems haunted by an apprehension that writing about war has become a precarious, untrustworthy activity.

The stringing out of 'gallant Howard' at the end of an overgrown alexandrine tells of Byron's anxieties about the heroic mode. It also suggests the displacement of the hero himself, the emptying of a central space that can no longer be filled unproblematically by the allegedly exceptional individual. Byron responds to this emptiness by activating the energies of self and adapting history for the purposes of self-analysis:[17]

> And Harold stands upon this place of skulls,
> The grave of France, the deadly Waterloo!
> How in an hour the power which gave annuls
> Its gifts, transferring fame as fleeting too!
> In 'pride of place' here last the eagle flew,
> Then tore with bloody talon the rent plain,
> Pierced by the shaft of banded nations through;

Ambition's life and labours all were vain;
He wears the shattered links of the world's broken chain.
(Childe Harold's Pilgrimage, iii, 18)

For Johnson, the stanza's penultimate line would always be the end of the matter, but Byron lingers in his disappointment into the thick vowels of his alexandrine. He needs every syllable he can find to come to terms with what has happened. This turning away from world to self, however, confers upon the latter a new heroic momentum.

Where, in the *Ode*, Byron rewrites Napoleon as Shakespearean tragic hero, here he absorbs him:

But quiet to quick bosoms is a hell,
And *there* hath been thy bane; there is a fire
And motion of the soul which will not dwell
In its own narrow being, but aspire
Beyond the fitting medium of desire;
And, but once kindled, quenchless evermore,
Preys upon high adventure, nor can tire
Of aught but rest; a fever at the core,
Fatal to him who bears, to all who ever bore.
(Childe Harold's Pilgrimage, iii, 42)

After the perfectly deployed semicolon of the second line (one of Byron's favoured dashes would not do here) the narrator abandons the second-person address that marks Napoleon's individuality, shifting instead to a generalized account of the Byronic psyche in which Napoleon is subsumed.[18] If the military 'hero' can no longer be relied upon to represent the traditions of virtue and honour, then his role will need to be reassigned. Byron's solution is to assume the burden himself, to become, as exiled poet, not just the custodian of heroic tradition but its uncertain agent. His present ('who bears') may be one of suffering, but at least it *is* a present, a submerged possibility, one, moreover, in direct correspondence with a past of 'all who ever bore'.

* * *

Byron's war poetry leading up to and concerning Waterloo demonstrates a strong attachment to a heroic tradition under pressure from unheroic modern realities and the poet's own sense of political urgency. Much of the poetry's tense thoughtfulness – and resistance to simple political paraphrase – is a consequence of Byron's inability to resolve these apparently contending impulses. This breakdown of tradition also turns

Byron inwards, most strikingly in the figure of the Byronic poet-hero, in search of answers. The problem with the Harold poet as tradition's embattled standard bearer, however, is his limited scope for analysis. The traditional virtues represented by the poetry of the past had not simply been abandoned and replaced by a corrupt modernity; they had been co-opted and subsumed at the level of rhetoric. The truth of political events was being falsely but persuasively claimed by the kinds of bad writing Byron saw as simultaneously misrepresenting the sublime and propping up legitimacy. His own earlier poetry, something the Byron of *Don Juan* often reflects upon critically, was too close to these problems to be part of the solution.

If Byron was going to revise the traditions of war writing he would first need to step outside of their agreed parameters. This would require a mode of poetry highly sensitized to its own representations. At Waterloo slaughter is tidied up in phrases such as 'thinn'd files'; at Ismail a decimated column of troops is described as 'now reduced [...] Into an elegant extract (much less massy) / Of heroism' (*Don Juan*, viii, 34). Both sidestep the blood and guts, but where the former does this as an inevitable consequence of rhetorical convention, the latter foregrounds and draws attention to the transformative nature of the written. This newly robust and reflexive written style was perfectly calibrated to register the distortions being forced upon the realities of war by writers that in Byron's view were motivated by entirely the wrong interests. Thus, also, the pointedly irrelevant choice of Juan as hero:

> Brave men were living before Agamemnon
>   And since, exceeding valorous and sage,
> A good deal like him too, though quite the same none;
>   But then they shone not on the poet's page,
> And so have been forgotten: – I condemn none,
>   But can't find any in the present age
> Fit for my poem (that is, for my new one);
> So, as I said, I'll take my friend Don Juan.
>
> (*Don Juan*, i, 5)

Byron's 'new' poem begins not by identifying contemporary heroic possibilities (such as those that had clustered around Napoleon) but by thinking through the processes of textual transmission. Crucial to this reimagining, as with the poet's visionary negotiation of 'infinite variety', will be reflexive acts of selection. Byron has (largely) ditched the role of elegist to think about how and why the individual emerges from the variety of 'Brave men' who have 'shone not on the poet's page'. His ironic choice of Juan, while reasserting his disappointment with an unheroic 'present age', also, however, marks the discovery of new comic, critical and formal energies. Juan may have no more character than the stilled hero of *The Siege of Corinth*, but his surrounding poetic environment is anything but listless. The poetry of endgame has been exchanged for a poetics of incipience.

As well as the selections upon which narrative depends, Byron also draws our attention to the critical possibilities of form. The now iconic misfitting of 'Juan' into the poem's rhyme scheme reflects modernity's heroic unfitness, a play on words resumed at Ismail when the poet struggles to fit the rapacious and (from an English poet's point of view, awkwardly named) Russian forces into his stanzas:[19]

> The Russians now were ready to attack;
>   But oh, ye Goddesses of war and glory!
> How shall I spell the name of each Cossacque
>   Who were immortal, could one tell their story?
> Alas! what to their memory can lack?
>   Achilles' self was not more grim and gory
> Than thousands of this new and polished nation,
> Whose names want nothing but – pronunciation.
>
> Still I'll record a few, if but to encrease
>   Our euphony – there was Strongenoff, and Strokonoff,
> Meknop, Serge Lwow, Arseniew of modern Greece,
>   And Tschitsshakoff, and Rougenoff, and Chokenoff,
> And others of twelve consonants a-piece;
>   And more might be found out, if I could poke enough
> Into gazettes; but Fame (capricious strumpet)
> It seems, has got an ear as well as trumpet.
>
> (Don Juan, vii, 14–15)

As well as the unfortunate Turkish city, the very possibility of poetry – both as an aesthetic object and as a carrying forward of the past – is under threat. These 'names', and the 'new and polished nation' from which they arise, are not fit material for poetry; they belong, rather, in the 'gazettes' that Byron can barely bring himself to 'poke' into.

We might conclude from this that Byron has grown up into a proto-Marxist who now understood the writer's role strictly in terms of demystification and social progress.[20] There is something to this, but Byron's poetry is not so easily claimed for such unwavering positions. He remained healthily suspicions of the democratic and thus wary of the ends of unmasking; he also, for all *Don Juan*'s textual meltdown, remained deeply invested in traditional ideas of heroic virtue. The war poetry of *Don Juan* is not bent on annihilation, but wants to strike honest balances and make clear-sighted distinctions between good and bad acts of military intervention. Cooke captures this aspect of the siege cantos in describing them as Byron's 'most profound statement of counter-heroic principles, specifically deflating the hero of mere power, specifically celebrating the life of courage and virtue'.[21] If the poem rejects the military efforts of conquest as 'nothing but a child of Murder's rattles' (*Don Juan*, viii, 4), it also picks out counterexamples, such as the Tartar Khan, one of the 'truly brave' who defends his family and city to the last. He is an instance of how 'Compassion breathes along the savage mind' (*Don Juan*, viii, 106), of how virtue can emerge in the direst circumstances, and may even depend upon them.

Compare the poem's presentation of Leonidas and Washington:

Whose every battle-field is holy ground,
    Which breathes of nations saved, not worlds undone.
How sweetly on the ear such echoes sound!
    While the mere victor's may appal or stun
The servile and the vain, such names will be
A watchword till the future shall be free.

(*Don Juan*, viii, 5)

Where the names of the Russian aggressors are not and do not fit, the names of true heroism sound 'sweetly on the ear'; each is a 'watchword' that it is the poet's duty to preserve and transmit. Such names, which invoke moral beauty by association, are for Byron inherently pleasing; they are aesthetic objects in their own right. If the war poetry of *Don Juan* delves deeper than its predecessors into a sceptical critique of language and textual presence, then it is also claims that words can be instinct with virtue.

As is often the case, Byron is playing something of a double game. On the one hand he is determined to expose a false, modern heroics based in irresponsible acts of selection. On the other he still insists upon poetry's traditional right to elegy. The two aims are by no means incompatible, but their mutual presence means that Byron was involved in building structures very similar to those he was also in the process of toppling. Indeed, Byron has been accused of blundering badly here, notably with respect to his sudden (and admittedly rather odd) digression, amidst the flames of Ismail, on the idyllic life of Daniel Boone, the 'back-woodsman of Kentucky' (*Don Juan*, viii, 61),[22] who is presented as an ideal of rustic goodness and simplicity:

Crime came not near him – she is not the child
    Of Solitude; health shrank not from him – for
Her home is in the rarely-trodden wild,
    Where if men seek her not, and death be more
Their choice than life, forgive them, as beguiled
    By habit to what their own hearts abhor –
In cities caged. The present case in point I
Cite is, that Boon lived hunting up to ninety;

And what's still stranger, left behind a name
    For which men vainly decimate the throng,
Not only famous but of that *good* fame,
    Without which Glory's but a tavern song –
Simple, serene, the antipodes of shame,
    Which hate nor envy e'er could tinge with wrong;
An active hermit, even in age the child
Of Nature, or the Man of Ross run wild.

                                      (*Don Juan*, viii, 62–3)

Where Johnson forges the name bequeathed into a warning, Byron still
holds to the possibility that names 'left behind' can be emblems of pure
virtue. Of course, the fact that he has to swerve so dramatically from his
main subject to find such a name does not seem promising. It suggests an
unwilling admission on Byron's part, as Kelsall has it, 'that the vestiges
of incorruptibility are now beyond the Atlantic, and retreating ever
further westward'.[23] In saying this, virtue is not for Byron so strictly a
question of geography or indeed of the immediate present. Also in mind
here is the informing vitality of literary tradition, specifically represented
by Pope's 'Man of Ross', a figure of pure goodness whose very presence
magically banishes 'variance' and 'contest'.[24] What is perhaps more
striking than the allusion, however, is the risk Byron was prepared to
take in asserting the continuity of virtue within poetic writing. While
assembling an effective satire aimed at specific, deserving examples of
(morally) bad writing, he was also determined to keep in mind the
ideas of origin that validate true poetry. Whether he could find a more
convincing and relevant way of doing this than by swerving away to the
ultramontane figure of Boone remains to be seen.

                              * * *

The siege cantos of *Don Juan* relentlessly associate the politics of war
with the politics of authorship:

The Russian batteries were incomplete,
   Because they were constructed in a hurry;
Thus the same cause which makes a verse want feet,
   And throws a cloud o'er Longman and John Murray,
When the sale of new books is not so fleet
   As they who print them think it necessary,
May likewise put off for a time what story
Sometimes calls 'murder,' and at others 'glory.'

                                  (*Don Juan*, vii, 26)

The shoddiness of the Russian batteries, and the rushed rapacity it implies, flows into a reflection on the decline of poetry under the pressure of political and market forces. Driven by a common principle of gain, the arts of war and literature have both abandoned the honesty of genuine craft. In the case of the Russians this poor workmanship is briefly if darkly merciful in putting off 'for a time' widespread loss of life. The literary equivalent – the war poetry that is being hacked out for all the wrong reasons – suffers from a lack of moral clarity. Unlike Byron's scrupulously reflexive narratives such stories are not honest about their acts of selection; they cannot be trusted, therefore, to distinguish 'murder' from 'glory'.

High on Byron's list of targets, again, was Wordsworth, who Byron attacked not just as a mistaken poet of the sublime but as a dishonest poet of war. The two failings, for Byron, were closely linked, the 'narrowness' or written misapprehension of the beyond detected in *The Excursion* following a similar pattern to the questionably selective post-Waterloo *Thanksgiving Odes* of 1816. The two longest of these poems imagine the post-victory celebrations back in a Britain that glows with patriotic sanctity:

But Thou art foremost in the field: – there stand:
Receive the triumph destined to thy hand!
All States have glorified themselves; – their claims
Are weighed by Providence, in balance even;
And now, in preference to the mightiest names,
To thee the exterminating sword is given.[25]

Scott had ushered the rank and file into his poem's background imagery, but Wordsworth goes a step further by losing even the 'mightiest names' of Waterloo in a blinding blaze of divine glory. God himself, with 'exterminating sword' in hand, becomes agent of, as well as justification for, military conflict. God even assumes a parental responsibility for killing:

But Thy most dreaded instrument,
In working out a pure intent,
Is Man – arrayed for mutual slaughter,
 - Yea, Carnage is thy daughter![26]

Byron could hardly be expected to miss the opportunity:

The columns were in movement one and all,
   But of the portion which attacked by water,
Thicker than leaves the lives began to fall,
   Though led by Arseniew, that great son of Slaughter,
As brave as ever faced both bomb and ball.
   'Carnage' (so Wordsworth tells you) 'is God's daughter:'
If *he* speak truth, she is Christ's sister, and
Just now behaved as in the Holy Land.

                                        (*Don Juan*, viii, 9)

Wordsworth's maladroit earnestness, his carelessness with human life and his unwitting travesty of Christianity are simultaneously deplored. What links these failings with the Wordsworthian sublime for Byron is their closed-down, sham evocation of the text's prevenient object. What is on the page, in both cases, does not stand in an honest relation to what the page cannot directly comprehend. True visionary process has been hijacked, respectively, by a Romantic rhetoric of ego and by establishment forces that have turned Wordsworth's coat and, through him, churned out a bankrupt theology of smug, nationalistic violence. By way of riposte, Byron deploys a typically deft and expansive joke ('she is Christ's sister') that follows Wordsworth's logic in order to haul it back into a semblance of the complexity it blithely overlooks.

The most important text for the spinning out of Byron's critical vision in the siege cantos of *Don Juan* is Castelnau's *Essai sur l'Histoire ancienne et moderne de la Nouvelle Russie* (1820). This was Byron's main historical source for the siege cantos, one he followed 'very closely to ensure his story's accuracy in all particulars'.[27] Byron uses Castelnau, however, to do more than get his facts right. By playing off an apparently factual but in fact politically interested account of the siege he could explore the swerves and deceptions that occur during the transmission of historical events.[28] Typically, Byron is interested not just in the events of narrative but in the moral dynamics of their selection:

'If' (says the historian here) 'I could report
   All that the Russians did upon this day,
I think that several volumes would fall short,

> And I should still have many things to say;'
> And so he says no more – but pays his court
>   To some distinguished strangers in that fray;
> The Prince de Ligne, and Langeron, and Damas,
> Names great as any that the roll of Fame has.
>
> (*Don Juan*, vii, 32)

Castelnau is right, of course, to say that he cannot describe everything that has happened during the siege simply because such events will always outstrip the capacities of the written. His reflexiveness, however, is revealed to be corrupt due to its obsequious logic. The space he does have has not been used, as it should be according to Byron's ethics of vision, to assemble a simulacrum of human and political reality (a 'miniature' or 'outline'); it is dominated, rather, by the author's paying court to the 'Prince de Ligne' and other powerful, although not necessarily heroic, figures.

The workings and limitations of historical narrative are never far from Byron's thoughts as he constructs his account of the siege:

> History can only take things in the gross;
>   But could we know them in detail, perchance
> In balancing the profit and the loss,
>   War's merit it by no means might enhance,
>
> (*Don Juan*, viii, 3)

It may be that an 'outline is the best' for the purposes of responsible visionary and imaginative writing, but this is not the same as taking things 'in the gross'.[29] Our narratives can never comprehend complex events in their full 'detail', but to know this is to inherit a responsibility, one with respect to which both Wordsworth and Castelnau have been found grossly wanting. War, Byron's narrator recognizes, is inescapably a textual construct, a fact also apparent to Sardanapalus in his exchanges with his brave – but textually uncritical – advisor Salemenes:

> SARDAPALUS. I understand thee – thou wouldst have me go
>   Forth as a conqueror. By all the stars
>   Which the Chaldeans read! the restless slaves
>   Deserve that I should curse them with their wishes,
>   And lead them forth to glory.
> SALEMENES.   Wherefore not?
>   Semiramis – a woman only – led
>   These our Assyrians to the solar shores
>   Of Ganges.
> SARDAPALUS. 'Tis most true. And *how* returned?

SALEMENES. Why, like a *man* – a hero; baffled, but
   Not vanquish'd. With but twenty guards, she made
   Good her retreat to Bactria.
                    And how many
   Left she behind in India to the vultures?
SALEMENES. Our annals say not.
SARDAPALUS.   Then I will say for them –
   That she had better woven within her palace
   Some twenty garments, than with twenty guards
   Have fled to Bactria, leaving to the ravens,
   And wolves, and men – the fiercer of the three,
   Her myriads of fond subjects. Is *this* glory?
   Then let me live in ignominy ever.

                    (*Sardanapalus*, I, ii, 121–39)

The heroism of an apparently masculine woman is offered as a spur to an apparently feminine and dilatory ruler. Sardanapalus's response, however, is not one of cowardice or lazy luxuriousness but of critical reading. Where the Assyrian 'annals' from which Salemenes draws are at pains to record and celebrate the event described, they are less forthcoming about the general loss of life upon which 'Glory' generally depends. Sardanapalus's response to this, rather like the narrator of *Don Juan*, is to draw attention to the gaps in the narrative to which he is being made subject. By speaking 'for them' he becomes a revisionary author, one concerned with correcting the processes of interested textual manipulation.

Similar processes are again explored, darkly and brilliantly, in the figure of Suwarrow, the commander of the Russian forces at Ismail. For Castelnau, Suwarrow is the great conquering hero; for Byron he is a rather more complex figure. Unlike Sardanapalus, Suwarrow has the right qualities to get the job done, qualities that in other circumstances might have made him a Leonidas or Washington. The line between greatness and infamy, as Byron had learned with Napoleon, can be a very fine one:

A single step into the right had made
This man the Washington of worlds betrayed;
A single step into the wrong has given
His name a doubt to all the winds of heaven;

                (*The Age of Bronze*, 233–6)

Unlike Napoleon's, however, Suwarrow's career has provided few opportunities to step into the right, and his immersion in butchery has eroded any moral sensibility he may have had ('habit sears / Men's hearts against whole millions' (*Don Juan*, vii, 69)). Where Lara, the Byronic nobleman, evades the taint of his corrupt homeland – 'long absence from his native clime / Had left him stainless of oppression's crime' (*Lara*, ii, 170–1) – Suwarrow is a grotesque emanation of the modern imperialist state. He is also an aspiring poet. On finally overrunning Ismail, he 'threw', we are told, 'Into a Russian couplet rather dull / The whole gazette of thousands whom he slew' (*Don Juan*, ix, 60). A hideously careless written compression of human life links Suwarrow with Wordsworth and also, more explicitly, with the 'gross' historian encountered above:

> Suwarrow, – who but saw things in the gross,
>   Being much too gross to see them in detail,
> Who calculated life as so much dross,
>   And as the wind a widowed nation's wail,
> And cared as little for his army's loss
>   (So that their efforts should at length prevail)
> As wife and friends did for the boils of Job, –
> What was't to him to hear two women sob?
>
> (*Don Juan*, vii, 77)

Like Castelnau, Suwarrow is guilty of a profound failure to see 'in detail', something Byron connects simultaneously with a weak apprehension of literary form and with an allegiance to the grotesque forces of tyranny, specifically, in Suwarrow's case, Catherine the Great, to whom he sends his poem as tribute. The narrator's wide-scoping role, in response to this, is one of ironic counterbalance. He offsets Suwarrow's mis-scripting of his soldiers as so much 'dross' with a telling allusion to Job, the type of the afflicted and neglected Christian hero. He also reorganizes the traditional geographies of eulogy to emphasize the human facts of collateral damage. Where we might expect the poet to save his most striking images for his main character or hero, Byron's lyric tribute, in the form of the haunting, echoing 'as the wind a widowed nation's wail', is directed offstage.

This insistence on the innocent victim repeatedly complicates the claims of rhetoric, tradition and even grammatical order:

> The town was entered: first one column made
>   Its sanguinary way good – then another;
> The reeking bayonet and the flashing blade
>   Clashed 'gainst the scymitar, and babe and mother
> With distant shrieks were heard Heaven to upbraid; –
>   Still closer sulphury clouds began to smother

The breath of Morn and Man, where foot by foot
The maddened Turks their city still dispute.

(*Don Juan*, viii, 69)

'The reeking bayonet', 'flashing blade' and clashing 'scymitar' are recalled
from the same collective memory bank as *Lara*'s 'And flash the scimitars,
and rings the steel' (*Lara*, ii, 363). What is different here is the manner
in which Byron brings the 'babe and mother' up close to the edge of
his otherwise conventional 'blade'. Separated from 'Clashed' only by the
comma after 'scymitar', and hidden from their intended verb ('upbraid')
by the enjambment, the defenceless pair, in a stanza that compels rapid
reading, seem to invite an illogical but ghoulish misapprehension. The
easily stumbled upon clash of 'scymitar' with 'babe and mother' amidst
the ringing echoes of 'bayonet' – 'blade' – 'babe' is as disturbing as it
is logically incorrect.

The narrative of *Lara*, as well as an eye for disturbing detail, has a
strong pictorial feel in its aestheticized framing of war's aftermath:

Day glimmers on the dying and the dead,
The cloven cuirass, and the helmless head;
The war-horse masterless is on the earth,
And that last gasp hath burst his bloody girth;

(*Lara*, ii, 394–5)

Compare this to *Don Juan*, and its critical concern with its own subject
matter:

But here I leave the general concern,
    To track our hero on his path of fame:
He must his laurels separately earn;
    For fifty thousand heroes, name by name,
Though all deserving equally to turn
    A couplet, or an elegy to claim,
Would form a lengthy lexicon of glory,
And what is worse still, a much longer story.

(*Don Juan*, viii, 17)

The narrator's decision to 'leave the general concern' in order to
concentrate on Juan ('we must give the greater number / To the
Gazette' (*Don Juan*, viii, 18)) should immediately put us on our guard
because it mimics the strategies of Castelnau (Byron even recycles the
latter's excuse of not having enough space). It also recalls and further
problematizes Byron's decision to zoom away to Boone at a point where
his responsibilities seem to lie elsewhere. What is happening is that

in order to make us think Byron has morphed into the object of his own critique. He raises, to the highest possible pitch, the issue of trust between reader and author by probing the relation between immediate narrative moment and the 'much longer story' of which his fragments ceaselessly give notice.

Acts of selection and extraction crop up in the siege cantos with unwavering regularity. Here, an apparently heroic senior officer rescues a Prince:

> Also the General Markow, Brigadier,
>   Insisting on removal of *the Prince*
> Amidst some groaning thousands dying near,–
>   All common fellows, who might writhe, and wince,
> And shriek for water into a deaf ear, –
>   The General Markow, who could thus evince
> His sympathy for rank, by the same token,
> To teach him greater, had his own leg broken.
>
> (*Don Juan*, viii, 11)

As Cochran notes, Byron takes the incident directly from Castelnau.[30] What he adds to the latter's less than democratic account are the 'common fellows' placed in the centre of the stanza, an addition that allows him to highlight the coercive strategies of his source. Where Castelnau's reader is encouraged to approve Markow's actions, Byron's reader is confronted with a more problematic reading experience. The *Prince* may be distinguished on the page, but, rather like Bowles's capitalized absolutes, his distinction is forced and hollow. Our attention (unless we have a 'deaf ear') is more likely to be grabbed by the arresting literary effects that follow, the drawn out vowels and piercing alliteration that commemorate the writhing and wincing 'thousands dying near'. If, in the cant-ridden world of Castlereagh and Castelnau, the conventions of heroic writing can no longer be trusted, we can, Byron suggests, still put our faith in the clear-sightedness and craft of the genuine poet. Realigned with a linguistic past that Byron both cherishes and questions, the small-scale but resounding immediacies of lyric writing are brilliantly reasserted.

Byron's anxieties about the hearing of his readers were well founded, especially when it comes to the tricky but fundamental question of Juan's heroism. On the one hand, Byron's least likely hero is an admirably brave soldier, particularly when compared with his mercenary colleague Johnson, who runs away when the odds become unpromising. On the other, he seems scarcely admirable in that he is not defending his home from invaders (as Conrad, for instance, does in *The Corsair*), but has enlisted in a foreign army for no other apparent reason than to quench 'The thirst / Of Glory' (*Don Juan*, viii, 52). There can be nothing glorious, however, about Juan and Johnson's willingness 'To burn a town which never did them harm' (*Don Juan*, vii, 76). The problem, as usual, is the absence of a corresponding act of mind to regulate martial action. Juan and his colleague fight 'thoughtlessly enough to win, / To their *two* selves, *one* whole bright bulletin' (*Don Juan*, viii, 19). Their lack of reflection befits them only for the most debased forms of war writing, the bulletins and gazettes that reconstitute chaotic slaughter as neat lists of names.

War, luckily for Juan, has a habit of throwing up opportunities for redemption. His occurs when he encounters the orphaned Turkish child Leila in grave danger at the hands of the brutish Russian invaders. At the risk of his own life Juan gallantly saves the girl from destruction, thus mitigating, as more than one commentator has pointed out, his otherwise suspect contributions to the siege.[31] Thorslev may be right in saying that Juan 'does not seem at all to share a common paternity' with the majority of Byronic heroes,[32] but his rescue of Leila, nonetheless, places him right at the centre of Byronic heroic consciousness. His act of courage recalls Byron's own (alleged) heroism in saving a young Turkish woman from being drowned,[33] an episode the poet, who traded on intriguing overlaps between autobiography and fiction, had refigured in *The Giaour* (1813), where the eponymous hero avenges the drowning of his beloved (also called Leila) by the Turk Hassan. The incident also recalls *The Corsair* when Conrad heroically conveys Gulnare 'From reeking pile and combat's wreck – away –' during a 'pause compassion snatched from war' (*The Corsair*, ii, 222, 227). Juan, it seems, has stepped back towards the right by acting upon his poem's wisdom: the 'drying up a single tear has more / Of honest fame, than shedding seas of gore' (*Don Juan*, viii, 3).

What Cronin refers to as a 'sentimental [...] episode',[34] however, is in fact a radical challenge to our conditioning as readers. The manner of Byron's narration cuts against the emotionalism often drawn by such incidents. After two powerful stanzas (*Don Juan*, viii, 87–8) describing the devastating effects of the Russian victory, the narrator becomes exhausted with his 'awful topic' and, once again, leaves the 'general concern' in order to 'track' his hero:

And one good action in the midst of crimes
   Is 'quite refreshing,' in the affected phrase
Of these ambrosial, Pharisaic times,

> With all their pretty milk-and-water ways,
> And may serve therefore to bedew these rhymes,
>   A little scorched at present with the blaze
> Of conquest and its consequences, which
> Make Epic poesy so rare and rich.
>
> Upon a taken bastion where there lay
>   Thousands of slaughtered men, a yet warm group
> Of murdered women, who had found their way
>   To this vain refuge, made the good heart droop
> And shudder; – while, as beautiful as May,
>   A female child of ten years tried to stoop
> And hide her little palpitating breast
> Amidst the bodies lulled in bloody rest.
>
> (Don Juan, viii, 90–1)

As well as being Castelnau's stock-in-trade, such myopic closing in on 'one good action in the midst of crimes' is also associated with other questionable, 'pretty milk-and-water' writers of these 'Pharisaic times'. This sounds like Wordsworth again, who, as well as being a hypocrite (in Byron's view), was a fond bedewer of war.[35]

Byron, by way of contrast, wants to look at things as steadily as possible while encouraging his reader to do the same:

> If here and there some transient trait of pity
>   Was shown, and some more noble heart broke through
> Its bloody bond, and saved perhaps some pretty
>   Child, or an aged, helpless man or two –
> What's this in one annihilated city,
>   Where thousand loves, and ties, and duties grow?
> Cockneys of London! Muscadins of Paris!
> Just ponder what a pious pastime war is.
>
> (Don Juan, viii, 124)

We may not want to hear it, but the 'pretty / Child' does not rescue us from, or even balance out, the discomforts of Byron's war writing. Like her rescuer, Leila is nothing more than a rhetorical device, one picked out from a ready-made and overlarge pile of such things. When she has served her purpose (to make the reader ponder) she is thrown away again:

> But first of little Leila we'll dispose;
>   For like a day-dawn she was young and pure,
> Or, like the old comparison of snows,

Which are more pure than pleasant to be sure.

(*Don Juan*, xii, 41)

Leila dissolves back into a tired poeticism with which *Don Juan* takes issue. Byron takes us to the edge and throws the scabbard from it. Yet to dismiss the moral doggerel of dawning day, purity and snow, is not to call time on poetry. The fires of Ismail may burn away the kinds of still-seductive Romantic rhetoric that for Byron had been subsumed by the enemies of thought, but much remains for the ear and eye of the undistracted reader. The 'yet warm group / Of murdered women' that form the background to Juan's heroic act, to give one immediate example, still demand to be heard. That horribly incongruous reminder of female tenderness in the warmth of newly dead flesh and the suggestion, in 'lulled in bloody rest', of the mother's lullaby, arrest us in the margins of an event that wants us to think seriously about marginality. The call of the lyric voice and the unstated claim of form adapt the logic of vision to an immediate, pressing need for collective political thought.

Notes

1 *Shelley's Poetry and Prose*, 520.
2 See Wendy Hinde, *Castlereagh* (London: Collins, 1981), esp. 12–86.
3 Kelsall, *Byron's Politics*, 88–9.
4 *Percy Bysshe Shelley: The Major Works*, ed. Zachary Leader and Michael O'Neill (Oxford: Oxford University Press, 2003), 625. Shelley used Paine's 'We pity the plumage, but forget the dying bird' as an epigraph for his pamphlet, which argues that the Princess's public mourning has been disproportionate and, implicitly, that such outpourings distract from real public issues, such as the Government's brutal treatment of the so-called 'Pentridge Three'.
5 Compare Byron's later attack on the 'parts of speech' of that 'long Spout / Of blood and water, leaden Castlereagh' (*Don Juan*, ix, 49–50).
6 *CPW*, V, 196. 'Modesty has fled hearts and taken refuge on lips' and 'The more depraved our conduct, the more careful our words become; people believe they can reacquire through language what has been lost in virtue.' I quote the translations from *CPW*, V, 720.
7 Wordsworth wrote a pamphlet (*On the Convention of Cintra*, 1808) against what he perceived to be British weakness. His sentiments were shared by Southey. See J. R. Watson, *Romanticism and War: A Study of British Romantic Period Writers and the Napoleonic Wars* (London: Palgrave Macmillan, 2003), 125. Also see Philip Shaw, 'Byron and War, Sketches of Spain: Love and War in *Childe Harold's Pilgrimage*', in *Palgrave Advances in Byron Studies*, ed. Jane Stabler (Basingstoke: Palgrave Macmillan, 2007), 213–33.
8 Also see Nigel Leask, *British Romantic Writers and the East: Anxieties of Empire* (Cambridge: Cambridge University Press, 1992), 54–67.

9 Michael O'Neill, '"A Magic Voice and Verse": Byron's Approaches to the Ode, 1814–16', *The Byron Journal*, vol. 34, no. 2 (2006), 101–14.

10 Simon Bainbridge, *Napoleon and English Romanticism* (Cambridge: Cambridge University Press, 1995), 145, 149.

11 *The Vanity of Human Wishes*, 213–14. Taken from *Samuel Johnson: The Complete English Poems*, ed. J. D. Fleeman (Harmondsworth: Penguin, 1971).

12 Byron would return to Charles XII in *Mazeppa* (1819), which draws not from Johnson but Voltaire's *Histoire de Charles XII* (1772) and which is more concerned with Charles the man than Charles as moral exemplar.

13 William Gifford urged Byron to cut some of the poem's more graphic sections, including these lines.

14 See Leslie A. Marchand, *Byron: A Portrait* (London: Pimlico, 1993; first published 1971), 236.

15 *The Field of Waterloo*, xxi. Taken from *The Poetical Works of Walter Scott*, ed. J. Logie Robertson (London: Oxford University Press, 1904).

16 Scott approximates the conventions of Napoleonic war painting, which tends to draw the eye to a single heroic figure centrally positioned within a generalized and often chaotic wider scene. Prominent examples include Benjamin West's 'The Death of Nelson' (1806) and John Singleton Copley's 'The Death of Major Pierson' (1783).

17 Compare Andrew Rutherford, '*Childe Harold's Pilgrimage*, Canto III', in *Byron: A Casebook*, ed. John D. Jump (London: Macmillan, 1973), 181–98 (192) and McGann, *Fiery Dust*, 33.

18 Compare Marchand, *Byron: A Portrait*, 237.

19 Also see Peter Cochran, 'Byron and Castelnau's *History of New Russia*', *The Keats–Shelley Review*, vol. 8 (1993–4), 48–70.

20 Byron's 'position is implicit in all of his mature poetry; he believed that social amelioration would be possible only when existing values assumed to be natural and universal were understood as being historically and socially determined, serving specific political ends that were not necessarily in the best interests of the people'. Daniel P. Watkins, *A Materialist Critique of English Romantic Drama* (Gainesville: University of Florida Press, 1993), 141.

21 *The Blind Man Traces the Circle*, 186. Similarly, Shaw writes that 'Byron is both attracted to and disgusted by war, impelled on one hand by youthful "ardour", constrained on the other by "repugnance to a Life absolutely & exclusively devoted to Carnage" [*BLJ*, i, 118]'. Shaw, 'Byron and War', 214.

22 'While attacking the cant of glory', Byron, by turning to Boone, 'has lapsed into another equally offensive form of cant'. Rutherford, *Byron: A Critical Study*, 181.

23 Kelsall, *Byron's Politics*, 156.

24 *Epistle to Bathurst*, 271–2. Pope celebrates the life of John Kyrle, who (according to Pope's note) lived to ninety, an age at which Byron's Boone was still hunting.

25 *Ode, The Morning of the Day Appointed for a General Thanksgiving. January 18, 1816*, 153–8. Wordsworth is quoted from *The Poetical Works of William Wordsworth*, ed. E. de Selincourt and Helen Darbishire (Oxford: Clarendon Press, 1954).

26 *Ode, 1815*. These are the original lines composed in 1816 and read by Byron. They were replaced, in 1845, by the less sanguinary couplet: 'But Man is Thy most awful instrument, / In working out a pure intent'.

27 Rutherford, *Byron: A Critical Study*, 172. Also see *CPW*, 723.

28 Compare Cochran, 'Byron and Castelnau's *History of New Russia*', 48.

29 The primary meaning of 'gross' here is 'concerned with large masses or outlines; general, opposed to *particular*' (*OED*), although, of course, the more pejorative sense of the word lurks close in warning.

30 See Cochran, 'Byron and Castelnau's *History of New Russia*', 18.

31 By 'rescuing the "moslem orphan" Leila [Juan demonstrates] the capacity to put principles before the hot intoxication of mayhem and plunder' (Cooke, *The Blind Man Traces the Circle*, 195). Juan's 'unmitigated and unjustifiable slaughter' is balanced by his 'determination to preserve the orphaned Leila', an act which establishes 'a brighter, fresher image of military action that transcends the merely brutal savagery' (Mellor, *English Romantic Irony*, 51, 68).

32 Peter L. Thorslev, Jr., *The Byronic Hero: Types and Prototypes* (Minneapolis: University of Minnesota Press, 1962), 13.

33 See Marchand, *Byron: A Portrait*, 89–90.

34 Cronin, *Paper Pellets*, 201.

35 'Clear-sighted Honour, and his staid Compeers, / Along a track of most unnatural years; / In execution of heroic deeds / Whose memory, spotless as the crystal beads / Of morning dew upon the untrodden meads, / Shall live enrolled above the starry spheres' (*Ode* […], *Thanksgiving*, 57–64).

Coda: 'In short'

In short, I deny nothing, but doubt everything' (*BLJ*, ii, 136)

The first two – easily ignored – words here are important. To understand Byron as a thinker we need to pay close attention not just to his direct philosophical claims, but to the self-conscious forming of his articulations. 'In short' is more than throat clearing because it acknowledges the fragmentary relation of the utterance to the eternity of thought in which it participates. Something of this is also recognized in the form of the claim itself which acknowledges the intellectual force of scepticism but also the possibilities that attend scepticism's self-cancellation. Doubt is an encompassing inevitability for the thoughtful life, yet its very thoroughness offers to conjure us away from its apparent entrapment. This moment, in which for Byron philosophy ('she too much rejects') and truth part ways, is, as this book has argued, the opening act of Byronic poetics. Writing, for Byron, whether prose literary criticism or visionary poetry, must understand its own compacted provisionality in the face of what it cannot hope to capture. What is written is only a miniature or outline or sketch of what writing acknowledges. This shortfall is refigured as hope in the person of a reader who, during Byron's post-John Murray years, is both invested in and mistrusted to an unprecedented extent. Where poetic agency in these terms is seen to be misunderstood or misappropriated, Byron turns the logic of vision to the purposes of satire. 'Lake School' sublimity is for Byron a mock-up, something claimed by the author rather than offered to the reader. It misconstrues the sublime by failing to reach a poetics of the concrete. 'Cant Poetical' and 'Cant Political' being closely linked for Byron, the problem is reformulated, in the siege cantos of *Don Juan* and elsewhere, as one of political dishonesty. The corrupt historian's failure to acknowledge the relation between narrative and world is an act of moral violence that is also a desecration of the poet's obligation to see.

Across these negotiations, the visionary tradition permeates and is transmuted through Byron's thought, connecting up the poet's Romantic durability with his energies as a literary critic, satirist and political commentator. This unprecious, immediate and mobile sense of vision is not, as is sometimes thought, a less serious version of what we get from Byron's major contemporaries. It is, rather, the evolution of a Romantic paradigm seen as already drying up into its own language. It is not like Blake's sense of vision because it is happy to see in concrete and pugnaciously ironic ways. Byron sees, in other words, that looking at real things directly and being ironic about them can be visionary when this looking also glimpses that which evades words and thus makes irony real.

In the tradition of several critics quoted in it, this book makes a case for taking Byron seriously as a thinker. In doing this it tries to avoid reading the poetry into the service of a single philosophical, historical or political position. Of course, it would not be desirable to do this entirely because Byron does make commitments, he does stand for things and believe things directly; but we need to understand that these commitments are altered in our denaturing of them (our removal of them from poetry). Our understanding of Byron's poetry, I think, continues to suffer from the claims upon it, especially where those claims are generated by a careerist or market-led need for sheer and clear novelty. Byron already exists – we don't need a new one. The originality business, where it involves rewriting Byron as a philosopher, involves an especial misapprehension because Byron, again as this book has argued, self-consciously inhabits a tradition (one he found bits of in Horace, Montaigne, Pope, Johnson, Shelley and others) that identifies the unique articulations of poetry as irreducibly distinct from the narratives of argument. The *reading* of Byron's poetry, it follows from this, becomes a primary mode of critical argumentation because it is only in accepting Byron's invitation to think, read and imagine that we can comprehend the depth of his (philosophical, political, historical-ongoing) legacy. We must partake as well as behold, otherwise we have not understood what Byron is urging us (not) to do.

The visionary poet is in flux across Byron's works; there is the wise, embattled seer of *The Prophecy of Dante*; there is the naïve, frustrated rationalist of *Cain*; there is also the serio-comic narrator of *Don Juan* who presides over an encounter between a newly theorized sublime and a spectacularly concretized and politically aware poetic practice. Things look different again in *The Vision of Judgment*, which, as Byron's most self-contained and precise satire, seems far from dependent upon or even interested in the beyondness its title ironically invokes. Its brilliance depends precisely upon the tangible economy of its post-Miltonic inventiveness. Thus the angel tasked with recording human 'vice' and 'woe' who 'had stripp'd off both his wings in quills, / And yet was in arrear of human ills' (*The Vision of Judgment*, 3) calls for no visionary anxiety concerning the translation of divine into human. Such matters seem gloriously irrelevant to a sharply comic poetry that appears to have other priorities than ministering to the beyond:

> Saint Peter sat by the celestial gate,
>   And nodded o'er his keys; when, lo! there came
> A wond'rous noise he had not heard of late—
>   A rushing sound of wind, and stream, and flame;
> In short, a roar of things extremely great,
>   Which would have made aught save a saint exclaim;
> But he, with first a start and then a wink,
> Said, 'There's another star gone out, I think!'
>   (*The Vision of Judgment*, 16)

What is unseen here, it would seem, is not some inexpressible sublime, but the cretinous bluster surrounding the death of George III back on earth. Byron's 'In short' is not in any obvious way about drawing our attention to the provisionality of the written; it appears to signal, rather, a form of ironic impatience to get on with being (so impressively) in control.

The profound problems situated so humbly and movingly by Milton's Raphael are turned, here in the description of another archangel (Michael), to the purposes of immediate satire:

> And from the gate thrown open issued beaming
>   A beautiful and mighty Thing of Light,
> Radiant with glory, like a banner streaming
>   Victorious from some world-o'erthrowing fight:
> My poor comparisons must needs be teeming
>   With earthly likenesses, for here the night
> Of clay obscures our best conceptions, saving
> Johanna Southcote, or Bob Southey raving.
>   (*The Vision of Judgment*, 28)

Byron's poet is a long way from the existential angst of Cain. He glories in his acknowledged darkness and mire. He delights in getting his hands dirty, in moulding and working the clay he has been bequeathed into some of his filthiest jokes, notably this one about those 'damn'd souls' who are allowed to 'range freely':

They are proud of this—as very well they may,
    It being a sort of knighthood, or gilt key
Stuck in their loins; or like to an 'entré'
    Up the back stairs, or such free-masonry:
I borrow my comparisons from clay,
    Being clay myself. Let not those spirits be
Offended with such base low likenesses;
    We know their posts are nobler far than these.

(The Vision of Judgment, 54)

Poet and language, rather than stumbling into the frustrating misalignment of the 'voiceless thought', become one down in the dirt.

Yet clay is not just dirt; it is also the material of origin. If we are down in the mire then we are at least alive and real and able to create amidst a semantic plurality that resists the incursions of cant. Poetry is thus not just a way of attacking people but a way of seeing and thinking and recreating our lives. It tells us first that language can kill us and second that language can save us. More important than Byron's being disgusting here, then, are the terms of his disgust. It is Byron who is offended in *The Vision of Judgment* – by Southey – and not just because of the latter's suggestions about his personal life. Southey disgusts Byron because he represents bad poetry with no distinctness or outline but also no sense of the ethics of the fragment; his writing only hawks the deceits of those who would have us for their own ends. The bad poet can't be brief, even ironically. He can't sketch or outline things because he only deals, in full, in what he has been told to say. He is 'multo-scribbling Southey' (*The Vision of Judgment*, 65), all plenitude, no responsibility.

Southey's sham celebration of George III, which is of a piece with the monarch's funereal opulence, is a spectacular performance of cant:

He died! – his death made no great stir on earth;
    His burial made some pomp; there was profusion
Of velvet, gilding, brass, and no great dearth
    Of aught but tears—save those shed by collusion;
For these things may be bought at their true worth:
    Of elegy there was the due infusion—
Bought also; and the torches, cloaks and banners,
Heralds, and relics of old Gothic manners,

Form'd a sepulchral melo-drame. Of all
    The fools who flock'd to swell or see the show,
Who cared about the corpse? The funeral
    Made the attraction, and the black the woe.

There throbb'd not there a thought which pierced the pall;
   And when the gorgeous coffin was laid low,
It seemed the mockery of hell to fold
The rottenness of eighty years in gold.

                    (*The Vision of Judgment*, 9–10)

Amidst this groundless 'profusion', everything is misunderstood; the mystery of death is lost to the spectacle of burial as the honesty of poetry is lost to the falseness of purchased 'elegy'. There is no voice here to pierce the 'pall' of moral idiocy that hangs over the scene like the rich tapestries covering the coffin.

Byron wished that Wordsworth would change his lakes for ocean. This was not, of course, a desire for him to write more, only for him to think more about the contending claims of rhetoric and form as means of addressing the sublime. As well as a moral and political failure, the attempt to write or think boundlessness (Byron thinks about what this might mean in *Cain*) is a failure of poetics. Southey's eternal productivity is a silly case in point:

He said—(I only give the heads)—he said,
   He meant no harm in scribbling; 'twas his way
Upon all topics; 'twas, besides, his bread,
   Of which he butter'd both sides; 'twould delay
Too long the assembly (he was pleased to dread)
   And take up rather more time than a day,
To name his works—he would but cite a few—
Wat Tyler—Rhymes on Blenheim—Waterloo.

He had written praises of a regicide;
   He had written praises of all kings whatever;
He had written for republics far and wide,
   And then against them bitterer than ever;
For pantisocracy he once had cried
   Aloud, a scheme less moral than 'twas clever;
Then grew a hearty antijacobin—
Had turn'd his coat—and would have turn'd his skin.

He had sung against all battles, and again
   In their high praise and glory: he had called
Reviewing 'the ungentle craft,' and then
   Become as base a critic as ere crawl'd—
Fed, paid, and pamper'd by the very men
   By whom his muse and morals had been maul'd:

He had written much blank verse, and blanker prose,
And more of both than any body knows.

(The Vision of Judgment, 96–8)

Here are two acts of summary. Southey's – 'he would but cite a few'
– which serves only to betray the moral chaos over which he presides.
His unwittingly honest selection from his own bulging *oeuvre* speaks
only of self-interest and political complicity. There is no craft or
integrity to his brevity. This is being 'visionary' in the way Johanna
Southcote is visionary in that everything is present and complete and
interpreted in its haziness, but also meaningless because it doesn't
stand for anything. Byron hates this and returns to it (recall *Don
Juan*, iii, 95) because it travesties the dynamics of vision he establishes
in the textures and forms of his own best work. His own speaking
in short – 'I only give the heads' – is thus by contrast a gesture of
ironic control generated in rigorous, undepressed and unfinished
acceptance. Byron, that is, draws attention to the provisionality of his
critique, but then challenges any sense of restriction in the satirical
plenitude that follows.

Where Southey's proliferations constitute a travesty of the beyond,
the Byronic 'in short' stands in an honest relation to what the poet is
tasked with outlining. In not being an argument, but in trusting to the
semantics of its own forms, the poem becomes about the possibility of
real thought:

> And this is not a theologic tract,
>   To prove with Hebrew and with Arabic
> If Job be allegory or a fact,
>   But a true narrative; and thus I pick
> From out the whole but such and such an act
>   As sets aside the slightest thought of trick.
> 'Tis every tittle true, beyond suspicion,
> And accurate as any other vision.

(The Vision of Judgment, 34)

Byron is not a philosopher; he can spin off 'tract' and fact' as a rhyme,
but he cannot obey the imperatives that such words deploy over the
world. His interest is in a different kind of truth-telling, one that comes
through the selective processes that define his role as narrative poet. No
vision can be 'accurate', but visions can occupy and emerge from a spirit
of truthfulness that, as far as Byron was concerned, only the forms of
literature can host and preserve. The poet must acknowledge the limits
of poetic facture. He must understand that he can only pick things out

from 'the whole' to make something that is no more – or less – true than 'any other vision'. When this is done, however, he will find himself at liberty in a real and meaningful sense. He will have understood and helped his readers to understand something about the world and the lies it tells us about thought. In so doing he might cajole us into taking a second look.

Bibliography

Aarsleff, Hans, *From Locke to Saussure: Essays on the Study of Language and Intellectual History* (London: Athlone, 1982).

Abrams, M. H., *Natural Supernaturalism: Tradition and Revolution in Romantic Literature* (Oxford: Oxford University Press, 1971).

———, *The Mirror and the Lamp: Romantic Theory and the Critical Tradition* (New York: Oxford University Press, 1953).

Adorno, Theodor, W., *Notes to Literature*, ed. Rolf Tiedemann; trans. Shierry Weber Nicholsen, 2 vols (New York: Columbia University Press, 1991).

Alighieri, Dante, *The Divine Comedy*, trans. C. H. Sisson; notes by David H. Higgins (Oxford: Oxford University Press, 1993).

Amarasinghe, Upali, *Dryden and Pope in the Early Nineteenth Century: A Study of Changing Literary Taste* (Cambridge: Cambridge University Press, 1962).

Annas, Julia, and Jonathan Barnes, *The Modes of Scepticism: Ancient Texts and Modern Interpretations* (Cambridge: Cambridge University Press, 1985).

Arnold, Matthew, 'Lectures and Essays in Criticism', ed. R. H. Super (Ann Arbor: The University of Michigan Press, 1962).

———, 'English Literature and Irish Politics', vol. 9 of *Complete Prose Works*, ed. R. H. Super (Ann Arbor: University of Michigan Press, 1973).

Attridge, Derek, *The Singularity of Literature* (London: Routledge, 2004).

Bakhtin, Mikhail, *Rabelais and His World*, trans. Hélène Iswolsky (Bloomington: Indiana University Press, 1984).

Bainbridge, Simon, *Napoleon and English Romanticism* (Cambridge: Cambridge University Press, 1995).

Balfour, Ian, *The Rhetoric of Romantic Prophecy* (Stanford: Stanford University Press, 2002).

Barfoot, C. C., and Theo D'haen (eds), *Centennial Hauntings: Pope, Byron and Eliot in the year '88* (Amsterdam: Rodopi, 1990).

Barton, Anne, *Landmarks of World Literature: Don Juan* (Cambridge: Cambridge University Press, 1992).

Bate, W. J., et al. (eds), *The Yale Edition of the Works of Samuel Johnson*, 16 vols (New Haven: Yale University Press, 1973).

Beatty, Bernard, 'Calvin in Islam: A Reading of *Lara* and *The Giaour*', *Romanticism*, vol. 5.1 (1999), pp. 70–86.

———, *Byron's Don Juan* (London: Croom Helm, 1985).

Beaty, Frederick L., *Byron the Satirist* (DeKalb: Northern Illinois University Press, 1985).

———, 'Byron on Joanna Southcott and Undeserved Salvation', *Keats-Shelley Journal*, 26 (1977), pp. 34–38.

Bennet, Betty T. (ed.), *The Letters of Mary Wollstonecraft Shelley*, 3 vols (Baltimore: Johns Hopkins University Press, 1980–88).

Bernard, John Peter (Revd) et al., *A General Dictionary, Historical and Critical: in which A New and Accurate TRANSLATION of that of the Celebrated Mr. Bayle*, 10 vols (London, 1734–41).

Bernhard Jackson, Emily, *The Development of Byron's Philosophy of Knowledge* (Basingstoke: Palgrave Macmillan, 2010).

Blackstone, Bernard, *Byron: A Survey* (London: Longman, 1975).

Blake, William, *The Complete Poems,* ed. W. H. Stevenson, 2nd edition (London: Longman, 1989).

Bloom, Harold, *The Anxiety of Influence* (New York: Oxford University Press, 1973).

———, *The Visionary Company: A Reading of English Romantic Poetry* (London: Faber, 1962).

Bond, Donald F. (ed.), *The Spectator*, 5 vols (Oxford: Clarendon Press, 1965).

Bone, Drummond (ed.), *The Cambridge Companion to Byron* (Cambridge: Cambridge University Press, 2005).

Booth, Wayne C., *A Rhetoric of Irony* (Chicago: University of Chicago Press, 1974).

Bostetter, Edward E., *The Romantic Ventriloquists: Wordsworth, Coleridge, Keats, Shelley, Byron* (Seattle: University of Washington Press, 1963).

Bowles, William Lisle (ed.), *The Works of Alexander Pope*, 10 vols (London, 1806).

Bowles, William Lisle, *The Invariable Principles of Poetry: In a Letter addressed to Thomas Campbell, Esq; Occasioned by some Critical Observations in his Specimens of British Poets, Particularly relating to the Poetical Character of POPE* (London: Longman, 1819).

Bullitt, John M., *Jonathan Swift and the Anatomy of Satire* (Cambridge: Harvard University Press, 1953).

Burnyeat, Myles (ed.), *The Skeptical Tradition* (Berkeley: University of California Press, 1983).

Butler, E. M., *Byron and Goethe* (London: Bowes, 1956).

Brush, Craig B., *Montaigne and Bayle: Variations on the Theme of Skepticism*, International Archives of the History of Ideas, vol. 14 (The Hague: Nijhoff, 1966).

Butt, John (ed.), *The Twickenham Edition of the Poems of Alexander Pope*, 11 vols (London: Methuen, 1943–69).

Campbell, Thomas, *Specimens of the British Poets; with Biographical and Critical Notices, and an Essay on English Poetry*, 7 vols (London: John Murray, 1819).

Cavell, Stanley, *Must we Mean what we Say? A Book of Essays* (Cambridge: Cambridge University Press, 1976).

Clingham, Greg (ed.), *The Cambridge Companion to Samuel Johnson* (Cambridge: Cambridge University Press, 1997).

Chandler, James, 'The Pope Controversy: Romantic Poetics and the English Canon', *Critical Enquiry*, vol. 10, no. 3 (1984), pp. 481–509.

Cheeke, Stephen, *Byron and Place: History, Translation, Nostalgia* (Basingstoke: Palgrave Macmillan, 2003).

Christensen, Jerome, *Lord Byron's Strength: Writing and Commercial Society* (Baltimore: Johns Hopkins University Press, 1993).

Cochran, Peter, 'Byron and Castelnau's *History of New Russia*', *The Keats–Shelley Review*, vol. 8 (1993–4), pp. 48–70.

Cooke, M. G., *The Blind Man Traces the Circle: On the Patterns and Philosophy of Byron's Poetry* (Princeton: Princeton University Press, 1969).

Cooper, Andrew M., *Doubt and Identity in Romantic Poetry* (New Haven: Yale University Press, 1988).

Corbett, Martyn, *Byron and Tragedy* (New York: St. Martin's, 1988).

Cotton, Charles (trans.), *Essays of Michael Seigneur de Montaigne*, 4th edn, 3 vols (London, 1711).

Cronin, Richard (ed.), *1798: The Year of the Lyrical Ballads* (London: Macmillan, 1998).

Cronin, Richard, *Paper Pellets: British Literary Culture after Waterloo* (Oxford: Oxford University Press, 2010).

Curran, Stuart, *Poetic Form and British Romanticism* (Oxford: Oxford University Press, 1986).

Curtis, Paul, M. (ed.), *Revue de l'Universiténde Moncton: Des actes sèlectionnés du 30e Congrès international sur Byron*, 'Byron and the Romantic Sublime' (Moncton: Université de Moncton, 2005).

Dando, Joel Allan, 'The Poet as Critic: Byron in his Letters and Journals. Case Studies of Shakespeare and Johnson' (unpublished doctoral thesis, Harvard University, 1985).

DeMaria, Jr, Robert, *Samuel Johnson and the Life of Reading* (Baltimore: Johns Hopkins University Press, 1997).

Diogenes Laertius, *Lives of the Eminent Philosophers*, Loeb Classical Library, trans. R. D. Hicks, 2 vols (London: Heineman, 1965).

Dryden, John, *Of Dramatic Poesy and Other Critical Essays*, ed. George Watson, 2 vols (London: Dent, 1962).

Drummond, Sir William, *Oedipus Judaicus* (London: Valpy, 1811).

Eddy, Donald D. (ed.), *The Literary Magazine* (1756–58), 3 vols (New York: Garland, 1978).

Eagleton, Terry, *Criticism and Ideology: A Study in Marxist Literary Theory* (London: Verso, 2006).

Eliot, T. S., *On Poetry and Poets* (London: Faber and Faber, 1957).

———, *Poems Written in Early Youth*, ed. Valerie Eliot (London: Faber, 1967).

Elledge, Paul W., *Byron and the Dynamics of Metaphor* (Nashville: Vanderbilt University Press, 1968).

Empson, William, *The Structure of Complex Words* (Harmondsworth: Penguin, 1995).

England, A. B., *Byron's Don Juan and Eighteenth Century Literature* (Lewisburg: Bucknell University Press, 1975).

Erskine-Hill, Howard, *The Augustan Idea in English Literature* (London: Arnold, 1983).

Fairer, David (ed.), *The Correspondence of Thomas Warton* (London: University of Georgia Press, 1995).

Fleeman, J. D. (ed.), *Samuel Johnson: The Complete English Poems* (Harmondsworth: Penguin, 1971).

Foot, Michael, *The Politics of Paradise: a vindication of Byron* (London: Collins, 1988).

Furniss, Tom, *Edmund Burke's Aesthetic Ideology: Language, Gender and Political Economy in Revolution* (Cambridge: Cambridge University Press, 1993).

Furst, Lilian R., *Fictions of Romantic Irony in European Narrative, 1760–1857* (London: Macmillan, 1984).

Fussell, Paul, *The Rhetorical World of Augustan Humanism: Ethics and Imagery from Swift to Burke* (Oxford: Clarendon Press, 1965).

Garber, Frederick, *Self, Text, and Romantic Irony: The Example of Byron* (Princeton: Princeton University Press, 1988).

Garnett, David (ed.), *The Novels of Thomas Love Peacock* (London: Rupert Hart-Davis, 1948).

Gibbon, Edward, *Memoirs of My Life*, ed. Georges A. Bonnard (London: Nelson, 1966).

Gibson, John, 'Between Truth and Triviality', *British Journal of Aesthetics*, vol. 43, no. 3 (July 2003), pp. 224–37.

Gleckner, F., *Byron and the Ruins of Paradise* (Baltimore: Johns Hopkins University Press, 1968).

Gleckner, Robert, and Bernard Beatty (eds), *The Plays of Lord Byron: Critical Essays* (Liverpool: Liverpool University Press, 1997).

Goethe, Johann Wolfgang von, *Faust Part One*, trans. David Luke (Oxford: Oxford University Press, 1987).

Greenblatt, Stephen, et al. (eds), *The Norton Shakespeare* (New York: Norton, 1997).

Greever, Garland (ed.), *A Wiltshire Parson and his Friends: The Correspondence of William Lisle Bowles* (London: Constable, 1926).

Griffin, Robert J., *Wordsworth's Pope: A Study in Literary Historiography* (Cambridge: Cambridge University Press, 1995).

Griggs, Earl Leslie (ed.), *Collected Letters of Samuel Taylor Coleridge*, 6 vols (Oxford: Clarendon Press, 1956–71).

Hamilton, Sir William (ed.), *The Collected Works of Dugald Stewart*, 11 vols (Edinburgh: Constable, 1854–60).

Hammond, Paul, and David Hopkins (eds), *The Poems of John Dryden*, 4 vols (London: Longman, 1995–2000).

Hill, George Birkbeck (ed.), *Boswell's Life of Johnson: together with Boswell's Journal of a Tour to the Hebrides and Johnson's Diary of a Journey into North Wales*, rev. L. F. Powell, 7 vols (Oxford: Clarendon Press, 1934–50).

Hinde, Wendy, *Castlereagh* (London: Collins, 1981).

Hirst, Wolf Z., *Byron, The Bible and Religion: Essays from the Twelfth International Byron Seminar* (Newark: University of Delaware Press, 1991).

Hoagwood, Terence Allan, *Byron's Dialectic: Skepticism and the Critique of Culture* (Lewisburg: Bucknell University Press, 1993).

Howe, P. P. (ed.), *The Complete Works of William Hazlitt*, 21 vols (London: Dent, 1930–34).

Hume, David, *An Enquiry Concerning Human Understanding*, ed. Tom L. Beauchamp (Oxford: Oxford University Press, 1999).

Hume, David, *Essays: Moral, Political, and Literary*, ed. Eugene F. Miller, rev. edn. (Indianapolis: Liberty, 1987).

Jarvis, Simon, *Adorno: A Critical Introduction* (Cambridge: Polity, 1998).

Jump, John D. (ed.), *Byron: A Casebook* (London: Macmillan, 1973).

Johnson, Samuel, *A Dictionary of the English Language*, 2 vols (London: J. Johnson, 1806).

———, *Lives of the English Poets*, ed. George Birkbeck Hill, 3 vols (Oxford: Clarendon Press, 1905).

Jones, Frederick L. (ed.), *The Letters of Percy Bysshe Shelley*, 2 vols (Oxford: Clarendon Press, 1964).

Joseph, M. K., *Byron the Poet* (London: Gollancz, 1964).

Keach, William, *Shelley's Style* (New York: Methuen, 1984).

Keats, John, *Complete Poems*, ed. Jack Stillinger (Massachusetts: Harvard University Press, 1982).

Kenny, Anthony, *Action, Emotion and Will* (Bristol: Thoemmes, 1994).

Kelsall, Malcolm, *Byron's Politics* (Brighton: Harvester, 1987).

Kirkland Jr, Richard I., 'Byron's Reading of Montaigne: A Leigh Hunt Letter', *Keats-Shelley Journal*, 30 (1981), pp. 47–51.

Korshin, Paul J. (ed.), *The Age of Johnson: A Scholarly Annual* (New York: AMS), VI (1996).

Langford, Paul (ed.), *The Writings and Speeches of Edmund Burke* (Oxford: Clarendon Press, 1989).

Leader, Zachary, and Michael O'Neill (eds), *Percy Bysshe Shelley: The Major Works* (Oxford: Oxford University Press, 2003).

Leask, Nigel, *British Romantic Writers and the East: Anxieties of Empire* (Cambridge: Cambridge University Press, 1992).

Leavis, F. R., *Revaluation* (New York: Norton, 1936).

Leedy, Paul, 'Genres Criticism and the Significance of Warton's Essay on Pope', *The Journal of English and Germanic Philology*, 45 (1946), pp. 140–46.

Leighton, Angela, *On Form: Poetry, Aestheticism, and the Legacy of a Word* (Oxford: Oxford University Press, 2007).

Locke, John, *An Essay Concerning Human Understanding*, ed. Peter H. Nidditch (Oxford: Clarendon Press, 1975).

———, *Of the Conduct of the Understanding*, 1706 facsimile (Bristol: Thoemmes, 1993).

Lovell Jr, Ernest J. (ed.) *Medwin's Conversations of Lord Byron* (Princeton: Princeton University Press, 1966).

MacClintock, William Darnall, *Joseph Warton's Essay on Pope: A History of the Five Editions* (Chapel Hill: University of North Carolina Press, 1933).

MacLean, Kenneth, *John Locke and English Literature of the Eighteenth Century* (New York: Russell, 1962).

Marchand, Leslie A., *Byron: A Biography*, 3 vols (London: John Murray, 1957).

———, *Byron's Poetry: A Critical Introduction* (London: John Murray, 1965).

Marjarum, Edward Wayne, *Byron as Skeptic and Believer*, Princeton Studies in English, 16 (Princeton: Princeton University Press, 1938).

Martin, Philip W., *Byron: a Poet Before His Public* (Cambridge: Cambridge University Press, 1982).

Martindale, Charles, and David Hopkins (eds), *Horace Made New: Horatian Influences on British Writing from the Renaissance to the Twentieth Century* (Cambridge: Cambridge University Press, 1993).

Mendelson, Edward (ed.), *The English Auden: Poems, Essays and Dramatic Writings 1927–1939* (London: Faber, 1977).

McGann, Jerome J., *Fiery Dust: Byron's Poetic Development* (Chicago: Chicago University Press, 1968).

———, *Don Juan in Context* (London: John Murray, 1976).

———, *The Romantic Ideology: a Critical Investigation* (Chicago: University of Chicago Press, 1983).

———, *The Beauty of Inflections: Literary Investigations in Historical Method and Theory* (Oxford: Clarendon Press, 1988).

———, *Byron and Romanticism* (Cambridge: Cambridge University Press, 2002).

Mellor, Anne K., *English Romantic Irony* (Cambridge: Harvard University Press, 1980).

Midgley, Mary, *Beast and Man: The Roots of Human Nature* (London: Routledge, 1995).

———, *Science and Poetry* (London: Routledge, 2001).

Mole, Tom, *Byron's Romantic Celebrity: Industrial Culture and the Hermeneutic of Intimacy* (Basingstoke: Palgrave Macmillan, 2007).

Morton, Tim, *Shelley and the Revolution in Taste: The Body and the Natural World* (Cambridge: Cambridge University Press, 1994).

Nicholson, Andrew (ed.), *Lord Byron: The Complete Miscellaneous Prose* (Oxford: Clarendon Press, 1991).

O'Neill, Michael, '"A Magic Voice and Verse": Byron's Approaches to the Ode, 1814–16', *The Byron Journal*, vol. 34, no. 2 (2006), pp. 101–14.

———, *Romanticism and the Self-Conscious Poem* (Oxford: Oxford University Press, 1997).

Park, Roy, *Hazlitt and the Spirit of the Age: Abstraction and Critical Theory* (Oxford: Clarendon Press, 1971).

Parker, G. F., *Johnson's Shakespeare* (Oxford: Clarendon Press, 1989). *Scepticism and Literature: An Essay on Pope, Hume, Sterne, and Johnson* (Oxford: Oxford University Press, 2003).

Partridge, Eric (ed.), *The Three Wartons: A Choice of Verse* (London: Scholaris Press, 1927).

Partridge, Eric, *Shakespeare's Bawdy* (London: Routledge, 1993).

Paulin, Tom, *The Day Star of Liberty: William Hazlitt's Radical Style* (London: Faber, 1998).

Pittock, Joan, *The Ascendancy of Taste: The Achievement of Joseph and Thomas Warton* (London: Routledge, 1973).

Popkin, Richard H., *The History of Scepticism from Erasmus to Spinoza* (California: California University Press, 1979).

———, *The High Road to Pyrrhonism,* ed. Richard A. Watson and James E. Force (Austin Hill: San Diego, 1980).

Popkin, Richard H. (ed.), *Scepticism in the Enlightenment*, International Archives of the History of Ideas, 152 (Kluwer: Dordrecht, 1997) .

Popkin, Richard H., and Arjo Vanderjagt (eds), *Scepticism and Irreligion in the Seventeenth and Eighteenth Centuries* (Leiden: Brill, 1993).

Porter, Roy, *The Greatest Benefit to Mankind: A Medical History of Humanity from Antiquity to the Present* (London: Harper Collins, 1997).

Prior, Matthew, *Dialogues of the Dead and Other Works in Prose and Verse*, ed. A. R. Waller (Cambridge: Cambridge University Press, 1907).

Quennell, Peter, *Byron: The Years of Fame* (London: Collins, 1943).

Raizis, Marius Byron (ed.), *Byron and the Mediterranean World* (Athens: Hellenic Byron Society, 1995).

Rawes, Alan (ed.), *Romanticism and Form* (Basingstoke: Palgrave Macmillan, 2007).

Redford, Bruce (ed.), *The Letters of Samuel Johnson*, 5 vols (Oxford: Clarendon Press, 1992–94).

Reiman, Donald H., *Intervals of Inspiration: The Skeptical Tradition and the Psychology of Romanticism* (Florida: Penkevill, 1988).

Reiman, Donald H., and Neil Fraistat (eds), *Shelley's Poetry and Prose* (New York: Norton, 2002).

Reiman, Donald H. (ed.), *The Romantics Reviewed: Contemporary Reviews of British Romantic Writers*, 9 vols (New York: Garland, 1972).

Richards, I. A., *The Philosophy of Rhetoric* (London: Oxford University Press, 1936).

Richetti, John, *Philosophical Writings: Locke, Berkeley, Hume* (Cambridge, MA: Harvard University Press, 1983).

Ricks, Christopher, *Allusion to the Poets* (Oxford: Oxford University Press, 2002).

———, *Keats and Embarrassment* (Oxford: Clarendon Press, 1974).

Rollins, Hyder Edward (ed.), *The Letters of John Keats*, 2 vols (Cambridge: Cambridge University Press, 1958).

Roscoe, William (ed.), *The Works of Alexander Pope*, 10 vols (London, 1824–5).

Rosen, F., *Bentham, Byron, and Greece: Constitutionalism, Nationalism, and Early Liberal Political Thought* (Oxford: Clarendon Press, 1992).

Rudd, Niall (trans.), *Horace Satires and Epistles / Persius Satires* (Harmondsworth: Penguin, 2005).

Russell, Bertrand, *History of Western Philosophy and its Connections with Political and Social Circumstances from the Earliest Times to the Present Day* (London: Unwin, 1946).

Russell, D. A., and Michael Winterbottom (eds), *Classical Literary Criticism*, Oxford World's Classics (Oxford: Oxford University Press, 1998).

Rutherford, Andrew (ed.), *Lord Byron: The Critical Heritage* (London: Routledge, 1995).

Rutherford, Andrew (ed.), *Byron: Augustan and Romantic* (London: Macmillan, 1990).

Rutherford, Andrew, *Byron: A Critical Study* (Edinburgh: Oliver and Boyd, 1962).

Sextus Empiricus, *Outlines of Pyrrhonism*, Loeb Classical Library, trans. R. G. Bury, vol 1 of 4 (London Heinemann, 1933–49).

Schlegel, Friedrich von, *Dialogue on Poetry and Literary Aphorisms*, trans. Ernst Behler and Roman Struc (University Park: Pennsylvania State University Press, 1968).

Shaftesbury, Anthony, Earl of, *Characteristics of Men, Manners, Opinions, Times*, etc., ed. John M. Robertson, 2 vols (London: Richards, 1900).

Shilstone, Frederick W., *Byron and the Myth of Tradition* (Lincoln: University of Nebraska Press, 1988).

Simpson, David, *Irony and Authority in Romantic Poetry* (London: Macmillan, 1979).

———, *Romanticism, Nationalism, and the Revolt against Theory* (Chicago: University of Chicago Press, 1993).

Sontag, Susan, *Illness as Metaphor* and *Aids and its Metaphors* (Harmondsworth: Penguin, 1991).

Soskice, Janet, *Metaphor and Religious Language* (Oxford: Clarendon Press, 1987).

Spence, Joseph, *Anecdotes, Observations, and Characters, of Books and Men. Collected from the Conversations of Mr. Pope, and other Eminent Persons of his time* (London: John Murray, 1820).

Squirrell, R., *An Essay on Indigestion and its Consequences, or Advice to Persons Affected with Debility of the Digestive Organs, Nervous Disorders, Gout, Dropsy, &c.* (London: Murray and Highley, 1795).

Stabler, Jane, *Byron, Poetics and History* (Cambridge: Cambridge University Press, 2002).

Stabler, Jane (ed.), *Palgrave Advances in Byron Studies* (Basingstoke: Palgrave Macmillan, 2007).

Staël Holstein, Baroness, *Germany* (translated from the French), 3 vols (London: John Murray, 1813).

Steffan, Truman Guy and Willis W. Pratt (eds), *Byron's Don Juan* (*Variorum Edition*), 4 vols (Austin: University of Texas Press, 1957).

Steffan, Truman Guy, *Lord Byron's Cain* (Austin: University of Texas Press, 1968).

Steiner, George, *The Death of Tragedy* (London: Faber, 1961).

Sterne, Laurence, *The Life and Opinions of Tristram Shandy, Gentleman*, Florida Edition, ed. Melvyn New and Joan New, 3 vols (Florida: Florida University Press, 1978).

Striker, Gisela, 'The Ten Tropes of Aenesidemus', in *The Skeptical Tradition*, ed. Myles Burnyeat (Berkeley: University of California Press, 1983).

Stroud, Barry, *The Significance of Philosophical Scepticism* (Oxford: Clarendon Press, 1984).

Swift, Jonathan, *Gulliver's Travels* (*1726*), vol. 11 of *The Prose Works of Jonathan Swift*, ed. Herbert Davis (Oxford: Blackwell, 1941).

———, *A Tale of a Tub*, to which is added *The Battle of the Books* and the *Mechanical Operation of the Spirit*, ed. A. C. Guthkelch and D. Nichol Smith, 2nd edition (Oxford: Clarendon Press, 1958).

Thorslev Jr, Peter L., *The Byronic Hero: Types and Prototypes* (Minneapolis: University of Minnesota Press, 1962).

Vance, John A., *Joseph and Thomas Warton* (Boston: Twayne, 1983).

van Doren, Carl, *The Life of Thomas Love Peacock* (New York: Russell, 1966).

Van Rennes, J. J., *Bowles, Byron and the Pope-Controversy* (Amsterdam: Paris, 1927).

Voltaire, *Letters concerning the English Nation*, The World's Classics, ed. Nicholas Cronk (Oxford: Oxford University Press, 1994).

Wain, John, *Samuel Johnson* (London: Macmillan, 1974).

————, 'Byron: The Search for Identity', in *Essays on Literature and Ideas* (London: Macmillan, 1963), pp. 85–101.

Warton, Joseph, *The Works of Alexander Pope*, 8 vols (London, 1797).

————, *An Essay on the Genius and Writings of Pope*, 2 vols, 5th edn (London, 1806).

Watkins, Daniel P., *A Materialist Critique of English Romantic Drama* (Gainesville: University of Florida Press, 1993).

Watson, J. R., *Romanticism and War: A Study of British Romantic Period Writers and the Napoleonic Wars* (London: Palgrave Macmillan, 2003).

Weiskel, Thomas, *The Romantic Sublime: Studies in the Psychology of Transcendence* (Baltimore: Johns Hopkins University Press, 1976).

West, Paul (ed.), *Byron: A Collection of Critical Essays* (Englewood Cliffs, NJ: Prentice Hall, 1963).

Williams, Raymond, *Keywords: A Vocabulary of Culture and Society* (Glasgow: Fontana, 1976).

————, *Culture and Society 1780–1950* (Harmondsworth: Penguin, 1979).

Wimsatt Jr, W. K., *The Prose Style of Samuel Johnson*, Yale Studies in English, vol. 94 (New Haven: Yale University Press, 1941).

Wilson Knight, G., *The Burning Oracle* (Oxford: Oxford University Press, 1939).

Wolfson, Susan J., *Formal Charges: The Shaping of Poetry in British Romanticism* (Stanford, CA: Stanford University Press, 1997).

Woodhouse, D. R. S., 'Shades of Pope: Byron's Development as a Satirist' (unpublished Cambridge University thesis, 1996).

Wooll, John, *Biographical Memoirs of the late Revd Joseph Warton D. D.* (London, 1806).

Index